Early Learning and Development

Cultural–historical concepts in play

Early Learning and Development provides a unique synthesis of cultural–historical theory from Vygotsky, Elkonin and Leontiev in the 20th century to the ground-breaking research of scholars such as Siraj-Blatchford, Kratsova and Hedegaard today. It demonstrates how development and learning are culturally embedded and institutionally defined, and it reflects specifically upon the implications for the early childhood profession.

Divided into parts, with succinct chapters that build upon knowledge progressively, the book discusses the everyday lives of children at home, in the community, at preschool and at school in the context of child development and pedagogy. The book explicitly problematises the foundations of early childhood education, inviting postgraduates, researchers and academics to drill down into specific areas of international discourse, and extending upper-level undergraduates beyond the fundamental underpinnings of their learning. Ultimately *Early Learning and Development* offers new models of 'conceptual play' practice and theory within a globally resonant, cultural–historical framework.

Marilyn Fleer MEd, MA (Science and Technology), PhD (Philosophy/Education) holds the Foundation Chair of Early Childhood Education at Monash University, Australia, and is the President of the International Society of Cultural Activity Research (ISCAR). Her research interests focus on early years learning and development, with special attention to pedagogy, culture, science and technology. More recently she has investigated child development in the contexts of home and school.

Early Learning and Development

Cultural–historical concepts in play

Marilyn Fleer

CAMBRIDGE
UNIVERSITY PRESS

CAMBRIDGE UNIVERSITY PRESS
Cambridge, New York, Melbourne, Madrid, Cape Town, Singapore,
São Paulo, Delhi, Dubai, Tokyo

Cambridge University Press
477 Williamstown Road, Port Melbourne, VIC 3207, Australia

Published in the United States of America by Cambridge University Press, New York

www.cambridge.org
Information on this title: www.cambridge.org/9780521122658

First published 2010

Cover design by Sardine Design.
Typeset by Aptara Corp.
Printed in Australia by Ligare Pty Ltd.

A catalogue record for this publication is available from the British Library

National Library of Australia Cataloguing in Publication data
Fleer, Marilyn.
Early learning and development : cultural–historical concepts in play / Marilyn Fleer.
9780521122658 (pbk.)
Includes index.
Bibliography.
Child development.
Early childhood education.
Play.
372.21

ISBN 978-0-521-12265-8 Paperback

This book is dedicated to my late father, Franz Johannes Fleer
1931–2008.

Foreword

IN THE FIELD of early childhood education, one is presented with a dilemma – whether to guide and educate young children in relation to already established values or whether to give children room to become people in their own right. How do we engage and orient children towards the world through play activity? Fleer confronts this dilemma by drawing on the cultural–historical research tradition evolved from Vygotsky's theory and shows a way forward, a way, although rather complex, that views the child as both engaged and self-initiating, while at the same time as part of a collective cultural tradition. This dilemma starts the moment the child is born.

When, in the early 1970s, I was a newly educated researcher in developmental psychology and had had my first child, what do you think came to mind? To document the child's development, of course. I was inspired by several great men in child psychology. In the 1970s infant research started to show that babies were more competent than had been previously conceptualised in child psychology (Bruner 1968, 1999). This work inspired me, so together with a more experienced colleague, I decided to make a video of my first child from six weeks onwards and to follow him over the next two years. My colleague was a professor and an experienced clinical child psychologist. She suggested using tasks from Cattell's Infant Intelligence Scale to interact with my young son. I agreed. At that time video was a rather new tool for doing research, so we asked the technicians at the department of psychology to help us.

The first day of video recording came and I arrived with my son. Video technique did not always function well in those days, so it took some time to become organised. I waited in my lab with my son. After a while he started to become a little fussy looking at the bright light that was needed to make the recordings. Finally, we could start. He had to follow different objects with his eyes, react to different sounds by turning his head, and so forth. My son did not focus well on these tasks, rather, he was more interested in his mother. Consequently, I had to turn him so that his back was to me to help him become more attentive to the tasks. When we got through the testing I was exhausted and the child was tired. The next day my colleague came with a smile and told me the IQ of my six week old child. I was so amazed that she had scored the tasks, as I had never for one moment thought this was the aim. I was upset because I did not want to reduce the activity we had videoed to a score; for me, it was the child's competence to act as a six-week-old that was interesting.

I looked closely at the video material, and made a qualitative description of all the activities he was involved in, and noted what he was oriented towards. It was easy to see that the child oriented himself towards the light, was interested in his mother, and followed the technician and the tester as they moved around. But the objects the mother showed him did not catch the same interest. To get him to concentrate in the test setting we gave him a pacifier, but then he concentrated on sucking and not on the tester and her tasks. In this research situation what I came to realise was that I had entered naively into a scientific tradition in which one thinks that one can find the child's biological capacities as objective entities. This event was the fuel that made me orient my approach as a researcher in developmental psychology to the child's perspective, and to the theoretical writings of Vygotsky, who provided a framework for orienting research and education towards the complexity of the child's social situation. This situation involves more than just looking at the child; it also seeks to examine how one enters into an evaluation of the conditions that are expressed through the child's activity, conditions that are both cultural and historical. I dropped the idea of recording my son's development of competences and instead started to orient my research towards the everyday life activities of small children and their social and material conditions. I find the same spirit in Fleer's approach and theoretical discussion throughout this book.

Vygotsky's theory encompasses an educational and a wholeness perspective on children's development. It includes the complexity of children in their everyday life activities and how caregivers enter into a relationship with children to create children's developmental life course. Every caregiver, whether a parent or educational professional, enters into this complexity because they are motivated to do a good job. As a parent one wants the best for one's children; as a pedagogue or teacher one also wants the best for the children in one's care. To do one's best is not easy. Parents and caregivers take over procedures developed by an earlier generation and modify them in relation to the demands of the institutions and society they live in today. To create a quality educational experience is not so simple that it can be reduced to scientific or educational procedures. It implies an understanding of the social situation of the child as well as how this social situation is nested in traditions with different values of what education should provide and what knowledge is. The aim of educational science is to explicate and to modify accepted procedures and create new procedures and tools in the form of models of what can contribute to children's development and models of what is high-quality education. Fleer enters into this complexity with her discussions of valued curriculum concepts in early childhood education and of how the goal of education has to be related to what is seen as valuable forms of thinking and knowledge. Based on these discussions she provides models of good education that build on a conceptualisation of child development as an integrated whole.

Vygotsky argued for a wholeness approach in research and education of children (Vygotsky 1998; Hedegaard & Fleer 2008), an approach that researchers and educators have to take seriously if they want to better understand and provide a fuller, more encompassing support for children's development in relation to UNESCO's stated goals about children's rights. This implies that the child's relation to other people, the material world, community cultures and societal traditions should be included in an early childhood approach to education. The whole – the individual and the collective – has to be conceptualised together. Instead of building knowledge up from small building block, Fleer advocates that educators have to enter into the complexity of combining young children's everyday life with theoretical concepts to create conceptual models that can guide their interaction. It is valuable that she takes the child's as well as the teacher's perspective in this discussion, and in so doing thereby makes a contribution to education that brings the phenomenological understanding of the subject's orientation in the world into the cultural–historical tradition and surpasses the sometimes too functional view on Vygotsky's work, which she also criticises, an approach Vygotsky started himself by introducing the concept of the child's 'social situation of development' (1998), a concept he did not develop effectively because of his untimely death.

It is due time to start to conceptualise early childhood education from a wholeness perspective (Chaiklin & Hedegaard 2008). It is clearly evident that national boards for planning early childhood education conceptualise upbringing of children within institutions earlier and earlier. As more and more women enter the workforce an increased demand for childcare becomes evident. Significantly, most people in industrial and information societies conceptualise child development not as an unfolding event that refines inborn capacities, but rather as an appropriation and recreation of cultural competences that are social, emotional and cognitive. As such, upbringing and the education of young children has to transcend parents' responsibility and become a societal demand for education. Approaches to this problem have tended to move school education to earlier ages so that children start their formal educational experience younger and younger. This is reflected in research about literacy and maths learning in early ages and in curriculum plans in maths and literacy for younger children. To take the existing ideas and methods from school education into early childhood education the way it has been created for older children will be damaging for these young children. This generation who now starts in preschool and kindergarten will not get the possibility for exploring the world and social relations in play if these activities are not supported through the curriculum. When young children do not have the possibility to play and instead are expected to follow a kind of early school curriculum that focuses on learning for the acquisition of competences, it creates problems for them. The logic of what is important for young children to learn needs to be analysed. Instead of school teaching being pressed downwards to younger ages, the emotional and creative aspects of children's competence, so important for their development of social and cognitive competence, should be emphasised, yet this has long been forgotten and it is this that Fleer is up against.

Fleer gives solutions for these problems in advocating for a play approach to early childhood education. She advocates for educators to reflect on the education and knowledge they provide for young children and recommends that this should be different from the institutionalised curriculum of school. She gives us ideas that draw upon a newer version of the cultural–historical approach to play-based curriculum for how one can create educational approaches that build on play. Education creates the conditions for young children to orient themselves to the emotional and creative aspects of activities, elements that are central for the development of young children's social and cognitive competences.

I hope the richness in this book will lead to discussion of early childhood education both in scientific and educational communities as well as becoming a tool for educators for solving problems of education of young children.

Professor Mariane Hedegaard
University of Copenhagen, Denmark
2009

Contents

List of figures

List of tables

Acknowledgements

V ALUABLE FEEDBACK on the early versions of this manuscript were provided by Professor Joy Cullen, Dr Suzy Edwards, Liang Li and Dr Peter deVries. Their insights, which led to improving the quality of the book, are greatly appreciated.

Monash University support over two sabbaticals and an untiring belief in the importance of early childhood education made this ambitious project achievable. I am particularly indebted to Professor Sue Willis and Peter Lawford for providing the kind of leadership that supports research and scholarship within the Faculty of Education. I am also incredibly grateful to Carolyn Nye and Amanda Banks for generating a working context at Peninsula campus that makes undertaking enormous and intellectually demanding tasks doable. The expertise provided by Draga Tomas in laying out the manuscript is very much appreciated.

I wish to also acknowledge the mentoring received from international scholars who have come to Monash to work with me and my colleagues on important concepts for progressing thinking about learning and development: they are Professors Anne Edwards, Seth Chaiklin, Elena Kravtsova, Gennady Kravtsov, but particularly Professor Mariane Hedegaard, who has generously supported my learning through a range of writing projects and our joint research endeavour. Her wise counsel on many occasions, so kindly offered, has accelerated and improved my own work.

Last, but not least, the commissioning editor, Debbie Lee, who has been extremely helpful and so very easy to work with over the duration of the development of the proposal and the manuscript. Her support enabled this manuscript to become published.

Contributions to specific chapters and sections are also acknowledged and detailed below.

PARTS 1 AND 2

An Australian Research Council (Discovery) grant funded the research which has been drawn upon to build the arguments presented in the chapters that make up Parts 1 and 2 of this book. Dick Gunstone was the co-researcher named on the application. Avis Ridgway made an enormous contribution to the project by acting as the main field officer in the research project. Carol Fleer provided specialist expertise to the project through transcribing video and audiotapes. The time given by the preschool staff, children and their families is also acknowledged. The results of this research are reported in M. Fleer (2009); understanding the dialectical relations between everyday concepts and scientific concepts within play-based programs are reported in *Research in Science Education*, 39(2), 281–306 and supporting conceptual consciousness or learning in a roundabout way in *International Journal of Science Education*, 31(8), 1069–90.

CHAPTER 3

The Department of Education, Employment and Workplace Relations provided funding for the development of a set of early learning resources that are cited in this chapter. Consortium leaders were Professor Bridie Raban and myself. It was through this project that it was possible to undertake some fundamental research in numeracy, and into conceptual understandings of literacy and numeracy by staff. The overall results and theorisation are reported in M. Fleer and B. Raban (2007); early childhood literacy and numeracy in *Building Good Practice*, Canberra: Early Childhood Australia; and in M. Fleer and B. Raban (2006), A cultural–historical analysis of concept formation in early education settings: Conceptual consciousness for the child or only the adult? *European Early Childhood Education Research Journal*, 14(2), 69–80.

PART 3

The prestigious Margaret Trembath Research Scholarship fund provided financial assistance for the research reported in the chapters in Part 3. Gloria Quinones provided invaluable support to this project by accompanying me on all field trips to the family home and in videotaping most of the school and centre observations. Carol Fleer has supported this project by assisting with downloading tapes and undertaking some transcriptions of the video clips. The methodological approach to the coding was conceptualised by Professor Mariane Hedegaard, and is reported in M. Hedegaard and M. Fleer (2008), *Study Children: A cultural–historical approach to research*, Berkshire: Open University Press. The findings of the study are reported in M. Fleer and M. Hedegaard (forthcoming), Development as participation in everyday activities across different institutions: A child's changing relations to reality, *Mind, Culture and Activity*.

CHAPTER 13

Some sections of this chapter make reference to data from research reported in M. Fleer and C. Richardson (2009), Cultural–historical assessment: Mapping the transformation of understanding. In A. Anning, J. Cullen and M. Fleer (eds), *Early Childhood Education. Society and culture* (2nd edn), London: Sage, pp. 130–44, and M. Fleer and C. Richardson (2003), Collective mediated assessment: Moving towards a sociocultural approach to assessing children's learning, *Journal of Australian Research in Early Childhood Education*, 10(1), pp. 41–55 and S. Farquhar and M. Fleer (2007), Developmental colonisation of early childhood education in Aotearoa/New Zealand and Australia, In L. Keesing-Styles and H. Hedges, *Theorising Early Childhood Practice. Merging dialogues*, Castle Hill: Pademelon Press, pp. 27–50.

Part 1
Learning and development in play

1

A political–pedagogical landscape

Society and its institutions are not stable, unchanging structures. Emerging economic, political and cultural changes modify the ways people act and interact, and these changes also may have significant influences on human cultural development. However, the influence of changing societal structures on human activity and development is not a deterministic process. It depends on how these changes are perceived and how people cope with them. The recent transition of the global society into a knowledge economy is changing people's interactions, including their expectations, and the demands that are made on people.

(van Oers, 2009: 213)

INTRODUCTION

Over the past 10 years there has been unprecedented research interest in early childhood education around the globe. Longstanding and recent economic arguments (e.g., Heckman & Masterov, 2007; McCain & Mustard, 1999, 2002) have caught the eye of policy and departmental administrators in many countries. Economic arguments have centred on the rates of return in relation to investment in education. Age has become an important criterion in the investment analysis, with early education, particularly for the disadvantaged (usually defined as a low socioeconomic community), yielding the best economic returns for a society (see Heckman & Masterov, 2007). At the same time, research from neuroscience has made concrete (e.g., National Research Council and Institute of Medicine, 2000; Shore, 1997) what early childhood educators have known through their own research and practice for over a 100 years: that a quality early childhood experience for a child has a profound effect upon the child's schooling outcomes (Belfield, Nores, Barnett & Schweinhart, 2005; Sylva et al., 2004; Wylie & Thompson, 2003; Wylie et al., 2006) and their later life chances (Mitchell, Wylie & Carr, 2008; Schweinhart & Weikart, 1997, 1998, 1999; Schweinhart, Weikart & Larner, 1986). Although early childhood specialists have not been accorded Nobel prize status for their pedagogical and family-centred work, economic analyses have been more effective in getting the community to sit up and take notice (see Heckman & Masterov, 2007), and these latter arguments have been most influential in framing international reviews of early childhood care and education policy and in shaping country directions (e.g., Mitchell, Wylie & Carr, 2008; National Research Council, 2001; OECD 2006). These are important and significant changes in the political landscape of the global early childhood education community.

In this book the changing political context of early childhood education is acknowledged, but the evidence base from a pedagogical, rather than an economic, perspective is re-examined. The recently introduced concept of **sustained shared thinking** (Siraj-Blatchford, 2007) is discussed in relation to Vygotsky's (1987a) theoretical writings on everyday concepts and scientific concepts (both of which will be discussed in full later in this chapter and throughout this book). It is argued that knowing about sustained shared thinking is not enough and efforts directed to this area (Siraj-Blatchford & Manni, 2008; Siraj-Blatchford & Sylva, 2004) begin the important work needed for transforming pedagogy in the early years (Siraj-Blatchford, 2007). However, a deeper theoretical understanding of concept formation is needed to fully appreciate how the social process of teaching turns everyday practice into the conscious realisation of concepts that children use to transform their everyday lives, an important goal of this book.

In this book the focus is on conceptual development, where the term *concept* includes traditional knowledges formed through discipline or subject matter content. The term *concepts* may also encompass other valued knowledges that are supported through early childhood curriculum (see chapter 4).[1] Throughout this book the theoretical ideas build into a model of pedagogy for concept formation within play-based settings. Through a deeper theoretical discussion of key concepts in early childhood education, this book strives to reclaim the early childhood territory and provide a pedagogical discourse for navigating our way through the contemporary political landscape. It also makes explicit the core concepts in pedagogy, which empirical evidence has shown to make a difference to children's learning. Empirical material is used to show how concept formation occurs in early childhood education. It is argued that the early childhood profession now faces a new political–pedagogical landscape that has foregrounded concept formation and as a profession we must respond by researching and theorising how concept formation occurs within play-based programs. In the OECD report *Starting Strong II* (2006), for instance, the authors have mapped pedagogical practices in relation to political imperatives within particular countries and shown a continuum between social pedagogical approaches and programs that focus on traditional values such as social and emotional development (see chapter 4), and those that focus on school subjects (e.g., literacy and numeracy) termed by the OECD as a preprimary approach. How can early childhood professionals continue to support social outcomes and pedagogy at the same time as realising literacy and numeracy outcomes in the preschool years? Attention will be devoted to this theoretical challenge throughout this book.

MAKING A BIG DIFFERENCE

The increased international attention on early childhood education has proffered a promise of making a difference to the lives of disadvantaged families. For instance, in the OECD (2006) report on early childhood education and care, the authors state that

> Children at risk of educational failure are the object of a variety of policies and programs that seek to address the challenge through early education interventions, and increasingly through a comprehensive service approach focusing on the home and community environments (Haire & Radhakrishnan, 2004; Tremblay et al., 2004)...Children from low socioeconomic status (SES) families are less likely, statistically, to develop the same level of skills and intellectual capital as children from high SES backgrounds. Feinstein (2003) finds, for example, that a 13% difference in cognitive development exits at 22 months of age between British children from high and low SES backgrounds. By the age of 10 years...an average gap of 28% in cognitive development is recorded (p. 34).

Making a difference to the lives of children from low SES families is a significant and important goal for a society to strive for, and a huge responsibility for the early childhood field to shoulder. The relational links between poverty and quality early childhood education established in the research literature provide hope. But these relational links are based on a quality educational program being delivered. It is only in recent times that we have come to appreciate the complexity of what quality early childhood education means (David, 2005; Farquhar, 2003; Urban, 2005) and to begin to determine what are the indicators of quality education (Alton-Lee, 2003; Weber, 2002) that make the biggest difference for preschool-aged children (Siraj-Blatchford, 2009; Siraj-Blatchford & Sylva, 2004; Siraj-Blatchford et al., 2002, 2004).

One of the most significant factors to have been identified in determining quality and in making a big difference to learning for disadvantaged children has been the pedagogical approach of sustained shared thinking in play-based programs (Siraj-Blatchford, 2007). Siraj-Blatchford (2009), Sammons et al. (2002, 2007) and Siraj-Blatchford et al. (2002) have shown in their longitudinal research and case studies that staff with extensive teacher knowledge (as evidenced by tertiary education) produce the highest cognitive outcomes for children. This research has shown that teachers are a significant factor in determining concept formation. Siraj-Blatchford (2009) has identified among other factors that

- effective pedagogues have good curriculum knowledge and child development knowledge
- the most highly qualified staff provide the most direct teaching as well as the kind of interactions that guide but do not dominate children's thinking
- less qualified staff are better pedagogues when supervised and supported by qualified teachers (p. 156).

This work has highlighted 'play-based programs' and the importance of the 'mediating role of the teacher' through generating 'shared sustained conversations' with children (Siraj-Blatchford, 2007). Siraj-Blatchford and Sylva (2004), for instance, suggest that in programs where a balance between teacher-initiated and child-initiated group work and play activities exist, sustained shared thinking involves cognitive construction that has mutual 'understanding of the other' and where learning is achieved through a process of reflexive 'co-construction'. A necessary condition for this would be that both parties 'were *involved*, and, for the resultant learning to be worthwhile, that the content should be in some way *instructive*' (p. 720; emphasis in the original). This research is the single most important contribution to early childhood education reported in the literature in recent years. In introducing the concept of sustained shared thinking, the question that needs to be asked is: sustained shared thinking about what?

Historically, the early childhood profession has been strong on process but weak on articulating (and, indeed, understanding) cognitive content (see Cullen, 1996, 2009; Hedges & Cullen, 2005). Evidence for this has been seen through the numerous critiques of early childhood teachers' knowledge base in a range of learning areas (notably teacher knowledge of concepts), with findings that demonstrate very limited understandings of concepts in science (Appleton, 2006; Traianou, 2006), in literacy (Raban & Ure, 2000), with variability in findings noted for mathematics (Darling-Hammond, 2000) and a correspondingly low level of confidence and limited engagement in programming for these areas (Garbett, 2003). Conceptual knowledge has tended to be strongest in child development knowledge and learning theories, in child and family sociology, and in methodologies associated with child study (Fleer & Raban, 2006). Traditionally, these knowledges have been framed from a maturational perspective, drawing primarily upon traditional psychology to inform their framing (e.g., Blaise, 2009; Dahlberg, Moss & Pence, 1999; Edwards, 2009). Chapter 3 will reconsider these claims and examine the conceptual knowledge of teachers in detail.

WHAT KIND OF PROGRAM PROMOTES SUSTAINED SHARED THINKING?

The second part of Siraj-Blatchford's (2007) statement on what makes the difference to children's learning focuses on the importance of sustained shared thinking occurring in play-based environments. Wood (2008) has suggested that 'the commitment to play in education settings has always been strong on ideology and rhetoric and weak, or at least problematic, in practice' (p. 6). Play has been narrowly theorised as maturational (play as a natural expression of children) (e.g., Bruce, 1991, 1997) or centrally as a pedagogical tool for framing how 'teaching occurs' in early childhood settings (e.g., Brock, 2009). Although a multitude of differing views about what constitutes play and therefore what we mean when we use this term as a pedagogical tool in early childhood education abound in the literature (see Wood & Attfield, 2005), much of this work sits in isolation of concepts or content knowledge. In bringing together sustained shared thinking with play, Siraj-Blatchford (2009) provides a significant relational understanding between pedagogy and content knowledge; this work is much more explicit about teaching than previously discussed in early childhood education. But herein lies an important theoretical problem. In what kind of play-based program does concept formation take place for children? In the following examples taken from a cultural–historical[2] study of concept formation (see Fleer, 2009a, for details of the study design), this theoretical problem is made concrete:

> A group of three girls is inside a wooden boat that is within the outdoor area of a rural preschool located near a fishing port. The teacher and the assistant teacher have been running a preschool program that involves coloured water, plastic containers, tubes, funnels and a series of bottles with pump action dispensers. Many of the children are in the outdoor area funnelling coloured water. The teacher has recorded in her program that she is teaching science using materials that will facilitate potion play. The assistant teacher is inside working with a group of children on an art activity and the teacher is moving equipment around the outdoor area to support the children's potion play. The three girls now move outside of the boat and cluster around a pump action dispenser bottle of red coloured water, several spoons and a soft toy Humpty Dumpty. The girls work together and generate a playscript that calls for them to dispense medicine to the Humpty, who has fallen off the wall.
>
> Jayde takes a lead in the play, initiating the playscript about Humpty Dumpty by announcing 'He [Humpty] fell off the wall again and this is a girl Humpty'. Five girls are now surrounding the soft toy. Chloe responds by picking up Humpty and sitting him on the seat again. She says, 'Humpty fell off the wall again'. Freya moves closer and picks up a spoon, places it under the dispenser of the coloured water bottle and says, 'Wait. I'll spray it. I have to spray it.' She fills the spoon with red liquid from the bottle. Jayde says in response, 'Oh hi, ah, Humpty Dumpty'. Another child joins the group. She says, 'Hello. How are you today?' to no one in particular. All the children look up at her, and then turn back to Humpty Dumpty lying on the seat. Freya passes the spoon to Jayde, saying 'Here you go'. The children dispense a spoon of red liquid to Humpty. Another child moves forward and says, 'Ah, let me see'. She touches Humpty Dumpty's arm and says, 'Touch it here'. Jayde says, 'Yes, he's dead, he's dead. I knew he, he's dead'.

In this particular play scenario the group of children brings together the well-known narrative of 'Humpty Dumpty' with their everyday under-standings of medicine. Their playscript focuses on healing Humpty Dumpty who has fallen off the wall. Potions for these children are not about materials and their properties to be gleaned through mixing (e.g., density of substances, as planned by the teacher), but rather it is about medicine and caring for people in the community. This play example is not illustrative of the conceptual focus in science that the teacher had hoped for or had assumed would be generated through playing with the materials.

In this particular centre, the teacher has a clear view of how learning should be framed for children. She believes that the materials she provides should suggest the play, and therefore generate the learning for children. In the interview she stated:

> There [are] children coming out and in [of play]...when[ever] they want... I really liked the independence... I did not set up one thing... the children did it all themselves... and I was really pleased with that because I just think people set things up too much for the children.
>
> (interview with Teacher A)

The teacher, through providing a range of materials, did seek to generate scientific learning through play. Through organising the theme of potions she provided a range of materials for the children for mixing substances so that they could learn about how materials behave and how they do or do not mix. This was her learning intention. Her pedagogical approach was to allow the materials to do the teaching of the scientific concepts. This is not an unusual view of learning pedagogy in early childhood education, as Siraj-Blatchford (2009) has shown in her research. It is also not unusual in science education, as a discovery learning approach (Karpov, 2003) also seeks to allow children to focus on discovering the learning concepts through 'playing with the materials/equipment'. However, as Vygotsky (1966) has argued, 'It is vital to discover exactly what this activity does for development, that is, how the imaginary situation can assist in the child's development' (p. 9). As hoped by the teacher, the materials scattered around the preschool did indeed suggest possibilities for the children's play. The children generated an imaginary situation in which the spoons and coloured water (potions) were used to medicate Humpty who, of course, kept falling off the wall (as the rhyme suggests) and who required continual medical assistance. The plungers were useful for dispensing medicine, and the coloured water in the bottles was ideal for representing medicine. The children's play did focus on the materials within the bottles, but it did not lead to thinking about mixing the substances.

The play that resulted enabled the children to follow the rules for giving and receiving medicine as the children would have experienced it in their own lives. As Vygotsky (1966) has argued, 'there is no such thing as play without rules and the child's particular attitude toward them' (p. 9). The children used the known narrative of 'Humpty Dumpty' to collectively build the playscript. The addition of the line 'Humpty fell off the wall again' enabled all the children to participate in administering medication. It signalled to all the players that the repetition of medicating Humpty was possible in this game. This additional action statement enabled the play to continue. The additional action statement sat within the predetermined playscript, which was an imitation of administering medicine in everyday life through the imaginary and known rhyme 'Humpty Dumpty'. Clearly, 'Only actions which fit these rules are acceptable to the play situation' (Vygotsky, 1966: 9; see chapter 7 for a fuller discussion of these ideas).

In keeping with the teacher's philosophy, the materials alone provided the stimulus for the play. The children generated their own playscripts, and the teacher did not participate in the children's play. The imaginary situation that resulted enabled the children to explore relevant daily activities through play, as suggested by Vygotsky (1966): 'What passes unnoticed by the child in real life becomes a rule of behavior in play' (p. 9). Through administering medicine the children were coming to understand the actions performed by adults as they give medication to their children. They were consciously exploring the rules of being compliant as you receive your medication, and through this getting better and being ready to fall off the wall again, so that the play could continue. The play activity clearly held, and generated, motives for the children (see chapter 2 for a detailed discussion of motives, imitation and consciousness of concepts through play). It is also a real example of the kind of imaginary play that stems from children's everyday lives, where taking medicine is usually an unpleasant but necessary part of life with rules and expectations that could be imitated by the children in their play. As stated by Vygotsky (1966):

> I think that wherever there is an imaginary situation in play there are rules. Not rules which are formulated in advance and which change during the course of play, but rules stemming from the imaginary situation. Therefore to imagine that a child can behave in an imaginary situation without rules, i.e., as he behaves in a real situation, is simply impossible (p. 10).

The rules of the imaginary situation framed the children's play activity. The narrative did not lend itself to consciously exploring the mixing of substances. Because the teacher's philosophy was framed within a non-interventionist role, it is unlikely that this particular play activity would have moved towards the mixing of substances without new directions being introduced (e.g., This medicine is not working; we need to make our own medicine) (see chapters 3 and 9 for fuller discussion of this idea). The narrative within the play framed what actions were possible for the children, and through following those particular rules of play, the children's thinking was forged in particular directions.

THEORISING CONCEPT FORMATION IN PLAY

This play vignette, as illustrative of the theoretical problem of defining sustained shared thinking in play, can be better understood when we draw upon Vygotsky's (1987a) writings on concept formation and Hedegaard's theory of a double move (see Hedegaard & Chaiklin, 2005). Only a brief discussion is presented here (further discussion occurs in chapters 6 and 7). According to Vygotsky (1987a), concept formation should be thought about at two levels – an everyday level and a scientific[3] or academic level. At the everyday level, concepts are learnt as a result of interacting directly with the world – developing intuitive understandings of how to do things, such as administering medicine or caring for the sick. These are important everyday concepts about how the world works (e.g., its rules, expectations, social roles, etc.). At this level, children may not know the science behind their actions. It is unlikely that, for instance, a four year old child will have knowledge of the biology and chemistry associated with medicines. At the scientific or academic level, Vygotsky (1987a) argued that concepts are introduced to children through some form of instruction, that is, concepts are explicitly examined or taught to children. When these concepts are introduced to children away from their everyday experiences, they are, Vygotsky (1987a) argued, disembedded and hold little meaning for children (see chapter 3).

Vygotsky (1987a) suggested that everyday concepts and scientific concepts should be thought of as being **dialectically**[4] related to each other. Vygotsky (1987a) also argued that everyday contexts lay important foundations for learning scientific or school-based academic concepts. Developing everyday concepts in the context of children's everyday world is important not only for living but also for making sense of scientific ideas. Everyday experiences and the concepts that are learnt through them lay important foundations for scientific learning, in the same way as scientific concepts learned at school pave the way for thinking differently about everyday concepts. However, these two processes must be related. Thinking consciously about scientific concepts, while in an everyday context where important everyday concepts have been learnt, sets up an opportunity for transforming everyday practice.

As shown in the play vignette above, the children were further developing their everyday understandings of medicines and caring. In this example, there was no adult interacting with the children. When the teacher did seek to engage the children in scientific concepts during their play with the potion materials, the children showed no interest:

> The preschool teacher is squatting near the side of the sandpit and is observing two children who are actively playing with the materials that she has provided. The sandpit is located within the outdoor area of the preschool. There is a shelf near the sandpit that contains many different-sized containers. Three materials are provided for the children's use – a tin of shaving cream, a bottle of cooking oil and a bottle of vinegar. A plastic toy oven and stove are positioned next to the sandpit. A tap is nearby. Two children have taken a container from the shelf and have placed it on the cement edge that forms the boundary of the sandpit. Lana picks up the cooking oil bottle and studies it closely. She says, 'There. Baking [inaudible] oil experiment'. Lana takes the cooking oil and her container of water to the centre of the sandpit, where she collects some sand and puts it into her container. She swishes the container around. Molly joins her and watches as Lana adds cooking oil to her mixture. She is using the water, oil, shaving cream and sand to make a milkshake. Lana announces, 'Oh, this is working, babe', returns her container to the edge of the sandpit and immediately begins mixing the substances around with a spoon. She is pretending to be cooking meat.
>
> At this point the teacher enters the play. The teacher invites the children to notice how the sand, water and oil have separated out in the mixture. Each time she does this, the children observe closely and listen carefully, but their responses are in relation to the imaginary situation they have created – cooking meat and making milkshakes.

Over the whole observation Lana stayed focused on cooking her meat. The teacher attempted several times to move Lana and Molly's attention onto the materials. The teacher's initiatives are actively ignored by the children. In their play they have created an imaginary situation. As Vygotsky (1966) argued, 'The child sees one thing but acts different in relation to what he sees. Thus, a situation is reached in which the child begins to act independently of what he sees' (p. 22). Lana saw the materials in relation to cooking meat. While the oil was real and was used in the play for cooking, it was not used to lubricate a frying pan. Rather, the oil was mixed with the water and the shaving cream in a bowl, followed by the

Object		Meaning
(Meaning)	→	(Object)

Figure 1.1 The object–meaning relations

sprinkling in of sand. The sand represented meat to Lana, and this meat had to be cooked.

Similarly, Molly was influenced by the containers and materials provided for framing her play. Molly's mixing container was an old long glass container that had been originally used as the mixing bowl of a food-processor, which are sometimes used for making milkshakes; it is likely that the materials suggested this kind of play to Molly. The white shaving cream, the sand, the oil and the water were useful materials for pretending to make a milkshake. In the play of both children, it is possible to see how 'Action according to rules begins to be determined by ideas and not by objects themselves. This is such a reversal of the child's relationship to the real, immediate, concrete situation that it is hard to evaluate its full significance' (Vygotsky, 1966: 12). Object and meaning become inverted. Vygotsky (1966) has shown this as a fraction, where originally the object dominates in the fraction object–meaning; however, when the meaning dominates, such as when shaving cream becomes milk, the fraction becomes meaning–object.

The object acts as a pivot for meaning. The meaning as signified in the object dominates and determines the behaviour. Vygotsky (1966) states that a contradiction arises 'wherein the child operates with meaning severed from objects and actions, but in real action with real objects he operates with them in fusion' (p. 13). Vygotsky (1966) further argues that this is a transitional phase within play, in which 'situational constraints of early childhood' and thinking are 'totally free of real situations' (p. 13). Importantly, the children's imaginary play could not be penetrated by the teacher. The children respectfully interacted with her, answering her questions occasionally, or looking to what she was pointing at, but their imaginary situation of cooking continued. Once the imaginary situation had been developed by the children, it was difficult for the play to change or for the play to 'turn into an instructional situation' (Vygotsky, 1966: 12). The children would not engage in the concepts that the teacher had predetermined when selecting the materials.

This play vignette suggests that for concept formation to occur in the way that the teacher had intended, a different pedagogical framing was needed. The pedagogical framing needed to link to the concepts and with the children's prior experiences. The pedagogical framing also needed to occur before the children generated their own imaginary situation. A pedagogical problem had arisen: the teacher could not use the children's play to teach them about mixing substances. This is also relevant for the Humpty Dumpty play vignette, as there, too, the imaginary situation generated a narrative that was not related to mixing substances.

Here Hedegaard's work is useful for solving this pedagogical problem. Hedegaard and Chaiklin (2005) suggest that the most powerful learning contexts are those in which the professional keeps in mind the 'everyday context' and the 'concepts' when planning for learning. Hedegaard and Chaiklin (2005) have called this the **double move** in teaching. The double move conceptualises the relations between the child's everyday concepts and the concepts within the subject matter being investigated. Hedegaard (2002) has suggested that in order to transcend the learning experiences organised in classrooms and to connect with children's real world life, teachers need 'to acknowledge the student's personal everyday cognition' as a valuable fund of knowledge for building upon and developing. The challenge for the teacher is 'to create learning activities that connect subject matter knowledge with students' everyday cognition rooted in their activities both within and outside school' (Hedegaard, 2002: 23). School knowledge tends to be static and does 'not open up for a flexible combination and integration with the child's everyday concepts' (Hedegaard, 2002: 33). Hedegaard (2002) states that invariably learning experiences are grouped into disparate categories that belong to school subjects, and other learning is grouped as everyday experience. When everyday learning and schooled learning are kept separate children do not gain insights into how different forms of learning are connected. Rather, children 'appropriate knowledge of facts within different subject areas which are difficult to relate to one another' (Hedegaard, 2002: 33).

One of the challenges of traditional approaches to school knowledge is that 'the concept and context of school are not relevant for social practice outside school' (p. 51). How, for instance, can subject matter knowledge, with its long tradition within disciplines, be made relevant to young children in preschools and schools? A skilful teacher works with knowledge of the concepts and the everyday practices of the children. In introducing the concept of a double move in teaching, the school subject knowledge (scientific concept formation) and the importance of everyday cognition (everyday concept formation) become explicit in the teacher's mind. Hedegaard and Chaiklin (2005) realise Vygotsky's distinction between everyday concepts and scientific concepts through the double move and extend his theorisation by drawing upon Davydov's theoretical and pedagogical writings (see chapters 7 and 8), and note the importance of everyday life in home and community. Through the double move the teacher creates a teaching situation that is both engaging for children and situated within meaningful problem contexts. In expanding upon Hedegaard's work for preschool-aged children, I would argue that what is needed in play-based programs is a conceptual and a contextual intersubjectivity between the children and the teacher. When teachers wish to use play as a pedagogical tool for exploring or introducing particular concepts, then it becomes important for the teacher to first consider the everyday concepts that children have developed or are currently imitating through their play (e.g., administering medicines) and to think about the scientific concepts they want to introduce, that is, the teacher attains a level of psychological intersubjectivity with the children. The teacher can then consider what might be a motivating activity to conceptually engage the children to explore the scientific concept. As suggested previously, the teacher could generate an imaginary situation, such as, 'The medicine is not working on Humpty Dumpty. Let's research what we need to do and make our own. We have to know about mixing medicines (substances). What can we find out?' In this theorisation, we note that the children and the teacher can enact new practices together through play because they have achieved conceptual and contextual intersubjectivity. When intersubjectivity occurs (see chapter 6 for a successful example), it is possible for the teacher to move in and out of the imaginary situation. At these times, that teacher can engage in sustained shared thinking (Siraj-Blatchford, 2004) with children. This intersubjectivity between the child and the teacher forms part of what Kravtsova (2009a) has termed *Obshchenie* (see chapter 14). This theorisation can be considered as a model (see figure 1.2) and this helps explain how sustained shared thinking is possible in some contexts and not in others.

This model also makes explicit the role of the teacher in play when sustained shared thinking is desired or when new concepts are being introduced by the teacher. This model is not necessarily relevant for other forms of development, forms that result from valuable play that is focused only on the children's play agenda. This latter idea is discussed further in chapter 8.

In the Humpty and cooking vignettes, if the teacher had pedagogically framed the introduction of the materials with a particular purpose rather than letting the children work it out for themselves, the children would have been more focused on the intentions of the learning activity. The

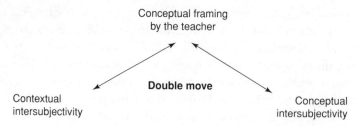

Figure 1.2 A pedagogical model for conceptual and contextual intersubjectivity during play

children would have been more receptive to the teacher entering their play. It is possible, then, that the children would have been more likely to allow the teacher to work with them on their project and they would have been more conceptually focused on the concepts that were being promoted through the play material. It should be noted though that the play episodes were valuable in their own right and are only viewed as problematic if the teacher believes she is using play as a pedagogical approach for concept formation in particular learning areas, such as science. In the next chapters, these ideas are considered further.

In Western communities we have assumed that the dominant activity of preschool children is play, but we have not clearly explicated what is meant when we use play as a pedagogical tool for supporting conceptual learning. The analysis of the play vignettes points to the problems that arise because we have not had a sufficiently robust understanding of the conceptual development of children during play or a theoretical model to explain conceptual development during play. It also demonstrates the significance of the relations between the mediating role of the teacher and the child's lived social world. When the teacher has a theoretical model for bringing together contexts and concepts, as shown in figure 1.2, it is possible for conceptual and contextual intersubjectivity to occur and greater insights into how sustained shared thinking happens during play (Siraj-Blatchford, 2007). The field of the teacher and the field of the child are foregrounded as a dialectical relationship, that is, it is not possible to consider the concept of 'a student' unless we have a teacher. Similarly, we cannot have the concept of 'a teacher' if we do not have students. They are two sides of the same coin. When the field of the teacher and the field of the child are added to figure 1.2, metaphorically, the child becomes one side of a coin, the teacher the other (see figure 1.3). They are dialectically related to each other. In contrast, Cartesian logic tends to focus on the inside of a person (i.e., the head) and outside of the person (i.e., the body

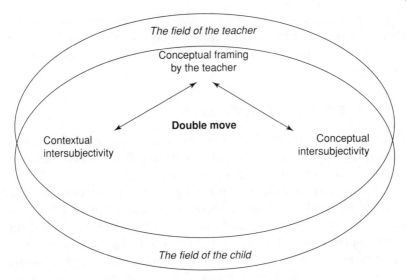

Figure 1.3 A dialectical model of conceptual and contextual intersubjectivity during play

acting on the social and material world). The mind–body split tends to separate out those features that dialectical logic assumes are acting in unity.

This new theorisation for pedagogically framing play enables teachers to more purposefully understand how play as a leading activity in European heritage communities leads to conceptual development in preschool aged children. Through this model we have a theoretically better understanding of how particular forms of pedagogy in early childhood education actually make the difference to children's school learning and life long opportunities, which were discussed at the beginning of this chapter. This pedagogical insight is much more theoretically and practically useful for explaining what makes the big difference in children's learning in early childhood settings. This model also positions early childhood professionals as having expert pedagogical and conceptual knowledge, rather than simply being variables in the discourse on economic returns for investing in the early years. The model presented here (figure 1.3) will build over subsequent chapters in this book (chapters 2–9).

SUMMARY

In this chapter the aim of the book was discussed in relation to a play vignette and a rudimentary model for theorising concept formation in play-based programs. Many early childhood professionals are currently working in contexts in which concept formation is highly valued; however, little guidance is available to support teachers working towards these new societal goals.

BOOK OVERVIEW

Throughout the first part of the book, learning and development in play is discussed, and the pedagogical practices that bring about concept formation in play-based settings are foregrounded.

In the second part of the book, play programs developed across countries that draw upon cultural–historical theory are presented. Cultural–historical theories of play are discussed in the context of those programs that deliberately support concept formation in play. The pedagogical model introduced in the first part of the book will be expanded in chapter 8, where the concept of conceptual play is introduced. In that chapter, the significance of imagination is foregrounded and new theoretical ideas, which support early childhood teachers in building concept formation through play, are presented.

In the final part of the book, the theoretical lens is broadened from concept formation in play to a cultural–historical discussion of child development. Cultural diversity is foregrounded in order to move beyond the existing colonising effect of traditional views of child learning and development. The book concludes with a discussion on the politics of knowledge and offers a new theory for early childhood pedagogy in which concept formation for young children is the focus of attention.

NOTES

1   The term *concept* should not be confused with teacher knowledge of concepts such as fine and gross motor development. Teacher understanding of fine and gross motor development represents conceptual knowledge. At the level of the child, this would be motor skill development and not conceptual development by the child.

2   The term *cultural–historical* has been used rather than *sociocultural*, because this term more accurately describes the body of literature that has been drawn upon to theorise play, learning and development; see also Hedegaard (1999) for an explanation of these two terms.

3   Note that Vygotsky used the term *scientific concept*. It does not simply mean concepts in science, but rather it captures a mature, disembedded concept found across disciplines, such as the arts, history, mathematics, literacy, etc. I have chosen to use Vygotsky's terminology of scientific concepts as I want to position concept formation in early childhood education discourse as a scientific endeavour and not to dumb down the

language of the profession, with the concomitant effect of reducing its status. The theoretical work being discussed in this book on concept formation within early childhood education should be located within the broader research and theoretical writing; the terminology used should reflect this.

4   *Dialectical logic* is used throughout this book but is not defined here because it would distract the reader from the focus of the book. But a definition that outlines how the term is interpreted and used in this book can be found in the glossary.

2 | Parallel conceptual worlds

When we say the child acts on the basis of imitation, we do not mean that he looks another person in the eye and imitates him. If today I see something and tomorrow do it, I do it on the basis of imitation. When the school child solves a problem at home on the basis of a model that he has been shown in class, he continues to act in collaboration, though at the moment the teacher is not standing near him. From a psychological perspective, the solution of the second problem is similar to this solution of a problem at home. It is a solution accomplished with the teachers help. This help – this aspect of collaboration – is invisibly present. It is contained in what looks from the outside like the child's independent solution of the problem.

(Vygotsky, 1987b: 216)

INTRODUCTION

Vygotsky (1966) put forward a dialectical view of play in which psychological functioning and external activity mutually constituted each other. Contrary to popular belief, he argued against an intellectualisation of the concept of play, but suggested that the cognitive dimensions of play could not be separated out from the affective dimensions of play (see also Levykh, 2008 for a related discussion of emotions and the Zone of Proximal Development – ZPD). He also argued that development in play could not be removed from the relations between internal psychological functioning and external activity. This dialectical approach to play provides an important alternative reading of play that goes beyond the dualism of a natural developmental view or a purely intentional educational play pedagogy (Wood, 2008).

In this chapter a theoretical discussion of play as a leading activity for European heritage children will be given (see also Kravtsov, 2008a, Kravtsova, 2008a). In line with Vygotsky's theoretical writings, this chapter uses dialectical logic to explicate play activity in relation to psychological functioning and pedagogical practices within play-based settings. The psychological concepts of 'motives' (Hedegaard, 2002; Kravtsov, 2009a; Leontiev, 1978), 'imitation' (Vygotsky, 1987b) and 'consciousness' (Vygotsky, 1966; 1997a) are viewed as foundational for understanding play activity; they are discussed in full in this chapter. These concepts should not be read from a maturational view of play, such as that put forward by Parten (1932, 1933), in which children progress in play complexity in relation to stages of development, such as from solitary play through to social pretend play. Rather a different view of play is featured in which dialectical logic is used.

The concepts of motives, imitation and consciousness will be discussed in the context of the play vignettes introduced in chapter 1, and through this a dialectical understanding of play will be outlined for play pedagogy in early childhood education. It is through this new view of play that it is possible to see how concepts are enacted through play.

IMITATION AND MOTIVES

One of the defining features of Vygotsky's theoretical position focuses on the significance of the social context. Vygotsky and Luria (1994) argued that 'Social forms of behaviour are more complicated and are in advance in their development in the child' (p. 153), that is, children engage in activities within their social world and through this interaction work collectively with others, often above what they could do independently. What is less well understood is that Vygotsky and Luria (1994) also argued that when these activities 'become individual, they are "lowered" and begin to function according to simpler laws' (p. 153). The concept of imitation is important here for understanding how this may be possible. Vygotsky (1998b) had a particular view of this concept, arguing not for an everyday reading of this term, but rather a specific psychological view that saw children 'socially primed to pay attention' to particular activities in their social world.

> Speaking of imitation, we do not have in mind a mechanical, automatic thoughtless imitation but sensible imitation based on understanding the imitative carrying out of some intellectual operation . . . Everything that the

child cannot do independently, but which he can be taught or which he can do with direction or cooperation or with the help of leading questions, we will include in the sphere of imitation.

(Vygotsky, 1998b: 202)

For instance, a toddling baby may see adults participating in a game of chess, but it is unlikely that the baby will focus its attention on the game of chess. The baby cannot imitate the actions of the adults moving chess pieces across a board. We are more likely to see a toddling baby holding a play spoon, offering food to another child or to a doll. The toddling baby has engaged in the process of being fed, something that is meaningful and contains particular social rules for eating. The baby imitates these socially meaningful actions knowing that the spoon and the doll are toys. As the baby experiences more over time the rules expand, so that feeding a toy doll now involves seating the doll, putting on a bib and having a cloth ready to wipe the doll's mouth. These social acts are significant in a family's everyday life and, as such, are the actions that a baby or young toddler will pay attention to. Vygotsky (1966) argued that, initially, imitation of this kind occurs without conscious realisations of the caring concepts that are associated with the actions being performed. The baby is operating at an interpsychological level only. These playscripts are based on the day-to-day life of the players, and it is only with older children that we observe the players engaged in more complexity, such as preparing the baby food or soothing the baby prior to feeding the doll – exhibiting intrapsychological functioning (Vygotsky, 1997b) of caring. Vygotsky (1966) argued that, initially, children imitate familiar and important activities, and through imitative action in play generate a motive for playing with these actions to generate deeper social meaning about the rules that frame the play (and their social world).

Considering the concept of imitation is not enough for understanding what occurs in play or how the play supports children's development. The concept of motives is important here and is dialectically related to imitation in play. Leontiev (1978) argued that

the object of an activity is its true motive. It is understood that the motive may be either material or ideal, either present in perception or existing only in the imagination or in thought. The main thing is that behind activity there should always be a need, that it should always answer one need or another.

(Leontiev, 1978: 62)

Leontiev (1978) suggested that in Vygotsky's general collective meaning of activity, researchers must consider specific activities 'each of which answers a definite need of the subject, is directed toward an object of this need, is extinguished as a result of its satisfaction, and is produced again perhaps in other, altogether changed conditions' (p. 62). The central idea in Leontiev's theory is that every activity is driven by distinct motives and these motives do not arise from within, but rather are the objects of the material world. Stetsenko and Arievitch (2004) argue that what Leontiev 'wanted to achieve by introducing the notion of object–motive was to convey the idea that human activities are always driven by something objectively existing in the world, rather than by some event and occurrence in the hidden realm of mental processes or human souls' (p. 482). As such, motives are socially produced within the human world and 'an individual activity bears the birthmarks of and reflects these collaborative practices, never becoming completely isolated from the social processes that give rise to it' (Stetsenko & Arievitch, 2004: 487). Stetsenko and Arievitch (2004) suggest that although the positioning of motives outside individuals seems counterintuitive, it is nevertheless a central and important concept in cultural–historical theory. As children grow they 'increasingly enter into connection with historically established human experience, and come to know objective reality with increasing breadth and depth' (Leontiev & Luria, 2005: 47).

If we return to the chess example, an older child may observe this activity and note that this is a valued family activity. The older child will notice what the baby does not, that there are particular actions governed by rules for playing chess. Through repeated viewings of chess in action, this experience has the potential to generate a motive for being a chess player (Leontiev, 1978). Imitation of chess play (without understanding the rules) is now possible. The motive in play is an important concept for understanding imitation in play activity. Motive defined in this way – as something generated through observing or participating in an activity, rather than as something that comes solely from within, is a powerful concept for understanding play. However, this theorisation does not take account of the child's perspective.

The child's perspective is evident in the theoretical writings of Elkonin (1999a–e). Elkonin (1999a), in returning to Vygotsky's original theorisation of activity, foregrounds the importance of the dialectical relations between the child and the object through the social. In particular, children's changing relations to their environment is foregrounded. The toddling baby, for instance, is oriented towards a spoon (object) and eating (social).

As the toddler gains more experience of the world, the child moves from a focus on eating implements (object) to how the objects are associated with caring activities in the preparation of meal times (social), thus making central the child's changing view of reality (and the objects). Children's theorisation of motives makes visible their perspective within the child–social–object relations, and is helpful for gaining a deeper understanding of children's lived world and their relation to it. Veresov (2006) suggests that in this theorisation, Vygotsky's concept of the social situation of development must be foregrounded (see Part 3 for further details of this concept):

> Vygotsky speaks here not of activity, let alone leading activity, but precisely of the *relations **between** the child and his social environment* . . . the latter is a form of relations of the child **and** society. The difference in contexts here is that while for Vygotsky the social situation of development is characterized by a definite leading type of relations between the child and social environment, for Leontiev a leading activity is a 'relation of the child **to** reality' . . . Through the child's changing relations to reality, the child acquires a 'qualitatively new *space of possibilities*'.
> (Veresov, 2006: 15, 22; emphasis added; Veresov's emphasis in bold)

Imitation and motives as concepts are important for theorising play and for explaining how particular play activity is generated and sustained. Motives as a psychological concept for understanding play provides an important direction for early childhood professionals interested in consciously considering how play influences children's development.

CONSCIOUSNESS OF CONCEPTS THROUGH PLAY ACTIVITY

In returning to the less well known position put forward by Vygotsky (1966) of when something becomes individual it is psychologically lowered, we can see that 'The presence of such generalised affects in play does not mean that the child himself understands the motives which give rise to the games or that he does it consciously' (p. 8). Consciousness as discussed by Vygotsky (1966) in relation to play is a very important concept. First, Vygotsky (1966) argued that consciousness 'originally arises from action' (pp. 7–8). Action is defined as someone being a participant in everyday life or through the child's imitation of everyday activities. As stated earlier, Vygotsky (1966) argued that 'What passes unnoticed by the child in real life becomes a rule of behavior in play' (p. 9). This is one of the most important ideas in Vygotsky's writings on play. In discussing a study by Scully, Vygotsky (1966) gives the example of two children who in real life are sisters and who pretend to be sisters in their play. In order to play at being sisters they must follow the rules of how sisters interact together and through this they make conscious the concept of sisterhood.

Vygotsky (1966) suggests that 'there is no such thing as play without rules and the child's particular attitude toward them' (p. 9) and only 'actions which fit these rules are acceptable to the play situation' (p. 9). Empirical evidence to support this can be found in recent contemporary research. In studies between visually impaired and sighted preschool children at play, Janson (2008) noted that sighted players became frustrated when blind children positioned themselves inaccurately within the play space or when their playscripts did not follow the expected social conventions, that is, the visually impaired children in their play did not follow the rules and conventions found in everyday practice for sighted children. Janson (2008) describes a play episode in which the visually impaired child, Pia, is acting as a train driver. Anna, a sighted child, plays with her. They have arranged a row of chairs to represent the train engine and the carriages. Pia sits in the carriage chairs to drive the train and makes movements with her body and hands to indicate the train motion and the turning on and off of the engine. This causes conflict for Anna, who tries to get her to sit in the first chair (the train engine), where the train driver would normally sit. The play does not progress because there is a difference in shared meaning and cognitive representations. Janson (2008) suggests that two conflicting ideas about what constitutes driving a train emerge, that is, where one is physically positioned matters and how the motion of the train feels is important. 'Anna is governed by a predominantly visual scheme. Driving a train means being placed on the driver's seat . . . to Pia, however, the symbol must preserve the moving sensation. Otherwise she *cannot feel* the train is running' (pp. 115–16; emphasis in original). Janson's (2008) study shows the significance of everyday life for informing play activity and for determining the rules of play: the children were following the rules of everyday life very closely for framing what could or could not occur within the play; their frame of reference was simply different.

As Vygotsky (1966) has noted, children are not free to play in what-ever way they wish. Everyday life determines and frames how play may occur. Shared understandings of these rules in play have been shown to be systematically communicated. Longstanding research has shown how metacommunicative strategies (see Bretherton, 1984) ensure that play

partners build shared intentions during play, and through this play partners add to the evolving playscripts. However, unlike developmental or
maturational theories of play, which would suggest that play is inter-
nally driven, a cultural–historical perspective would show that the rules
of everyday life and the child's experiences of everyday practice shape
how play is enacted (see chapter 9 for more details). Anna experienced
trains visually; Pia through movement and vibrations. 'The reason for this
is not the presence of some "deviant individual", but diversity in information, social perception and representation of everyday reality' (Janson,
2008: 117).

Vygotsky (1966) also argued that children involved in play do not
believe 'the fantasy they create, that would be a delusion' (p. 7), and that
they are strongly grounded in reality, which is contrary to popular opinion
and much writing on play in Western communities (Wood & Attfield,
2005). Evidence for Vygotsky's (1966) claims can be found in contemporary research by Sawyers and Carrick (2008), who argue that because most
research has 'relied exclusively on adults' (parents, teachers, researchers)
interpretations of children's play', some commonly accepted understandings about the nature of play are questionable. In their research into concepts in play, such as themes, roles, object substitution, fantasy/reality, and
pretence, Sawyers and Carrick (2008) videotaped the play of two 4 and
5 year olds each day over a period of four weeks. Using stimulated recall
of selected videoclips, the children were interviewed about the play concepts noted in the literature – themes (Garvey, 1977), roles (Fein, 1981),
object substitutions (Matthews, 1977) and reality/fantasy (Flavell, Flavell
& Green, 1987; Lillard, 1996). The findings problematise widely held
views about the nature of children's play. They state, among other things,
that 'While watching the videotapes of the children, we repeatedly asked
the question, "Who are you pretending to be here?" or "Are you pretending
to be someone?"', and found that, 'Surprisingly, the children most often
replied that they were not pretending to be someone' (p. 147). Sawyers and
Carrick (2008) argue that 'Unlike adults who see all role-playing as pretence, Skeeter and Hannah [children in their study] appear to be making
a distinction depending on the type of role' (p. 148). Further, the children
were consciously engaged in what they were doing: 'by imitating the people
at the ice cream store, she [Hannah] could convey the intent of her play
(serving ice cream), her role (employee), and her friend's role (customer)'
(p. 145). The findings of this study demonstrate that children have a strong
object–motive for imitating everyday life in their play, which supports the

importance of the concepts of imitation, motives and consciousness for studying play activity.

In returning to the play vignettes introduced in chapter 1, it is clear that the everyday life experiences of the children had generated the theme for their play – cooking and medicating. The object–motive in the Humpty Dumpty play was medicating; for the sandpit play it was cooking meat and making milkshakes. In both examples the children were consciously examining the everyday concepts of caring–medicating and cooking and displaying a strong object–motive for imitating everyday life. In most European heritage communities, it is unlikely that four year old children would have the opportunity to actually cook meat, make a milkshake or administer medicine. Observing these activities occurring in their own lives generates a powerful motive for participating in them, and in European heritage communities, this translates into pretending to do these everyday life tasks when at play (Bodrova, 2008). Karpov (2005), in citing Elkonin (1978), states that by the age of three years, children develop a strong interest in the world of social relations.

> The world of adults becomes very attractive for children, and they are looking forward to becoming a part of this world. In industrialised societies, however, children cannot fulfill their desire directly: They cannot be doctors or firefighters, that is why they 'penetrate' the world of adults by imitating and exploring social roles and relations in the course of sociodramatic play, Thus, the motive of sociodramatic play is 'to act like an adult'.
>
> (Elkonin, 1978, pp. 139–40)

With such a strong object–motive for participating in important life events, such as cooking and medicating, it is now easier to understand why the teacher discussed in chapter 1 had difficulty changing the conceptual focus of the children's attention to mixtures and mixing of substances. If we look in detail at the cooking example and study what the teacher said to the children when she entered the play, we can see that the children and the teacher were operating in parallel conceptual worlds, even though they were physically together looking at the same materials. The full details of the play vignette introduced in chapter 1 are analysed here.

LANA   I'm going to mix this . . .
TEACHER Hm–hm.
LANA   . . . all the way to the bottom, to the end.
TEACHER What does it smell like?

LANA   Um, cause I'm making meat.
TEACHER You're making . . . ?
LANA   Meat.
TEACHER Meat. Okay. (*Lana stops mixing and pours in oil*) More oil?

As was intended by the teacher, the children did mix the substances together. To Lana, the oil, the containers, the spoons and the oven close to the sandpit all afforded (Gibson, 1979) an opportunity for cooking. Lana immediately framed her play in this way. She had entered an imaginary world, where the rules of play were determined by what happens in real cooking events. But the teacher had other conceptual intentions in mind. In order to facilitate conceptual learning about mixing and mixtures, the teacher respectfully continues to observe the children and waits for another opportunity in which to enter the children's play so she can draw their attention to the layering of the substances that they are mixing. When Molly finds it difficult to close the lid to the food processor container she is using for her milkshake, the teacher seizes this moment and attempts to enter her play.

TEACHER Ah, that is hard to shut isn't it? (*Molly tries to push down lid*)
MOLLY   Hard to shut.
TEACHER So what are you going to do with it?
MOLLY   Shake it.
TEACHER What can you see Molly? What can you see? (*tilts container*)
MOLLY   Oh, water and oil.
TEACHER What's this at the top? (*Molly looks*) Can you see how something's at the top and there's other stuff at the bottom and then . . . ?
MOLLY   There's oil (*points to top*), there's, um, water (*points to middle*) . . .
TEACHER Yep.
MOLLY   . . . and there's sand (*points to bottom*).
TEACHER Why do you think it does that?
MOLLY   Cause I put it in there; I put them all in there.
TEACHER Yeah, but why do they all stay layered? I thought you shook it?

(*Molly starts shaking the container and does not respond to her question; the container is heavy and she struggles*)

MOLLY   I couldn't shake it properly.
TEACHER You can't shake it properly. Well how about we shake it together? (*shaking together*) Here we go. We're doing really well together, aren't we?

(*Molly and the teacher shake the container while Lana continues to add oil to her mixture*)

LANA   Yeah, we make some more different oil (*she goes to the shelf and oven looking for another container of oil, doesn't find any, so returns to her mixture and continues to add cooking oil to the bowl; the teacher stays focused on Molly's mixture*)

TEACHER Okay, let's have a look at it. (*looks at Molly's container*)

LANA   I make some more different oil. (*adds more oil; no one responds to her*)

TEACHER See, we shook that, didn't we Molly? But it's still the same.

As the teacher now turns her attention to Lana again, Lana says, 'I make some more'. The teacher looks into her bowl and Lana states, 'I make some different oil'. The teacher supports her efforts by saying, 'Okay, you made some different oil'. While Lana continues to mix her substances the teacher asks her about her mixture. As with Molly, Lana ignores the questions and stays focused on her cooking play.

LANA   Put a little bit . . . a little bit more sand (*grabs a handful of sand and puts it into bowl*) little bit, mix it all around (*picks up handful of sand with other hand and puts it into the bowl*). Lots of sand. (*mixes, then picks up oil and pours it into bowl*)

TEACHER A different type of oil.

Lana puts the oil container down and rearranges the containers she has gathered together. She opens up the oil container and adds more oil.

TEACHER (*as she observes Lana*) How come there's all these spots of it? (*points into the sprinkled sand*)

LANA   (*leans forward and looks into bowl*) Oh, cause that's my meat. (*stands up and walks away with oil*)

The strong object–motive for cooking and imitation of important activities in the children's everyday lives kept their conceptual focus of attention on cooking meat and making milkshakes, despite the teacher's attempts to use play as a pedagogical tool for supporting science learning. As is evident in this transcript, Lana concludes her interactions with the teacher by stating, 'Oh, cause that's my meat', despite her persistence in attempting to intervene gently and respectfully into Lana's and Molly's play. This highlights how strong the object–motive is for Lana. Motives, imitation and consciousness of concepts as psychological concepts explain what was occurring within the children's play, and are important theoretical concepts for understanding the relations between play and teaching. Figure 2.1 demonstrates the conceptual problem that arose as a result of the different pathways between the children's play and the teacher's pedagogical

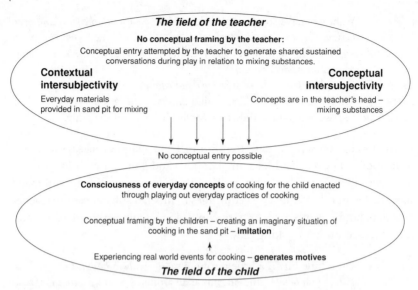

Figure 2.1 Children and teacher operating in parallel conceptual worlds

practice, that is, the teacher could not enter the children's play and focus the children's thinking on mixing substances.

Conceptual entry by the teacher was further complicated by the teacher's confusion about the specific scientific concepts she wanted to introduce to the children. On the final attempt to engage both children in science play, the teacher invited Lana to use the vinegar she had also made available for the children.

TEACHER So you don't want to use the vinegar Lana?
LANA   Yeah. Where's the vinegar? (*stops mixing*)
TEACHER It's over there.
LANA   (*turns and goes and gets a 2 litre plastic container*) Vinegar, vinegar.
TEACHER (*speaking to the research assistant*) Hope this doesn't explode. (*watches as Lana brings a plastic container back to mixing bowl and tries to take off the lid*) I don't know what happens with oil and vinegar. (*laughs*)

Having a clear conceptual view of the type of thinking being promoted through the introduction of the materials is clearly important for how a shared sustained conversation may evolve between a child and a teacher. It is also necessary for the double move (Hedegaard, 2002). Play-based programs have the potential to create contexts in which children's everyday cognition can be expressed, but for these programs to be

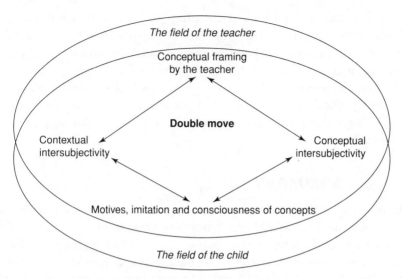

Figure 2.2 A pedagogical model for conceptual and contextual intersubjectivity during play

effective in building conceptual connections between the teacher and the children, pedagogical framing of the materials being provided is essential: play-based programs provide an effective pedagogical mechanism for teachers to simulate the play of everyday activities known and familiar to the children, and useful as sites for introducing concepts. These play events are motivating because children can imitate what matters to them in everyday life. During their play, children express everyday concepts. When teachers pedagogically frame the play through generating an imaginary situation based on knowing children's everyday concepts (conceptual and contextual intersubjectivity has been established by the teacher), they create a shared conceptual space in which sustained shared thinking is possible. It is at these moments within the play that concepts are consciously considered, interrogated and expanded. The children and the teacher are not operating in conceptually parallel worlds, but rather are aligned.

Figure 2.2 expands the model introduced in chapter 1 to include the psychological concepts of motives, imitation and consciousness of concepts within play-based programs. Here the object–motives associated with everyday activity are considered within the model of conceptual and contextual intersubjectivity.

This model is useful for teachers using play as a pedagogical tool for learning concepts. It contains the same elements as figure 2.1, but this model leads to conceptual and contextual intersubjectivity during play, while that shown in figure 2.1 does not allow the teacher to enter the children's imaginary world. Later in this book, this model is discussed further in relation to a study of a teacher who successfully organised learning in ways that foreground conceptual consciousness during play (see chapter 7).

SUMMARY

In this chapter a dialectical understanding of play activity in relation to concept formation was outlined. It was shown how motives, imitation and consciousness of concepts occur during play, and how teachers can draw upon these understandings to build conceptual and contextual intersubjectivity. The chapter also showed the significance of teacher conceptual connectedness with children, and how teachers and children may be operating in parallel conceptual worlds during imaginary play. Through the analysis of play vignettes it was shown how complicated it is to consider the dialectical relations between psychological functioning and pedagogical practice in play-based programs.

3

Teacher beliefs about teaching concepts

This [cultural–historical view] calls for greater involvement of early childhood teachers in children's play than most teachers are used to.

(Bodrova, 2008: 366)

INTRODUCTION

Through theoretical analysis and experimental research, Vygotsky argued that conscious awareness of concepts is only realised within a system that is 'based on specific relations of generality among concepts' (Vygotsky, 1987a: 197, vol. 1). In refuting Piaget's work on spontaneous concept formation, he suggested that the child's lack of awareness of concepts was not as a result of egocentrism, but rather of experimentation framed to remove the systems in which everyday concepts are embedded. He suggested that only within a system can concepts acquire conscious awareness. In the previous chapters, it was shown how important children's everyday conceptual system was as they pretended to cook and administer medicine. The conceptual system is kept intact and promoted through a play-based program.

In the first two chapters the research lens was predominantly on the children's thinking as they played. The children's thinking was analysed in relation to how the play had been pedagogically framed (or not) by the teacher. Through this relational analysis it was possible to show the significance of the teacher's philosophy in affording (or not) sustained shared thinking within the everyday conceptual system that was at the children's disposal (cooking, administering medicine). However, it is not just the children's conceptual system that is of importance here. In a cultural–historical view of learning, we cannot ignore the teacher's pedagogical system: they are dialectically related to each other.

In this chapter the research lens moves to the pedagogical system of teachers and their role in mediating concept formation. The chapter focuses on beliefs about teaching and the role of the teacher in children's learning. Through this, a new understanding of the early childhood professional is built and a theoretically different view of the teacher and teaching is presented.

THE CULTURAL CONSTRUCTION OF TEACHING IN EARLY CHILDHOOD SETTINGS

Goodfellow and Sumsion (2003), in their research into early childhood professional experience, foreground culture and personal beliefs as important dimensions of understanding the practice traditions found within early childhood education. They state that

> teachers' knowledge is situated not only within oneself and within one's practice, but it is also located within the knowledge base and culture of the early childhood teaching profession and, in turn, within the broader socio–cultural–political context.
>
> (Goodfellow & Sumsion, 2003: 68)

In order to understand an individual teacher and the process of teaching we must examine the context of the teacher. Yet to make personal and professional practice visible is not always easy (Schieffelin & Och, 1998). Working across cultures to examine one's own practices has been the subject of research by many scholars (e.g., Tobin, Wu & Davidson, 1998) and through this kind of study 'comparative material can lead us to reinterpret behaviours as cultural that we have assumed to be natural' (Schieffelin & Och, 1998: 50), thus making visible the diversity of practice traditions within early childhood education and teacher beliefs about pedagogy and what is valued knowledge within early childhood education.

In Japan, for instance, there is a strong belief by teachers about the importance of *shuudan seikatsu* (group life) (Holloway & Yamamoto, 2003). Small groups serve a pedagogical function where 'stronger students can help weaker ones' (p. 194). Small groups also provide a motivational function as 'it promotes a feeling of belonging to children and provides a way of encouraging the less motivated students to follow the lead of more motivated group members' (Holloway & Yamamoto, 2003: 194). Holloway and Yamamoto (2003) argue that Japanese educators believe that 'individual-capacity building' and 'group-community building' are complementary. As individuals develop, they are better able to contribute to the functioning of the group. In referring to Peak (1991) they state that the primary goal in the preschools was 'to help children develop the skills necessary for group life. At home, on the other hand, mothers expected children to express child-like dependence (*amae*), and placed little pressure on them to demonstrate mature, restrained behavior' (p. 200). Holloway and Yamamoto also outline that teachers divide large groups into smaller groups, naming these small groups and then referring to the small group rather than an individual. Individual tracking through assessment and testing are discouraged since this would highlight individual performance. Similarly, 'loose participatory control' is used, in which 'they call on children who raise their hands but not on those who do not, and they don't discourage children from making comments that are tangential to the topic'. In addition teachers commonly use a technique known as *idea piling*, 'in which the teacher accepts a "pile" of ideas about a topic, without ever specifying a correct answer', thus concealing the different abilities of children (Holloway & Yamamoto, 2003: 198). This research illustrates how beliefs about knowledge and pedagogy are grounded in societal values. Einardottir (2003) argues that 'raising teachers' awareness of their beliefs is an important aspect in curriculum development and teacher education' (p. 128).

Noticing the traditions of practice for preschool education that are valued within particular communities is the first step in ascertaining teacher beliefs about teaching concepts. What is also important is having the language to name and discuss those practice traditions. Einardottir (2003) notes the difficulty with undertaking this kind of work:

> Because much of what teachers believe about their work is tacit and they do not always possess language with which to describe their beliefs, it can be difficult to discover their beliefs. Direct questions such as: 'What is your philosophy of teaching?' are usually ineffective ways to discover beliefs.
>
> (Einardottir, 2003: 118)

Einardottir (2003) argues that 'the field of early childhood education will benefit from the global perspective attained through continued study of cultural differences among beliefs and practices of teachers around the world' (p. 128–9). This is taken up further in Part 2.

TEACHER BELIEFS ABOUT TEACHING AND LEARNING

As was noted in chapter 2, teacher belief about how young children learn has a strong bearing upon the type and amount of conceptual learning that is possible, as was evident in the cooking meat example (see Fleer, 2009b). When the teaching philosophy foregrounds materials and backgrounds the teacher's role in suggesting how the materials may be used or frame how children may think during play, then it is difficult for the teacher to enter into the children's conceptual space. Through interviewing the teacher and the teacher assistant about their philosophy and pedagogical practices, it is possible to better understand how the program was planned. The teacher who created the program on mixing substances believed that the children were learning 'in a round about way' (Teacher interview). Adult suggestions about how to think about the materials were not given because the teacher believed that the resources themselves would generate the learning opportunities. Interviews of the teacher assistant provided an alternative perspective. The assistant teacher was keen to introduce specific materials with a scientific purpose in mind and a way of interacting with the materials to make visible scientific ideas. 'I can see the situation that we need to produce something extra... to make... to help... the play along...' (Teacher assistant interview). The assistant teacher wanted to name what the children were experiencing (potions), while the teacher did not wish to guide the children in this way. 'I'd rather the children didn't say this is a potion... they didn't have a fixed word for it...' (Teacher interview). The assistant teacher saw her role as developing conversations with children so that they had 'a database of ideas' that they could draw upon.

> I really believe that the children with the biggest data base are the ones that have had a lot of conversation and I don't mean like an empty vessel that has to be filled with information... I don't like that thinking either... but I do believe that the adult has a role in extending it in whichever way they see fit to extend it.
>
> (Teacher assistant interview)

The assistant teacher foregrounded the relations between the children's everyday concepts and the need for introducing scientific concepts in ways that supported the children's motives and interest expressed through their

Table 3.1: *Summary of different perspectives*

Teacher's beliefs about teaching and learning	Assistant teacher's beliefs about teaching and learning
The teacher wanted to have a free flow program in which the environment was not set up. Mediation was planned through the provision of unstructured contexts and everyday materials.	The assistant teacher wanted a program in which scientific knowledge was mediated through staff interactions with children as they engaged with the set up environment.
The teacher was not focused on concepts, but rather on processes.	The teacher assistant believed it was important for a teacher to have in mind the concepts she wanted to actively explore with children – to make them conscious through play and with interactions with staff.

play. The assistant teacher's comments suggest that she was sensitive to the ideas, thinking and experiences that the children had at home. She valued the children's perspective and was mindful of furthering children's learning. The conditions she created for children's play took into account the children's motives and goals through the provision of other mediational tools, such as books and resources related to their play, which helped the children to move beyond their everyday concepts. She created a shared activity in which the children and she as the assistant teacher could be conceptually connected: 'I think really the children who hypothesise the best are the ones who have had some input . . . but doing something together, looking something up together, adding some information . . . that's a really important part of the process' (teacher assistant interview). The conditions she valued foreground the child's project and the assistant teacher's intentions. The different perspectives between the staff are summarised in table 3.1.

The divergent beliefs between the staff about teaching and learning foreground the importance of acknowledging teacher philosophy when considering what kinds of opportunities for sustained shared thinking may be possible within a play-based program. Teachers who believe in a free flow program with minimal intervention by the teacher will afford less opportunities for examining planned concepts, deeply or in a sustained way (see Fleer, 2009b). Teachers who frame conceptual opportunities through keeping in mind the everyday concepts and the scientific concepts will be conceptually connected to the children during their play. Conceptual connectedness will allow for sustained shared thinking. Vygotsky (1987a) argued that 'The fundamental difference between the problem which involves everyday concepts and that which involves scientific concepts is that the *child solves the latter with the teacher's help*' (p. 216; emphasis added). Table 3.1 shows that the teacher assistant takes an active role, guided by a belief of sensitively supporting scientific concept formation within the play based program. Raising children's awareness of the objects in play and consciously, but sensitively, considering the scientific concepts associated with their actions, is something the teacher assistant valued and looked out for during her interactions with children. Vygotsky (1987a) has shown the importance of the teacher's role in supporting concept formation within concrete action oriented contexts:

> The child gains conscious awareness of spontaneous concepts at a comparatively late point in the developmental process. His [*sic*] abilities for the verbal formulation and definition of concepts and his volitional use of the concept in establishing complex logical relationships with other concepts are not present in the initial stages of the developmental process. The child knows things. He has a concept of the object. What the concept itself represents remains vague for the child however. He has a concept of the object and is consciously aware of the object that is represented in the concept. He is not, however, consciously aware of the concept itself. He does not have conscious awareness of the act of thought that allows him to represent the object. In contrast, the development of scientific concepts begins with that which remains most underdeveloped in the spontaneous concept over the whole of the school age. It begins with work on the concept itself. It begins with work on the concept's verbal definition, with operations that presuppose the nonspontaneous application of this concept (p. 217).

Vygotsky points out how important it is for the teacher to make conscious to children scientific concepts, not as disembedded concepts removed from the child's world but rather as a process of bringing new insights into the objects the child is interacting with or the everyday activities that are being enacted through play within play-based programs. The orientation of children to scientific concepts through active engagement by the teacher with the child in these play-based situations has traditionally had little

The materials do the teaching

Teacher knowledge

Subject matter or discipline knowledge
science concepts

Child development knowledge – as a naturally
evolving process

Beliefs and practices

Observation of children –
(providing materials to match
children's developmental level)

Philosophy – drawing upon Piaget's
theory

Everyday activities in the centre – Materials introduced to frame learning

Figure 3.1 Common pedagogical model used for the material framing
of learning

support within many Western early childhood communities. This is due in
part to the theoretical underpinnings of many early childhood programs,
and this finding is now well understood in the Western literature (see
Bodrova, 2008). The legacy of Piaget's theoretical work could be heard
through the teacher's discussion (table 3.1, p. 37) of pedagogy and science
concepts. This legacy needs to also be understood as an interpretation, as
noted by Glick (1997):

> The era from the early 60s through to the late 70s saw many aspects of the
> Piagetian paradigm battered from a number of directions, not all of which
> were relevant to core Piagetian ideas. The issues were not so much Piagetian
> theory as intended by Piaget, but rather the way in which Piagetian theory
> was consumed by the English-speaking psychological establishment (p. ix,
> Foreword to vol. 4 of Vygotsky's collected works).

Staff assumptions about learning in the program on 'potions or mixtures'
featured the importance of providing rich environments where conceptual opportunities were embedded. The role of staff in raising conceptual
consciousness of children did not feature for the teacher, and this is consistent with the traditional non-interventionist philosophy strongly advocated
when Piaget's work was first introduced into early childhood education over
40 years ago (Fleer, 2005; Anning, Cullen & Fleer, 2009). This problem
is represented in figure 3.1.

In this pedagogical model, the materials provide the framing for concept formation. The role of the teacher as a conceptual mediator through interactions is de-emphasised. Contrary to Siraj-Blatchford's (2007) construct of sustained shared thinking, in this pedagogical model it would be unlikely to see teachers and children working together in an intellectual way to solve a problem, or clarify a concept or for teachers to extend a narrative in relation to embedded concepts. Siraj-Blatchford (2009) has argued that in Western societies there is a strong tradition of providing individualised, play-based programs, where 'adults should be non-directive' and 'facilitate' learning rather than 'teach' (p. 137). She argues that this 'general belief underpins notions of quality in early childhood education' (p. 137). Importantly, she argues that what has been missing in early childhood practice (and debate) has been a focus on considering the need for a more active teaching role in developing cognition. Research in this area is increasingly showing that some teachers are seeking other ways of framing curriculum (Edwards, 2005; Patterson & Fleet, 2003), or seeking new theoretical drivers for informing observations and assessment practices (Fleer & Richardson, 2003). Edwards (2003) and Fleer and Richardson (2004a) have suggested that early childhood education is currently in theoretical flux and looking for new perspectives and conceptual tools to support thinking and practices. As noted by Dockett and Sumsion (2004), 'critiquing the traditional narrow knowledge base of the field that was heavily grounded in [traditional] developmental psychology and an accompanying broadening of theoretical framework informing early childhood education research' (p. 11) are urgently needed. Raban et al. (2007) have shown the existing breadth of theoretical possibilities that have been influential in teacher thinking (maturational, behaviourism, psychodynamic, developmental, socio-constructivist, ecological systems). Adoption of alternatives to the naturally evolving maturational view of child development are variable across countries with no empirical work having been done (with the exception of Raban in Australia) to conclusively show any international trend.

RECONCEPTUALISING THE CONCEPT OF 'TEACHING'

One of the dilemmas facing a profession grounded in a social pedagogy approach with developmental outcomes is how much of a teacher should the early childhood professional become in their quest to make a difference to the cognitive outcomes of children from disadvantaged families (see chapter 1). Resistance to teaching in play-based programs has a long history in social pedagogical approaches where developmental outcomes are promoted (see Bodrova, 2008). Potentially, what is being imagined for teaching does not take account of other theoretical models of learning, and this thinking may be blocking other ways of conceptualising how teaching may be enacted. What is needed is a new model for teaching and a different way of thinking about the role of the teacher. Early childhood teachers need to reclaim their professional expertise as active agents in children's learning, and not be seen as passive providers of materials to foster developmental milestones, where the latter role not only de-emphasises their place in children's learning but also positions them badly within the mix of professions who now interact together to provide services to children and families (see Edwards, 2009).

Cultural–historical theory provides an alternative reading of learning and teaching that is useful for realising the two concurrent aims introduced in chapter 1 – how to maintain the valued social pedagogy as well as how to generate a more active teaching role for promoting concept formation. Vygotsky (1997b), in discussing the history of the development of the pointing gesture, illustrates nicely how this may be possible. He showed how pointing was 'simply an unsuccessful grasping movement directed toward an object and denoting a future action' (p. 104). It is through the adult recognising the infant's movement (intersubjectivity) as pointing that the context changes. 'In response to the unsuccessful grasping movement of the child, there arises a reaction not on the part of the object, but on the part of another person. In this way, others carry out the initial idea of the unsuccessful grasping movement' (p. 105). But this action is mediated through an adult who displays contextual and conceptual intersubjectivity (as discussed in chapter 1). Hence, the role of the adult in introducing the 'concept of pointing' is critical.

Vygotsky (1997b: 105) suggested that 'through others we become ourselves'. It is through social relations that mental functions develop. However, unlike developmental theory, which locates development within the individual (see part 3), cultural–historical theory positions development as occurring within the group through social interactions and it is through these social interactions that higher mental functions evolve for the individual. The individual and the collective are mutually constituted. A developmental view sees development as located within the self, reaching out to the external world, grasping for cognition. A cultural–historical view sees development as occurring through the external world, raising interest and motivation for the child to engage in the activities, to participate with others beyond what can be done alone, and only later to do this with meaning as cognition becomes internalised through social action (from interpsychological functioning to intrapsychological functioning). In the latter view of learning, the mediating role of the adult is crucial for realising cognition. In the former view, cognition must be found by the lone child, where the adult provides a space and not a conceptually framed conversation. In a cultural–historical view, cognition is generated through engaging in activities with others, building towards conscious realisation of the concepts in culturally meaningful situations. A contemporary empirical example to illustrate this can be seen in the work of van der Veer (2008).

In van der Veer's (2008) extensive discussion of research undertaken by Rodriquez and Moro (1999) into semiotic guidance by adults and the acquisition of different semiotic means of children, he examined the interactions of infants and adults with two commercial toys – one a brightly coloured plastic toy tip truck with inserts for matching and pushing a series of shapes into the tipper, the other a toy telephone with wheels and a dial mechanism. Rodriquez and Moro (1999) made observations of infants aged seven months, 10 months and 13 months and showed that at seven months, the infants did not know how to use the toys in the conventional way (e.g., to put the shapes into the holes of the tipper truck) and that the mothers actively showed the infants how to do this. They were also able to show that the conventional use of the toys was an entirely learnt process by the infants. At seven months (nonconventional) the infants hardly touched the toys, at 10 months (preconventional), they approximated the act of putting the shapes in the holes in the tipper truck and at the 13 months (conventional) they put the shapes into the holes. Their research demonstrated a significant amount of modelling on the adults' part, some of which was accompanied by language. This they termed *remote demonstration*. More difficult for the infants was the use of immediate demonstrations, where the child is shown the act and asked to do the same or continue to do it. Finally, signalling or pointing gestures on the part of the adult were the most difficult act for the infants. For instance, 35 per cent of infants watch the mother model the act, while only 8 per cent responded to the pointing or signalling gesture of the adult. Rodriguez and Moro (1999) argue that

> the effectiveness of the more abstract semiotic means (including language) increases because they are being repeatedly presented in conjunction with the more simple ones such as modeling . . . Children are introduced to various social practices with the help of various signs of ascending complexity when

they do not yet understand language. They do not simply discover or copy the conventional uses of objects, because this is beyond their abilities, but gradually introduced to them by their caregivers through the use of subtle and increasingly abstract semiotic means.

(van der Veer, 2008: 33–4)

This study demonstrates the importance of the mediation role of the adult.

In contrast, developmental theory has traditionally been thought about as human capacity fully primed, ready, semi-ready or is in a rudimentary form and through interacting with the world, human development unfolds through a predictable sequence (see Blaise, 2008; Berk, 1994; Berk & Winsler, 1995; Dahlberg, Moss & Pence, 1999). Vygotsky (1997b) argued that 'functions initially are formed in the group in the form of relations of the children, then they become mental functions of the individual' (p. 107). 'Area', for example, is a mathematical concept that children learn later in school. It is a higher order measurement concept that is useful for adults in undertaking many everyday tasks, such as buying land, replacing a flyscreen, landscaping with pebbles and purchasing fabric for sewing. Families can build foundational knowledge of this specific form of measurement through their interactions during everyday activities, such as when wiping down a table – wiping the whole area, right to the edges. When children participate in wiping down a table without any mediation by an adult, they intuitively build a sense of area, but without conscious realisation of the concept of area measurement, that is, they are unlikely to think about the surface area of the table as being a defined space that can be measured. Knowing that a space can be defined with a boundary and measured is a very powerful concept and foundational for higher level mathematics. Figure 3.2 (p. 44) shows this everyday practice and the relational everyday concept of area measurement.

From a developmental view, children would participate in the experience of wiping down the tables, but as was shown in the example of the teacher in this chapter, they would not necessarily discuss the area they were wiping or introduce the concept of area. This concept may be consciously considered by the teachers, but would be experientially learned by the children through the materials. But as has been shown in chapters 1 and 2, the children are unlikely to move into the same conceptual space as the teachers, if no mediation (e.g., through the teacher conceptually framing the activity) occurs for the children. A cultural–historical perspective would also see the children engaged in wiping the table with others, but the framing and narrative would be different. For sustained shared thinking to emerge,

Dad: Let's wipe the table together.

(using paper towels, the children wipe the table)

Dad: Did you wipe to the edge? We cover the whole surface!

When we talk about 'edge', 'top' and 'bottom', we can help children learn about area. Children often don't think about area. Helping children pay attention to it helps them later on when they will measure these surfaces and make comparisons.

Figure 3.2 'Top', 'bottom' and 'edge' are about area
(Fleer & Raban, 2007. Image © Commonwealth of Australia 2006).

teachers would not only discuss the boundary of the table by using words such as 'edge', but they would also be likely to make the concept of 'surface area' more visible through, for example, inviting the children to cover the whole surface area of the table while wiping. Later, they may spray the area when wiping ('Let's spray the whole area of the table'), and later still may actively discuss table sizes in relation to a range of tablecloths, actively modelling how to cover or measure the surface areas. The children would work together with the adult in the real performance of these everyday tasks, but with greater conscious awareness of the concept of surface area and the concept of measurement. Vygotsky (1987a) argued that through this process, the children's relationship to the object they are interacting with changes:

> Scientific concepts have a different relationship to the child's personal experience than spontaneous concepts. In school instruction [or early childhood practice], concepts emerge and develop along an entirely different path than they do in the child's personal experiences. The internal motive that moves

the child forward in the formation of scientific concepts are completely different than those that direct his [*sic*] thought in the formation of spontaneous concepts. When concepts are acquired in school, the child's thought is presented with different tasks than when his thought is left to itself. *In sum, scientific concepts differ from spontaneous concepts in that they have a different relationship to the child's experience*, in that they have a different relationship to the object that they represent, and in that they follow a different path from birth to final formation.

(p. 178; emphasis added)

What becomes apparent in a cultural–historical view of learning and development is that the role of the teacher is critical for promoting concept formation. But the role the adult takes is not about matching materials or activities to the children's current developmental level; rather it is to conceptually engage the children in activities well beyond what they could think about on their own. As noted by Vygotsky,

The teacher must orient his work not on yesterday's development in the child but on tomorrow's. Only then will he be able to use instruction to bring out those processes of development that now live in the zone of proximal development.

(1987a: 211; emphasis in the original)

Spending four years in a childcare centre wiping tables will not of its own accord introduce children to the concept of area or the concept of measurement. Similarly, it is also highly unlikely that the teacher who believes that wiping the table together with the children will on its own introduce the children to these concepts. The teacher may be thinking about the concept but, as was shown in chapters 1 and 2, the children may not. Children becoming conscious of the concepts is what is different:

What the child does learn in school . . . is conscious awareness of what he does. He learns to operate on the foundation of his capacities in a volitional manner. His capacity moves from an unconscious, automatic plane to a voluntary, intentional, and conscious plane.

(Vygotsky, 1987a: 206)

Vygotsky (1987a) also noted in his research into concept formation that 'The boundary that separates these two types of concepts [everyday concepts and scientific concepts] is fluid. In the actual course of development, it shifts back and forth many times' (p.177). Significantly, Vygotsky

(1987a) also argued that children's embedded everyday experiences were also foundational for building concept formation. Without experiencing life events or educational activities through engaging in activities, the foundations for concept formation would not be possible. 'The development of scientific concepts becomes possible only when the child's spontaneous concepts have achieved a certain degree of development. The beginning of school age characteristically attains this level of development' (p. 177). Further, Vygotsky (1987a) noted that not only do everyday concepts influence what might be possible to fully understand in terms of scientific concepts but that scientific concepts will influence how children make sense of everyday contexts and concepts. 'On the other hand, the emergence of higher types of concepts (e.g., Scientific concepts) will inevitably influence existing spontaneous concepts' (p. 177). Understanding the concept of area measurement is only possible through directly experiencing area through activity; how the child reacts within these everyday practices changes when scientific mediation on the part of the adult occurs. Children experience everyday situations differently when they pay attention to the idea of area and area measurement. Vygotsky (1987a) showed in his research that

> These two types of concepts are not encapsulated or isolated in the child's consciousness. They are not separated from one another by an impermeable wall nor do they flow in two isolated channels. They interact continually. This will inevitably lead to a situation where generalisations with a comparatively complex structure – such as scientific concepts – elicit changes in the structure of spontaneous concepts. Whether we refer to the development of spontaneous concepts or scientific ones, we are dealing with the development of a unified process of concept formation (p. 177).

Overall, what is particularly important for conceptual development is the mediating role of the teacher.

THE MEDIATING ROLE OF THE TEACHER

The mediating role of the early childhood professional in developing concept formation is clearly central to cultural–historical theory. This role is extremely complicated and requires exceptional skill and understanding on the part of the teacher. At what moments in play or everyday activity do teachers make conscious for children specific scientific concepts? Figure 2.2 showed conceptual and contextual intersubjectivity to

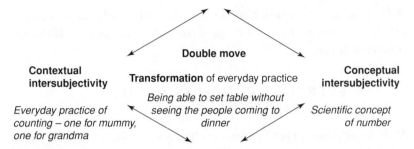

Figure 3.3 Child consciousness of concepts – example of a child setting the table for a dinner party

be important. But how do these dialectically related concepts interact in practice?

In figure 3.3 a model is introduced to show the mediating role of the early childhood teacher during concept formation for children. This model builds upon Hedegaard's (2002) concept of a double move in teaching; it does not replace existing teacher thinking about pedagogy, but rather seeks to transform the way teachers think about the conceptual work they do and make explicit and conscious how they can interact with children during sustained shared thinking during play. The model can be better understood through an example. Specifically, the knowledge system of mathematics is considered and shown through the concept of number.

SCIENTIFIC CONCEPT FORMATION IN MATHEMATICS

Concept formation that is planned or consciously considered by the early childhood teacher in this model is deemed as scientific concept formation (shown to the right in the model). These concepts are abstract and can be transported across contexts. For example, 'number' is a scientific concept, and knowing that in the process of counting the number the counter has identified represents the whole group of items signifies the concept of number. When someone has an isolated concept of number, they have attained empirical knowledge. The counter can trust this process to always give an accurate quantity (see Willis, 2002). They can also trust that when someone says there are six people coming to dinner, if six place settings are put out for dinner, then this will accurately represent the quantity predicted. The guests do not have to be physically seen before the table is set because the abstract concept of number can be worked with. When children have a concept of number they can consciously use this concept to help them think or act in a range of contexts within or outside the early childhood setting.

EVERYDAY CONCEPTS ABOUT MATHEMATICS

As discussed, concepts embedded in everyday situations and which support the child to undertake everyday things is deemed an everyday concept. In this case, children do not consciously think about the concepts they are using to support them, but rather are likely to participate with, or copy, other more knowledgeable individuals (imitation, as discussed by Vygotsky, 1987a). Sometimes children may count how many people are coming for dinner, but they won't apply this knowledge when they are setting the table, that is, they can engage in the counting activity, but have not yet developed a concept of quantity: the relational link between counting and quantity has not been established. They may think that the last number that they counted is connected to that numeral, rather than think about the whole group or quantity of people counted. For the child, the counting ritual is not linked to the concept of number, therefore they cannot consciously use counting when setting the table. Rather, the child is likely to set the table by referencing each person who is coming to dinner – one setting for Aunty, one for Uncle, one for Mummy, and so on.

BUILDING RELATIONAL KNOWLEDGE AND THINKING

The act of interlacing everyday concept formation and scientific concept formation (shown in the centre of the model as the double move) is possible when the early childhood teacher connects the scientific concept with the lived everyday practice of the child (in relation to knowledge systems; see next chapter for details). The child becomes conscious of the abstract concept being introduced and builds a working knowledge of how the abstract concept can transform their everyday practices. Being conscious that counting is about determining the quantity of a group (consciousness raising), for example, will transform children's everyday concepts of how they may set the table for guests at a birthday party (everyday practice). The everyday practice of setting the table – by matching one to one (plate and cutlery to person) – is an important everyday concept that lays the foundations for building scientific concept formation of number

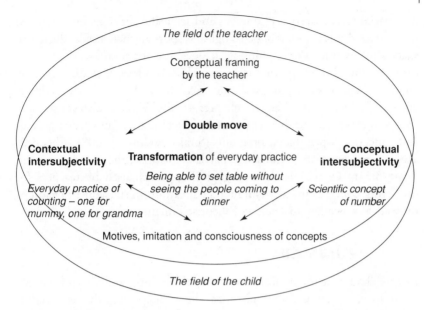

Figure 3.4 A dynamic pedagogical model for teacher and child consciousness of concepts

and quantity. Both are needed, but they can only interlace when there is consciousness on the part of the child and the transformation of everyday practice through the active connections between home and formal schooling are made. Consciousness and transformation are shown as central to the model. To successfully bring together everyday concepts and scientific concepts the teacher not only has to think about the materials and how they may be introduced to the child (contextual intersubjectivity) but must also think deliberately about conceptual intersubjectivity (concepts as part of a relational knowledge system). To generate conceptual intersubjectivity requires that the teacher knows about the children's everyday concepts, the concepts the teacher wants to introduce and what contexts and pedagogical framing are likely to generate a motive for engaging in concept formation. This idea was shown in the model created in chapter 2 and has been brought together into a new model, shown in figure 3.4. This is a high order pedagogical approach that is very different to simply providing resources that may suggest possibilities for concept formation. Supporting concept formation of subject matter knowledge in ways that are transformative for children is difficult work for teachers. It is complicated and requires great skill and a high level of knowledge about how to dialectically relate everyday concepts and scientific concepts in play-based programs. This is the kind of pedagogical work that teachers who engage in successful sustained shared thinking achieve. It is the skilful work of expert early childhood teachers who understand how to preserve traditional early childhood concepts that longstanding research has shown to make a difference to the lives of children (see chapter 4), and who can also consciously engage themselves and their children in subject matter knowledge systems and concepts in play-based programs (Siraj-Blatchford, 2009). This pedagogical expertise and knowledge partially theorised here and shown in figure 3.3 makes visible the pedagogical approach used by teachers for mediating concepts in early childhood education. In subsequent chapters, these ideas are taken up again and theorised further.

SUMMARY

In this chapter a theoretical discussion of teaching and the role of the teacher were given. Cultural–historical theory helps with the reconceptualising of teaching and the role of the teacher in programs that seek to introduce discipline knowledge alongside other valued knowledge. These constructs are not about replicating what is done in schools, but rather, early childhood teaching is about thinking and interacting conceptually with children in play-based programs. A pedagogical model for teacher–child interaction was introduced in this chapter to make explicit how teachers' work changes when they make conscious to themselves and to the children, valued concepts during play and everyday activities within early childhood centres.

4

Valued curriculum concepts in early childhood education

> Thinking and knowledge are anchored in societal practice and problem areas... [and] thinking as a process... proceeds in social practice 'by manual as well as symbolic tools' that a person shares with others in his [*sic*] everyday life.
>
> (Hedegaard, 2002: 22)

INTRODUCTION

The kind of knowledge that is valued within a community may be similar or dissimilar to that of other communities. Societies have different traditions for early childhood pedagogical knowledge and for the outcomes of learning during that period. In the social pedagogy tradition, 'all children should develop a desire and curiosity for learning, and confidence in their own learning, rather than achieving a pre-specified level of knowledge and proficiency' (Martin-Korpi 2005, cited in OECD, 2006: 60). Wagner and Einarsdottir (2006) argue that in the Nordic tradition,

> Child and family policies are based on Nordic ideology and traditions, emphasizing democracy, equality, freedom and emancipation, solidarity through cooperation and compromise, and a general concept of the 'good childhood,' or what life should be like for all children... Nordic people generally view childhood as important in its own right, not simply a platform from which to become an adult.
>
> (Wagner & Einarsdottir, 2006: 4, 6)

The OECD (2006) report contrasts the social pedagogy tradition with what it has termed 'a preprimary approach'. In countries that the OECD defined as tending to use a preprimary approach, it argued that curriculum in the early years is linked directly to the curriculum found in primary schools. Curricula are generally based on subject domains, such as literacy, numeracy and science. Countries such as Australia, Canada, France, Ireland, the Netherlands, the UK and the USA have tended to adopt this model, with some countries training graduates who can work across both the early childhood settings and primary schools (see OECD, 2006). Other countries, such as the USA, have focused on school readiness and have more sharply defined these content domains in their goals and curricula outcomes. In its report, the OECD (2006) suggested that the emphases noted in curriculum and pedagogy across countries should be viewed as sitting on a continuum of broadly developmental goals to focused cognitive goals.

Staff qualifications correspond well with this differing value base. Social pedagogues are found, for instance, in Austria, Denmark, Finland, Germany and Norway. Preprimary or primary teachers are seen in Australia, Canada, France, Ireland, the Netherlands, the UK and the USA. The OECD (2006) also notes that early childhood specialist or pedagogue with birth to six years training occurs in Austria, Belgium, the Czech Republic, Finland, Hungary, Italy, Mexico and Sweden. These traditions and expectations of what early childhood education will do for children and for society significantly influence what might be the expected outcomes of early education found in a particular society. What is valued in one community, such as early education for its own right, is very different from focusing on the concepts of early literacy and early numeracy. However, it must be acknowledged that what is valued at one point in time within a particular society, may quickly change, as noted by Wagner and Einarsdottir (2006):

> [I]ncreasing emphasis on academic learning (which many Nordic scholars and practitioners view as an 'invasion' from other countries) encroaches on both the value and the time for childhood play, as each Nordic country in turn produces national curriculum guidelines and restructures early childhood teacher preparation, often to more closely mirror professional preparation of elementary school teachers (p. 6).

Regardless of the kind of knowledge that is valued within a community, the early childhood professional has become increasingly mindful of what kinds of concepts underpin a social pedagogical approach and a preprimary approach. Are early childhood staff charged with delivering programs that support psychological concepts of 'agency' and 'self-worth' (Wagner &

Einarsdottir, 2006) or community-specific concepts of 'interdependence' (Rogoff, 2003), or are they now needing to focus on subject matter or discipline knowledge concepts such as numeracy and literacy? It should be noted that 'knowledge is not a mirror of the world, but rather collective experiences that are created through solving pressing societal problems connected to specific ways of living' (Hedegaard, 2002: 26). As such, particular forms of knowledge will prevail within communities for supporting their specific needs. Although there are clearly different knowledge traditions across communities, in this book, the concepts that are examined relate to subject matter knowledge and social pedagogical knowledge. Because subject matter knowledges have caused the greatest challenge for the field of early childhood education, a greater weighting has been directed to theorising this area. It is also noted that subject matter or discipline knowledge will influence those communities that have traditionally adopted a more social pedagogy approach, as has already been noted by Wagner and Einarsdottir (2006) for Nordic countries.

A review of the kinds of knowledge systems that are promoted across countries for the early childhood years is given in this chapter. Through document analysis of a selection of early childhood curriculum documents and an examination of commonly available resources in early childhood centres, it is hoped to make visible the knowledge systems that are promoted in many early childhood education programs. Subsequent chapters will take up the challenge of how learning and development are supported across these different knowledge systems.

DOMINANT KNOWLEDGE FORMS IN CURRICULA

Learning outcomes or educational goals for particular communities do and should vary, as they represent what is valued or what is sanctioned for children to learn while at school (see Hedegaard, 2009). Preschool education, like school education, also represents a particular form of valued community knowledge. Van Oers (2008) has clustered the diversity of learning goals into four discrete areas, categories that are also useful for analysing preschool curricula across cultural communities. The cultural–historical categories he has identified are

- learning to perform
- learning to make meaning
- learning to participate
- learning to be.

Learning to perform involves the children's appropriation of actions that are meaningful for them in a particular community. Specific motor development or perceptual learning, for example, can be classified as learning to perform. Subject matter or discipline knowledge and other specific concepts deemed important in a particular community are what constitute *learning to make meaning*. This categorisation of knowledge can be framed as learning the community's shared collective codes (e. g. numerals, number system). *Learning to participate* includes the learning of rules and tools of a particular community in order to participate independently or interdependently, creatively, critically or in whatever manner is valued within the community or across communities. Successful participation across a variety of contexts is deemed important. The learner's identity, as expressed through motives, ambitions, morals and aesthetic values, is the focus of learning in *learning to be*. Personal sense of these constructs is highly valued in this type of learning. Personal sense is often supported through narrative knowledge (see chapter 6).

When these categories are used for undertaking a content analysis of curricula, valued concepts become evident and provide for a better understanding of how particular communities sanction particular concepts in children's learning, and how particular curricula afford particular concepts. In this section the curricula from a range of countries are examined in relation to van Oers' (2008) categories in order to gain some insight into what is valued generally within the field of early learning. Curricula are expressed differently, and for some the *areas of learning* are identified; other curriculum writers have used *goals* or *aims*, and still others have used the term *outcomes*. However, when a general content analysis of what concepts are valued is undertaken, some interesting trends can be noticed (see summary in table 4.1).

Curricula examined are one state of Australia (Queensland), a province of Canada (Ontario), England, Hong Kong, Korea, Malawi, New Zealand and Sweden. While this analysis does not seek to be representative or to know what is actually the taught curriculum in these countries, it does give some insights into those concepts that dominate at the particular time when these curricula were developed. Most countries continue to refine and evolve their curricula, so this analysis seeks only to give a broad indication of trends at a particular moment in history.

In table 4.1 it is possible to notice that all countries have expressed the concepts of maths, language and science for learning to make meaning. Some countries, such as Australia, New Zealand and Sweden, have also

Table 4.1 *Valued early childhood curriculum concepts across a selection of countries at a particular moment in time*

Country	Learning to perform	Learning to make meaning	Learning to participate	Learning to be	Other concepts
Australia (Queensland; birth to school age) Creche and Kindergarten Association, 2006	e.g., experience environments that are responsible to our emotional and physical needs, promote our health and ensure our safety from harm.	from, e.g., numeracy, language and literacy, natural and built environments; we are of the present, with unique connections to the past and future.	in, e.g., family and community, democracy, safe, nurtured, respectful interactions, active participants, capable, researchers, open to new possibilities and perspectives, honour values, beliefs and traditions.	e.g., belonging, wellbeing, identity, valued and treated with dignity, justice, equity and respect, unique individuals, share our understanding, knowledge and thinking in many ways, active negotiators.	
England (nursery and reception aged children) Dept of Education and Employment, 2000	Physical development.	Communication, language and literacy, mathematical development, knowledge and understanding of the world.	Personal, social and emotional development.	Creative development.	
Hong Kong (preprimary) Curriculum Development Council, 2006	Physical fitness and health.	Language, early mathematics, science and technology, (understanding basic health and safety issues).	Self and society (family and society).	Arts: enjoy different creative works through senses and bodies, expression, imagination, express through different media, develop creativity, experience different cultures, emotional development, self-confidence.	

(cont.)

Table 4.1 (cont.)

Country	Learning to perform	Learning to make meaning	Learning to participate	Learning to be	Other concepts
Korea (kindergarten) Ministry of Education, 1999	Sensory skill and physical cognition, fundamental movement competence, health, safety.	Listening, speaking, becoming interested in reading and writing, scientific enquiry, logical–mathematical enquiry, creative enquiry.	Basic living habits, personal life, family life, group life, social phenomena and environment, exploration, expression, appreciation.	Appreciation, creative enquiry.	
Malawi Ministry of Gender and Community Services, 2003	Learning readiness: fine motor skills, gross motor skills, visual perception, auditory perception.	Mathematics (future interest in maths and science), health care and education (health education knowledge).	Social and interpersonal relationships, language for good development, Health care and education (physical wellbeing, toilet training, good health habits, care with play materials).	Creative expression, spiritual and moral development, environmental education (space for stimulating development).	Nutritional care by the adults: promotion of breast feeding, identifying junk food, knowledge of nutritious food and hygienic food supplements.
New Zealand (preschool and childcare children) Ministry of Education, 1996	Spatial, visual, linguistic, physical, musical, mathematical, personal, and social, non-verbal and verbal communication skills (listening skills), confidence in and control of their bodies.	Knowledge of body and functions, knowledge about how to keep safe, language skills, syntax and meaning, stories and symbols of their own and other cultures (this goal includes concepts of reading, writing and numeracy), living, physical and material worlds.	Self-help and self-care, emotional wellbeing, kept safe from harm, family and wider world, sense of place, routines, rituals and regular events, limits and boundaries of acceptable behaviour, creative and expressive, importance of spontaneous play, active exploration, thinking and reasoning.	Equitable learning opportunities, affirmed as individuals learn with others (first language is valued, enjoyment of verbal communication).	

	Physical	Cognitive/Academic	Social	Personal
Ontario (kindergarten) Ministry of Education, 2006	Large and small muscle development and control.	Language, mathematics, science and technology, health and safety practices, the arts: problem solving strategies when experimenting, basic knowledge and skills across arts, awareness of surroundings.	Personal and social development (self-awareness and self-reliance, social relationships).	Personal and social development (self-awareness), communicate ideas through various art forms, awareness of selves as artists.
Sweden (preschool) National Agency for Education, 2006	Motor skills, ability to coordinate, awareness of own body.	Health and wellbeing, differentiate shades of meaning in concepts, understanding the surrounding world, spoken language, communicate and express their thoughts, develop vocabulary and concepts, play with words, interest in written language, to build create and design using different materials and techniques, use mathematics, concept of number, measurement and form and time and space, nature and simple scientific phenomena.	Norms and values (openness, respect, solidarity and responsibility, take account of and empathise with others and willingness to help), participation in own culture, and feel respect for other cultures, understand that everyone is of equal value, respect and care for surrounding environment, function individually and in group, handle conflicts, understand rights, obligations and common rules, express thoughts and influence own situation, responsibility, democracy.	Identity, curiosity and enjoyment at the same time as ability to play and learn, autonomy and confidence (work out own position on different ethical dilemmas and fundamental questions of life), creative expression, cultural identity, ability to listen, reflect and express views.

Note: Brackets have been used in the content analysis where it has been necessary to include information at the second tier of concepts for the particular curriculum framework.

identified technology (materials, built environments, designing). Others have identified the arts and health as concepts of importance. England, Ontario, Malawi, Hong Kong and Korea have expressed these areas as discrete bodies of knowledge, while countries such as Australia, New Zealand and Sweden have discussed them as relational concepts referenced directly to the child's everyday world. In this latter analysis, the core concepts are most obscure in the New Zealand document and clearest in the Swedish document. Ontario provided the most detailed expression of concepts: educators in that country would not need to second guess the expected learning. In contrast, educators in New Zealand and Australia would require a great deal of discipline knowledge about mathematics, technology, science and language in order to prepare their programs. Malawi provided detailed contextual statements to educators and caregivers about the importance of the concepts for general child development.

Learning to perform focused primarily on children's fine and gross motor skills, and on body awareness; Malawi also included perception. All countries had extensive goals or outcomes related to learning to participate. Sweden had the most comprehensive and most sophisticated, detailing values of democracy. It also had the broadest definition for inclusion. Most other countries tended to focus on social participation, emotional wellbeing, being active members of family and community and developing personal abilities and skills. Cultural awareness featured in almost all countries.

The learning to be category was the most variable across the countries. Malawi and New Zealand made special mention of spiritual development, which was absent from all other countries except Sweden, which mentioned awareness of others' spirituality in relation to inclusion. Moral development, while absent from the others, was also included in both these countries. Self-awareness, cultural identity and creative expression featured across all the countries for this category. Hong Kong made special mention of creativity and creative pursuits being an important dimension of learning to be. Dignity, justice and equity for self and others were identified across the two categories of learning to participate and learning to be. A cultural–historical view of identity locates the self in relation to others, that is, how you participate within family and community is directly related to how you feel about yourself as a social member of that community, which in turn reflects your own sense of who you are, determining identity and defining it as a relational social construct; hence, these two categories identified by van Oers (2008) are difficult to separate in the analysis shown in table 4.1.

A further finding of the analysis of the curricula was that both Sweden and New Zealand (and to some extent Australia) had an overwhelming amount of curriculum content in the learning to participate category. The emphasis of content and detail for this area was vast compared with other countries; however, for Sweden there is an assumption that teachers have a great deal of knowledge about how to plan and action the value statements which form a central component of the Swedish curriculum.

Overall, the analysis undertaken here tends to suggest that all the countries reviewed link their preschool curriculum to discipline knowledge found in their school curricula, even Sweden. This finding contrasts with that of the OECD review (note that the analysis of curricula for Ontario, Sweden, Australia and the UK overlaps with the OECD country reviews). For those countries classified by the OECD as using a social pedagogy approach to curricula, the discipline knowledge (i.e. linked to school curriculum content) was embedded within the child's everyday practice rather than shown as disembedded and discrete forms of knowledge. What is important for our analysis is the identification of those curriculum concepts that are valued. In the countries reviewed here, they all valued similar concepts, but Sweden, Australia and New Zealand gave greater weight to learning to participate, and Hong Kong, Ontario, Korea and England weighted more towards learning to make meaning; the latter perhaps fell within what the OECD has named as a preprimary approach, the former a social pedagogy approach. Malawi was more equally distributed, and the Australian document was for one state only and therefore is not representative of all of Australia; similarly with Ontario being only one Canadian province.

As mentioned in the introduction to this chapter, what a society values and sanctions through its development of curricula will continue to change. Van Oers (2009) has argued that in the Netherlands changes in policy directions since the 1980s have focused the country's attention on the idea of a knowledge economy or knowledge society. With this change in thinking has come change in curriculum development for schools, with a flow-on effect to preschools. Curriculum is now focused on essential content within a regime of school and teacher accountability, resulting in frequent testing of concepts in order to strengthen the society's knowledge economy. In contrast, countries such as Hong Kong and Singapore, which have had a long tradition of discipline knowledge in their curricula, have noted the value of creativity and imagination as learning outcomes and have made curriculum changes that allow for the foregrounding of these processes within their education system – both for preschool and school.

EMBEDDED CONCEPTS IN EARLY CHILDHOOD PRACTICE

It is important to know what concepts are promoted through the use of curriculum documents within a particular community. It is also important to be mindful of what kinds of concepts are afforded through the traditional practices found within early childhood programs. An analysis of the commonly available preschool resources is particularly important because the dominant teacher philosophy in early childhood education centres (see chapter 3) was on the materials doing the teaching. Many materials commonly found in preschools, such as blocks, puzzles, construction kits and memory games, have been specifically designed for preschool education. What kinds of concepts do these resources promote? Many of these resources were designed a very long time ago, yet they are still standard purchases for preschools in many countries. Hedegaard (2007) suggests that in the 1980s cognitive psychology promoted the view that it was important to stimulate and challenge preschool children's cognitive development. During that time many educational materials that were closely aligned with the tasks contained in intelligence tests or were specifically created to prepare children for school were designed and produced for preschools. Hedegaard (2007) argues that the same design principles are still being adopted today for the production of resources and toys as well as for computer games. Hedegaard (2007) argues that these materials may be designed to lead to the 'appropriation of empirical concepts' only (pp. 272–3). Hedegaard (2007) states:

> If pedagogues and parents do not pay attention to playthings and educational play materials, but rather let commercial interest determine the choice, the child may appropriate skills and competencies that are inappropriate in relation to the child's everyday life, and this can be detrimental to the child's development of a theoretical orientation to his or her surroundings (p. 273).

What kinds of concepts are being promoted through the use of educational resources commonly available in preschools today? To answer this question, Hedegaard (2007) undertook a research project aimed at studying the effects of symbolic educational play materials on children aged three to five years in a Danish university play group for their social interaction and appropriation of conceptual competencies. One hundred educational materials, common to most preschools in Denmark, were analysed for material content, children's demonstrated competence or difficulties, and the children's intentions and social interactions. The types of materials included jigsaw puzzles, games with conceptual content such as picture lotto and dominos, self-controlling conceptual material, books, language games and logical reasoning games. Participant observation was used to gather data, with one researcher using the material with the child, another researcher making observations of the event.

Hedegaard (2007) argues that puzzles, lotto games, language games, etc. have been designed to train children in visual discrimination and object categorisation but do not help children build theoretical knowledge. Theoretical knowledge (see chapter 6) enables children to experiment with conceptual relationships between things, which enables them to be creative and encourages them to engage in symbolic play. Most of the play materials Hedegaard (2007) reviewed 'trained the children to pass intelligence tests but did not allow much creative experimentation or symbolic play activity' (p. 273). In analysing how children used the preschool resources, Hedegaard (2007) found that the materials encouraged visual discrimination, memory and manipulation, and that the content of the resources was not meaningful or relevant to the children's lives.

While preschool programs will vary within and between countries, Hedegaard's (2007) study points to the importance of ascertaining what concepts are embedded in the preschool resources predominantly used within specific communities. Being conscious of the concepts that are being promoted is important for considering not just the taught program but also the program that is enacted through the use of specifically designed preschool resources.

SUMMARY

In this chapter the kinds of concepts that are valued by society across a range of countries were presented. It was shown that there are different views on which concepts should be taught to preschool children. It was also noted that what is highly valued at one point in time is not static, and changes as societies change. Of significance is finding out the types of knowledge that are being promoted (e.g., empirical, theoretical, narrative; see chapters 6 and 7) and, through this, understanding the bases for the professional knowledge that are recorded and sanctioned in national curricula or through the production and use of particular preschool resources: we need to be conscious of the concepts and the kind of knowledge being built. The latter is taken up fully in the next three chapters.

Teacher knowledge of subject matter concepts

[L]earners *actively transform* the learning material included in these [cultural–historical] programs by means of certain object-related or mental actions. In the process of this kind of transformation, learners discover and distinguish in the learning material some essential or *general relationship*, and when they study it they can discover many particular appearances of the material . . . Curricula that provide for such directions of thought help to establish relationships with integrated systems of knowledge. The leading role in the appropriation of such knowledge belongs to the learners' *actions*.

(Davydov, 1999a: 135; emphasis in original)

INTRODUCTION

While a growing number of articles have been written about teacher knowledge of concepts (see Appleton, 2006), much of the research contained in them has concentrated upon discipline content knowledge devoid of the conceptual system in which the concepts were developed or are being used (Fleer, 2009b). In these articles, teacher knowledge of concepts in discipline areas has generally been researched against a checklist of concepts (e.g., Garbett, 2003), and great associated claims have been made about early childhood teachers' lack of knowledge. Research into teacher knowledge of subject matter concepts has not been examined in relation to everyday concepts and scientific concepts in specific subject areas (see chapter 3). Much of the research into early childhood teacher knowledge of concepts gives a rather limited reading of teacher concept knowledge within discipline areas (see Fleer, 2009b).

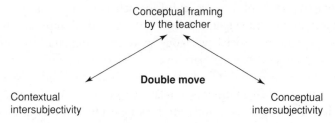

Figure 5.1 Concepts examined during professional development

For instance, concept formation was examined by Fleer and Raban (2006) in relation to teacher knowledge of literacy and numeracy in play-based programs. In their study, teachers were actively involved in examining their own conceptual knowledge. Professional development was the vehicle through which their knowledge was meaningfully interrogated. For example,

> Eight experienced early childhood professionals are assembled for a session on professional learning in the areas of literacy and numeracy. One of the staff members has a four year university degree, three of the staff have a diploma in children's services (a two year technical and further education course), and four staff have no formal qualifications. All the staff are from the same childcare centre. The previous day, the research team photographed and videotaped the children and staff interacting in the centre. From these data, the team produced a series of A4 sized photographs and these are displayed around the room. The team organised a workshop for the staff, but before they commenced the workshop, a brief presentation was given on everyday concepts, scientific concepts and the double move in teaching. The focus for professional learning was on concept formation in literacy and numeracy within their centre, and the staff discussed scientific concepts, everyday concepts and the double move in teaching, as shown in the model below (figure 5.1) (field notes).

With full teacher awareness of the theoretical model the staff discussed their knowledge of literacy and numeracy, but within the context of the learning activities undertaken the day before. The photographs and video clips of their practice were used as the stimulus for this individual and group interrogation of concepts in literacy and numeracy. Because concepts get their meaning in relation to practice (see Chaiklin & Hedegaard, 2009), it is important to discuss literacy and numeracy concepts in relation to the practices that are afforded through preschooling. Within the practice traditions of preschool, it is difficult for teachers to engage in discussions on subject matter knowledge because the traditional approach that has prevailed has been a social pedagogy with developmental outcomes. In the early childhood teacher narratives about concept formation, it was evident that, even with directed discussions about the children's everyday concepts and focused comments in relation to scientific concepts, teachers found it difficult to actively focus on making explicit in their interactions literacy and numeracy concept formation. Two general areas were noted as problematic for the field, and requiring more focused research attention: consciousness of concepts, and the general intellectual lives of the children within the centre. The significance of these for considering subject matter knowledge generation is the subject of this chapter.

CONSCIOUSNESS OF CONCEPTS

In the example of the eight teachers, the early childhood professionals' level of consciousness in relation to scientific concepts was high. As would be expected of educated and experienced professionals, they were skilled at being able to analyse centre-based activities as opportunities for concept formation. They actively identified a range of scientific concepts that could be afforded in almost any situation within the centre. Annie (teacher), for example, states that 'We were talking about the use of maths words at meal times: they might say more, no more, all gone, finished, things like that', or, as one group listed, 'Counting, sorting, rhymes' (Karen); another group stated, 'Picture identification, sounds, when we were thinking about Jane [staff member] with the babies, words, reading, drawing, listening skills, conversations and all that sort of stuff' (Sharon). These examples show how teachers can endow experience with scientific terminology and create meaning as is illustrative of narrative knowledge and methods (see chapter 6). This is consistent with social experience pedagogy discussed by Hedegaard (2002).

The teachers' high level of analysis in identifying opportunities for concept development in the centre activities is supportive of the outcomes of more extensive research undertaken elsewhere (see Siraj-Blatchford, 2009; Sammons et al., 2002; Siraj-Blatchford et al., 2002). What was surprising was that when concepts were identified, they were conscious in the minds of staff, but they were not necessarily made conscious to the children. Debbie, for example, talks about this phenomenon in relation to particular scientific concepts (referring to video clip of practice).

DEBBIE   I wasn't actually doing it [concept development], but I was thinking it . . .

GROUP   (*general laughter*) Honest!

DEBBIE   The kids were throwing the sand in a container, and I was thinking at the time . . .

ANNIE   Emptying and filling.

DEBBIE   Emptying and filling. How many things fit into the container that they were pouring the sand into?

This finding is consistent with early research by Hutt et al. (1989), Sylva et al. (2000) and Smith and Connolly (1980), who provided evidence of the limited cognitive interactions in early childhood centres at that time. Back in 1990, David showed in her extensive review of the literature that in staff–child interactions in early childhood settings there was strong evidence of dialogue being 'banal and cursory', requiring children to answer closed questions, provide labels and, as one child has put it, 'tell the teacher something they already know' (p. 115). Siraj-Blatchford (1999) has also noted this for the least effective preschools in the UK.

Returning to the concept of sustained shared thinking, it was noted in the example of the eight early childhood staff that the participants did not discuss the need for this kind of interaction with children. Raising the consciousness of scientific concepts among children did not feature, but rather staff discussed the centre contexts and activities, which, by the very nature of being there and available to children, were thought to provide concept formation. This is consistent with early childhood teacher philosophy (see chapters 2 and 3 where it was noted that the materials do the teaching). Staff were very skilled at analysing, naming and discussing, in broad terms, the scientific concepts that were possible to support within the centre. As such, consciousness of scientific concepts was evident for staff, but they were not necessarily made conscious to the children. This is an important finding because it points to the specific aspects of teacher philosophy and pedagogical practice that can be easily reconsidered for improving learning outcomes for preschool aged children, that is, it is not the environment that changes for the teachers but rather the teacher's relationship to it through consciously interacting conceptually with children within the planned contexts (see chapter 7).

THE INTELLECTUAL LIVES OF CHILDREN

When teachers make relevant concepts more conscious to children in their play, the intellectual lives of children within the centre can be increased.

Amanda states: 'We were just saying that it [potential for conceptual development] happens right from the start [of the day] when they have to find their locker, and put their bag away, and put their coat away, and things like that; everything is literacy, in some way.' As noted earlier, concept formation was thought to occur simply by experiencing it through routines. While the staff felt confident that by participating in the daily activities of the centre, scientific concept formation was being developed, staff simply named generic concepts such as 'counting, large, small, measurement, weights' (Jane). These routines had the potential to build everyday knowledge through foregrounding communication within the everyday experiences of the children. But this kind of attention on everyday knowledge was implied rather than actively constructed.

Analyses by staff of their centre or room did not focus on the details of scientific concept formation or how they could mediate these concepts in play. Talk mostly focused on tagging general centre activities. Importantly, the related system of concepts gained through engaging with the conceptual systems of literacy and numeracy were not considered by the teachers (see chapter 3 for a full discussion of this conceptual problem). Staff tended to discuss processes around engagement in the experiences rather than the specific scientific concepts being developed.

> With our group, they tip all the puzzle pieces out and can't put [them] back together, so what I am encouraging them to do, maybe take a few pieces away and then put them back. [For example], what Liang wanted to do, was tip it all about, so we had to start putting it back together, she's got this piece, I said, and she is saying 'It is a fish', 'So there is a fish's body, so where do you think his mouth should go?' She is pointing to his tail. 'The mouth might go down the other end', and so just trying to get her to do the puzzle (Paula).

Overall, the intellectual lives of the children tended to be driven by experiencing the activities in the centre. This finding is consistent with longstanding, but also more recent, research (Bruner, 1966; Hutt et al., 1989; Smith & Connolly, 1980; Siraj-Blatchford; 2009) (see also chapters 1 and 2). As identified by David (1990) so long ago:

> in some preschool settings, children under five are indeed being under-educated because insufficient cognitive demands are being made of them and, generally speaking, it is the adult intervention which presents this challenge in dialogue.
>
> (David, 1990: 87)

Research undertaken by Edwards and Mercer (1987) demonstrated that children's experiences in educational settings were situated within the here and now, and that dialogue never transcended the boundaries of the concrete or linked with disembedded concepts. All the experiences and scientific concepts that were discussed by the teachers above were framed within the context of embedded early childhood activities. The pedagogical model the teachers had adopted for supporting learning did not enable them to easily build concepts in play. That would have required some form of mediation on the part of the teacher.

SUMMARY

Taken together, the studies reported in this chapter point to the long standing and recent evidence for the position that the intellectual lives of children in centres are not being optimised due to teacher beliefs about their non-interventionist role within play-based programs for supporting concept formation.

While teachers may have conceptual knowledge of subject matter content, such as literacy and numeracy, they do not make these concepts conscious to children through the programs they plan and implement. It was also shown that teachers are skilled at analysing where the everyday concepts arise within play-based settings; however, the teachers discussed in this chapter did not mediate concept formation for their preschool aged children during play. The outcomes of research discussed in this and previous chapters clearly point towards the theoretical and pedagogical model being used rather than a deficiency in the knowledge base of early childhood teachers for promoting conceptual development in preschool aged children. In the next two chapters knowledge traditions and theories of thinking in relation to the school context and early childhood education are examined.

6 Empirical and narrative knowledge development in play

> Concepts are never defined in isolation, but rather derive their meaning from their relations to other concepts within a coherent theoretical system.
>
> (Falmagne, 1995: 205)

INTRODUCTION

Hedegaard (2009) suggests that societies value particular forms of knowledge and theories of thinking, and that these knowledges are usually represented through documents such as curriculum, assessment tools and licensing policies, through resource designs such as traditional preschool buildings and equipment, and through pedagogical beliefs and practices such as teacher philosophy, and theories of learning and development. As was shown in previous chapters, these documents, resources and practices make visible those concepts or conceptual systems that are promoted in schools and early childhood settings in particular societies. Some knowledge systems are being actively promoted by governments (see chapter 1); as a profession we need to analyse what these knowledge traditions offer for young children. Some knowledge systems have not been a part of early childhood education, so they require analysis in relation to the play-based programs that characterise the field.

Specifically, empirical knowledge, narrative knowledge and theoretical knowledge (and thinking) are under review in this and the next chapter. These knowledges are societally developed collective knowledge systems that are valued within Western science traditions. There are other knowledge systems, such as the arts, religion and spirituality (e.g., indigenous views of country) that societies or communities value and support. Some knowledges, such as empirical knowledge and paradigmatic thinking, pervade school education systems around the world; as discussed earlier, these knowledges and ways of thinking are becoming increasingly significant for preschool education.

Given the current political context, it is important that early childhood educators undertake a full analysis of these knowledges and theories of thinking. Only then is it possible to theorise pedagogical practice in relation to the changing knowledge traditions being actively promoted by a society. Undertaking this conceptual work is necessary because the outcome will allow the early childhood profession to frame practice from within the field, rather than have the field positioned to adopt a particular view of pedagogy developed from outside early childhood education. This is particularly urgent if the knowledge traditions being promoted come from the medical field, where empirical knowledge is dominant, or from economics, where a teacher is conceptualised as a variable in economic modelling. These points will be taken up again in the final chapter in this book.

THEORIES OF KNOWLEDGE AND THINKING

Hedegaard (1999) has argued that the theories about thinking and the knowledge traditions that dominate Western societies can be conceptualised as either '*internal cognitive processes within people*' (but framed as a social activity) or as 'an *integrated part of social activity between persons*' (p. 24; emphasis added). Hedegaard (1999) cleverly shows this conceptualisation through an analysis of theoretical and research literature, naming four traditions: cognitive situated approach, cultural daily life approach, sociocultural approach and cultural–historical approach.

A *cognitive situated approach* positions thinking as a function of the individual, where individuals are supported through a social context to individually manipulate information. According to Hedegaard (1999), researchers who have conceptualised this approach or who have contributed to this knowledge tradition include well-known scholars such as Greeno (1997, e.g.) and Resnick (1989, e.g.).

A *cultural daily life approach* foregrounds thinking as occurring within the practice of everyday activities such as learning and using street mathematics to buy and sell produce within a community. Hedegaard (1999) argues that researchers who have contributed to this conception of thinking include Lave (e.g., 1991), Wenger (Lave & Wenger, 1991) and Scribner (1990).

A *sociocultural communicative approach* derives its name from authors such as Wertsch (1998, e.g.), who have framed their view of thinking from the works of Vygotsky and Bakhtin. In a sociocultural theory of thinking and knowledge generation, the present social context bears the birthmarks of historically created ways of being and doing that shape what people pay attention to and how they participate in activities, mediate events and learning, and communicate with each other. History in the present moment becomes an important dimension of this theoretical approach to how thinking is shaped. Importantly, sociocultural communicative approach foregrounds narrative forms of knowledge within the subject matter of history. Hedegaard also cites Billing (1991, 1993) within this classification of thinking, and suggests that the procedure of argumentation (forms of negotiation, acceptance, rejection and critique) is an important social process within the subject area of rhetoric.

Hedegaard (1999) argues that these theories of thinking and knowledge generation found in the literature do have 'aspects which are important to integrate into a cultural-historical understanding of thinking' (p. 25). Importantly, she identifies

- the social aspect of thinking
- thinking that is situated and distributed
- thinking as formed within everyday practice
- thinking characterised by communication and argumentation.

Hedegaard (1999) argues that in addition to these, there is also the content of thinking as a form of knowledge and the motives created to engage in particular forms of thinking. These concepts are part of a cultural–historical approach and Hedegaard (1999) argues that they can be found in the theories of Vygotsky (e.g., 1987a), Elkonin (e.g., 1999d), Davydov (e.g., 2008), Lompscher (e.g., 1999) and Lompscher, 1999), to which list I would also add Hedegaard (e.g., 1990, 1995, 1998, 1999, 2009).

Hedegaard (1999) conceptualises societal forms of knowledge as those collective knowledges that are generated in daily situations, including the many different types of institutions that a child participates in, such as home, preschool, childcare, school, clubs, and so forth. Importantly, she argues that in some institutional contexts, knowledges have become dis-embedded from the practices and the original problem area that drove the problem solving and generated the solution (which now forms our collective knowledge and understanding). Facts presented in textbooks about a subject area or subject matter, for example, such as the names of the states within the USA or the working out of mathematical formulas, are divorced from the original problem that geographers or physicists were trying to solve. One original problem area that is currently contested but mathematically rich is the challenge of coming up with a theory of unity for the universe (Einstein's theory of relativity) and for particle theory (quantum mechanics). String theory is one solution: in recent times unity has been mathematically achieved (something Einstein tried to achieve but could only theorise), but with no concrete way of determining the accuracy of the theoretical models being put forward. This represents a problem formulation – developing a theory of everything. Hedegaard (1999) suggests that mathematical formulas devoid of the problem area have characterised those education systems that primarily rely upon textbook explanations (i.e., the presentation of facts). A cultural–historical view of thinking would centre on the personal aspect of a child's thinking in relation to the original problem formulation through some form of active exploration (see chapter 7). Hedegaard suggests that most knowledge traditions tend to provide examples of the original problem, and then give children facts as a way of answering the question that the problem area has generated (i.e., the teacher gives the children the answer verbally or through textbook reading). According to Hedegaard (1999), these kinds of knowledge (empirical) and thinking (paradigmatic) underpin the discipline knowledge taught in many traditional schools. Yet, as the previous chapters have shown, many governments (and researchers) are actively promoting discipline content knowledge for early childhood education. Within the context of the early childhood institutions, knowledge and thinking traditions have focused upon social processes and the generation of personal knowledge through the formulation of narrative thinking. Attention is now turned to these knowledges and ways of thinking.

EMPIRICAL AND NARRATIVE KNOWLEDGES

Western communities steeped in industrial history have evolved over time and have used empirical knowledge to inform their development. As noted above, empirical knowledge underpins curricula models and educational activity in many schools, and increasingly is included in preschool programs as 'pre-numeracy' and 'pre-literacy' (see chapter 4). Empirical knowledge is built upon observation, description and quantification and is founded on a belief that through observation, knowledge can be generated about the physical world and accurately represented. Through this process, similarities and differences can be noted and measured. Representation and measurement allows for the organisation, categorisation and ordering of knowledge into hierarchies. Empirical knowledge becomes disembedded from the context in which it was generated.

Linked with empirical knowledge is paradigmatic thinking. In paradigmatic thinking, individuals move beyond the observable through organising information into categories. Through sorting the directly observable into categories of similarities, it is possible to transcend the individual observation. Through paradigmatic thinking higher forms of abstraction are achieved as categories become combined and single elements disappear. Hedegaard (2002) argues that 'paradigmatic thinking method and empirical knowledge [have] arisen through the search for invariance and general laws which can be used to make prediction' (p. 27). Bruner (1986) has argued that many 'prosthetic devices' have been invented to carry out this work (p. 13). Hedegaard (2002) states that school subjects such as mathematics, physics and biology have all evolved from the natural sciences, and through moving them outside the problem areas that created these knowledges, empirical knowledge and paradigmatic thinking methods began to dominate schools:

> Empirical knowledge presupposes that people have the ability to use categories to represent their knowledge of the world. Categorizing and use of categories is a way of creating order and simplifying experiences so they can transcend a given context and be transferred to other situations. Empirical knowledge forms and thinking methods are linked to sensory discrimination. This kind of discrimination can both be trained and refined.
>
> (Hedegaard, 2002: 28)

Empirical knowledge converts statements of fact generated through observations into 'statements implying causality' (Bruner, 1986: 11) in the quest for the ultimate search of universal truth. Bruner (1986), in citing Richard Rorty, states that 'the epistemological question of how to know truth' preoccupies paradigmatic thinking, while 'the broader question of how we come to endow experience with meaning' is the question of poets and storytellers or those who use narrative knowledge (p. 12). Bruner (1986) has argued that 'The imaginative application of the paradigmatic model leads to good theory, tight analysis, logical proof, sound argument, and empirical discovery guided by reasoned hypothesis'. But paradigmatic 'imagination' (or intuition) is not the same as the imagination of the novelist or poet. Rather, it is 'the ability to see possible formal connections before one is able to prove them in any formal way' (p. 13).

Bruner (1986), in formulating narrative knowledge, was able to name knowledge that was located at a specific time and place and within a situated context. Narrative knowledge is generated through a concern for the human condition, that is, a story is sad or humorous or contains a lesson. Bruner (1986) argued that in comparison to paradigmatic thinking, very little is known about narrative modes of thinking. He suggested that this was due in part to a simultaneous focus on action, consciousness and the accompanying 'story grammar'. It was shown in this book (see chapter 1) that the children who were playing with Humpty Dumpty were acting out and evolving a well-known rhyme. Consciousness includes 'what those involved in the action know, think, or feel, or do not know, think, or feel' (p. 14). The children in the Humpty Dumpty play repeatedly allowed Humpty Dumpty to fall off the wall so that they could administer their medicine, something that many children do not enjoy receiving themselves, but could through medicating Humpty Dumpty consciously play with emotions and feelings. Narratives leave the knowledge of the real world as implicit and focus explicitly on creating a world of psychic realities, never testing them, but rather seeking to make them believable. Empirical knowledge is generated through paradigmatic thinking, where theories must be tested and verified. Narrative knowledge values multiple perspectives in which the world can be simultaneously understood through different lenses.

Narrative knowledge is created through the everyday lives of children and families, and narrative thinking is characteristic of how children communicate with each other and with their families and the broader community. Hedegaard (2002) states that in Danish elementary schools, narrative thinking methods have underpinned the 'experience pedagogy' (but as noted earlier, what is valued knowledge in Nordic countries is changing). As was shown in the previous chapter, narrative knowledge was also used by the Australian teachers to discuss the children's everyday lives within the childcare centre (e.g., routines) and to give insights into the everyday concepts the children were experiencing through the materials and resources provided, such as filling and emptying buckets of sand. But teachers did not conceptually frame these experienced, and hence the children's thinking remained at the everyday experiential level.

Early childhood teachers who have traditionally been educated as social pedagogues are now finding that they must also have additional expert empirical knowledge of literacy and numeracy (and, increasingly, other subject matter areas). Being positioned to promote cognitive outcomes creates a pedagogical problem for the profession. Very little is known about how concept formation of discipline or subject matter knowledge occurs within play-based programs in which narrative knowledge and method has dominated. Hedegaard (1999) advises that 'Narrative knowledge is a necessary and valid knowledge in subject matter teaching', but she argues that 'it has to be put inside a frame of theoretical knowledge' (see chapter 7) 'whereby it is possible to combine situated learning and concrete life situations with theoretical concepts of subject matter knowledge' (p. 28). Bringing subject matter knowledge and pedagogical knowledge together has a brief history in early childhood education, and very little is known about how to do this effectively in play-based programs (notable exceptions are Bodrova & Leong, 1998, 2001; Kravtsov & Kravtsova, 2009; Kravstova 2008a, 2008b; van Oers, 2009; see also chapters 8 and 9 for a discussion of these play-based programs). These ideas will be discussed further in the next chapter.

SUMMARY

In this chapter narrative knowledge and empirical knowledge were introduced and discussed in relation to conceptual development in discipline areas. It was shown that narrative knowledge is a valuable form of knowledge, but it needs to be framed differently if conceptual development is to be promoted during everyday learning experiences within early childhood centres.

Empirical knowledge and paradigmatic thinking assume that the world can be represented accurately and measured correctly. Hedegaard (1999) states that 'Knowledge in this tradition is conceptualised as mental building blocks that can be stacked up or conceptualized as puzzle pieces which can be collected . . . knowledge does not change unless the information is wrong' (p. 27). As Davydov (1999b) contends, this view of knowledge transforms into discrete subject stacking, in which different 'blocks of knowledge' are built for different 'subject areas' resulting in empirical knowledge in which 'the child ends up with concepts and skills from different subject domains which are difficult to relate to each other' or to their everyday lives outside of school (Hedegaard, 1999: 27). Hedegaard (1999) further states that 'Empirical knowledge influences a great deal of the everyday life of people in Western industrialised societies. The argument is not to dismiss this kind of knowledge but to subordinate it to theoretical knowledge' (p. 28). In the next chapter theoretical knowledge and thinking is discussed in order to determine if this kind of approach can be used in play-based programs for promoting conceptual development.

7

Children building theoretical knowledge in play

[I]t is the knowledge systems that dominate the practices children participate in at different ages. If we want to give children conceptual competence that is more oriented toward theoretical knowledge, we must make this part of their everyday practice. So parents and educators should change the practice traditions that the children participate in to change the conceptual competence the child will acquire. Play, as the key activity for preschool children, offers the possibility for such a development where the motivational aspect is also involved.

(Hedegaard, 2007: 275)

INTRODUCTION

In the previous chapter empirical knowledge and narrative knowledge were introduced, critiqued and contrasted to show how empirical knowledge and paradigmatic thinking in play may limit rather than expand learning opportunities for children. As was shown, empirical–rational thinking enables humans to group and classify things and phenomena within the world 'by comparing and pointing out the interrelations of genus and kind' (Davydov, 1999a: 131). Through this type of thinking, 'it is possible to solve the tasks of relating things to a certain class (genus) or, vice versa, divide a class into certain subclasses or kinds' (p. 131). However, Davydov (1999a) stated that humans have another kind of thought and knowledge – theoretical knowledge and theoretical thinking. Davydov (1999a) writes that people in society frequently meet demands that require a system analysis where it is necessary to understand the particular and the general simultaneously, a task that requires a different kind of logic. In this chapter, theoretical knowledge and thinking are introduced in order to realise a new pedagogy for the current political and educational climate, and to afford (Gibson, 1979) new ways of thinking and working within early childhood education. The focus of this chapter is children's theoretical knowledge as dialectically related to teacher contextual and conceptual intersubjectivity (introduced in chapter 1).

THEORETICAL KNOWLEDGE

Vygotsky (1929) wrote about knowledge construction and the development of logical reasoning through a discussion of Petrova's research (1925). Two examples are cited below, in which children are unable to use logical reasoning and concept formation, but rather rely upon direct observations alone.

Example 1

A girl of nine years, quite normal, is primitive.[1] She is asked, 'In a certain school some children write well and some can draw well. Do all children in this school write and draw well?' She answers, 'How do I know; what I *have not seen with my own eyes*, I am unable to explain. If I had seen it with my eyes ...'

(Vygotsky, 1929: 2; emphasis in original)

In this example, in which the child works in her second language, Vygotsky states that 'She displays her total inability to think in words, although she speaks, i.e. can use the words as [a] means of communication. She does not understand how one can draw conclusions from words instead of relying on one's own eyes' (p.2).

In the second example the child has not yet developed a scientific concept of 'tree', even though he can name individual trees.

Example 2

[A] primitive boys [*sic*] is asked, 'What is the difference between a tree and a lot [of trees]?' He answers, 'I have not seen a tree, nor do I know of any tree, upon my word'. Yet there is a lime tree growing just opposite his window. When you ask him, 'And what is this?', he will answer, 'This is a lime tree'.

(Vygotsky, 1929: 2)

Having a scientific concept of a tree or knowing that it is possible to think and analyse with words, enables members of a community to build new understandings. How teachers build this knowledge in play-based programs is an important subject of research, whose significance cannot be underestimated. Theoretical knowledge is a powerful cultural tool and important for children to gain through their preschool education.

It is through the appropriation and transformation of subject matter knowledge that children develop personal cognition. Knowledges and thinking epistemologies are developed to support the needs and problems found within particular societies. Subject matter knowledge is one form of societal knowledge that has been generated in Western society to support its communities. Theoretical knowledge methods enable children to explore the relational concepts that make up particular knowledge system, such as mathematics or Darwin's theory of evolution. Theoretical knowledge generates for children symbolic tools 'that they can use to analyse and understand the complex and changing world' (Hedegaard, 2002: 36).

Davydov (1999a) argues that theoretical thinking supports children in orienting themselves to the general relationships found within materials and phenomena. Through theoretical thinking, children develop theoretical consciousness. Davydov (1999a) writes that people in society frequently meet demands that require a system analysis where it is necessary to distinguish between main and second order elements, basic and derived components of general and particular dimensions, and the essence and the phenomenon itself. It is important not only to determine the characteristics of the system but also to find the links between them. In this way, linkages are made visible. In theoretical thinking, it is also possible to determine a phenomenon derived from the core characteristics and to notice or construct particular features from a general characteristic. In this way it is possible to see that a general and a particular (phenomenon and core) of a system may not be similar. Davydov (1999a) suggests that they are often contradictory to each other. He sites the example of an electric globe as a concrete and particular object (physically observable globe) where the essence is a system of movement of electrical power that is not visible to the human eye (p. 132). Determining the essence of the globe (electrical movement) helps the learner to understand the general phenomenon of electricity. In theoretical thinking, the task of the child is to determine the essence of something (particular object such as a globe) and then trace it back to a general phenomenon (movement of electrical power). Davydov (1999a) states that the learner's thought moves 'from the general to the particular within a material' (p. 135), and then from the particular to the general. Davydov (1999a) suggests that

Humans solve all these tasks by means of dialectical/theoretical thinking within which contradictions can be handled in objective systems, to find mutual relationships and transitions in such holistic systems (p. 132).

Davydov (1999a) argued that 'the goal of educating and developing all school and college students' capacity for dialectical thinking [should be] in *all* matters' (p. 132).

Davydov (2008) theorised his developmental instructional method (discussed fully in the next chapter) on the basis of school aged children, where ascending from the abstract to the concrete encompassed human sensibility, encompassing the origins of concepts during the teaching process, the idealisation of objects in imagination and models, and perceiving sense data as a conception of a whole movement into a cognitive act, that is, for school-aged children to be supported in thinking theoretically they must experience the material world through the lens of contemplation. Davydov (2008) further argues that 'The task of theoretical thinking is to rework the data of contemplation and conceptions in the form of a concept, and thereby to fully reproduce the system of internal connections that give rise to the given concreteness and reveal its essence' (p. 100). To establish the core elements or the essence of the concept, primary aged children need to reproduce the concrete into some form of abstraction. In order to reveal the essence of the concept within the concrete in the form of an abstraction, such as a model, Davydov (2008) argues that

- the content being explored should include elements of the history of the development of the particular concept as a holistic system, such as looking at the beaks of birds on the Galapagos Islands in relation to their natural habitat and food sources for the development of the concept of natural selection
- the program of learning should deliberately include contradictions within the relational holistic system in order to help children to see differentiation such as weather changes that result from dry and wet years and result in changed food sources available to Galapagos Islands birds
- the content of the abstraction should be simple but allow for the essential relations of the system to be noticed, such as in the relatively independent components of habitat (including climatic conditions), species-food source, which will enable children to determine the essential relations between differentiated parts within the system, for instance, changing weather conditions change the habitat, which has a direct relationship to which bird species (with beaks to crack open hard seeds) will survive.

These relational links hold the independent parts of the concrete system together.

Davydov notes that through contemplation about the real relations within a holistic system abstraction of the concrete is possible. He argues that initial abstraction can be named as *concrete abstraction, the concretely universal relation, the objective cell of the whole being studied* or simply *cell* (Davydov 2008):

> The abstract and the concrete are moments of the differentiation of the object itself, of reality itself, as reflected in consciousness, and already for this reason they are derivative of the process of thinking activity. Asserting the objectivity of both of these moments is an important feature of dialectics as logic (p. 101).

In essence, the system is perceived as a cell of its concreteness, that is, the concrete cell is both individual and real, and universal and abstract: the beaks of the birds on the Galapagos Islands are real and tangible, while at the same time they are also universal abstractions for the concept of natural selection. The beaks encompass the relational essence of natural selection (habitat–weather change, species, food source). When children study the birds of the Galapagos Islands over time within a holistic system, using a model of species, habitat and food sources to frame their contemplation of seemingly independent components, the essence of the concrete is revealed as a universal concept. The concreteness of birds' beaks is obvious, real and external, while the essence 'is usually characterised as mediated, as internal, as the basis of phenomena', and the phenomena or concrete 'lie on the surface of things, as it were, while essence is hidden from direct observation' (2008: 103). Davydov (2008) states:

> Thus, essence is an internal connection, which, as the single source, as the genetic basis, determines all the other particular features of the whole. These are objective connections, which, in their differentiation and manifestation, provide for the unity of all aspects of the whole – i.e. they give the object its concreteness. In this sense, essence is the universal determination of the object (p. 103).

In rising from the abstract to the concrete there is a continual process of analysis by the child, where specific aspects of abstraction are needed to progress thinking towards the concrete. Davydov (2008) argues that in theoretical thinking, the concrete appears twice. The dialectical nature of concreteness can be seen as the concrete context begins and ends the process of contemplation, while the essence of the concept is revealed as concurrently universal and particular. Davydov, in citing Engels, states paradoxically that 'the general law of the change of form of motion is much more concrete than any single "concrete" example of it' (p. 105).

Rising to the concrete encompasses the pedagogical principle of initially examining a holistic system and mentally ascending to this system in order to determine its specific nature. Through establishing the individual relations it is possible to observe its universal character. Through this kind of contemplation, children discover a general law. Consequently, a concept must reflect the process of its historical and scientific development. Significantly, 'Empirical thinking solves the task of cataloguing or classifying objects and phenomena. Theoretical thinking sets itself the goal of reproducing the essence of the object of study' (Davydov, 2008: 107). Ascent is the leading and primary thinking activity. It is through these forms of thinking and knowledge generation processes that social consciousness arises and historically formed universals become available for individuals to use within society.

GENERATING THEORETICAL KNOWLEDGE IN PLAY-BASED PROGRAMS

In play-based programs designed for very young children there are many opportunities for generating children's theoretical knowledge. However, as shown in previous chapters, entering children's imaginary and conceptual worlds requires skilful pedagogical framing by the teacher and a deliberate consideration of concepts. An example of successful pedagogical framing by an early childhood teacher (Jacqui) is given below to illustrate how to build theoretical knowledge and thinking in children (see Fleer, 2008, for details of the study design and findings). An example of pedagogical practice that builds theoretical knowledge in play-based programs is illustrated in the following vignette and is discussed throughout this chapter:

> Jacqui, a recent honours graduate in early childhood education, observes Christian crouched down close to the ground observing a bull ant. Jacqui is the head teacher of an early childhood centre located in a heavily treed and thick bushland area in southern Australia. The outdoor area has many indigenous plants, is teaming with birds and insects, and has the usual playground equipment. Jacqui has noticed over time that Christian, a five

year old child, spends a great deal of time watching the wildlife at the centre. Both his mother and father are scientists. On this particular occasion, Christian becomes distressed by a bull ant because he fears that one of the children will be bitten by the ant or that the ant will be hurt by the children. Jacqui immediately suggests to Christian that they relocate the bull ant to a more appropriate place in the outdoor area. This suggestion is accepted, so Jacqui and Christian take a piece of cardboard and carefully scoop up and capture the bull ant. They then quickly discuss an alternative location, and together transfer the ant to another area

(Summary of field notes and video observations, 21 February)

Through studying his local environment, Christian actively builds knowledge of the organisms in the outdoor area. Over repeated observations, Christian has identified the visual characteristics of bull ants, and the adults in his life have given the insect a language label that he can use. The term *bull ant* becomes an abbreviated form of the sensorially perceived insect he has been viewing. The identification and use of generic words to label repeated observations permit a form of abstract universal generality to be attributed to his sensory experience and this allows Christian to make generalised judgements. As a result, he knows that the ant is not in the right place and makes judgements about what might happen if it stays where it is (a child might be bitten or the ant might be hurt). Davydov (1990) suggests that verbally expressed forms of activity become the subject matter for the 'senses of theoreticians' (p. 246). These begin as 'flashing impressions', in which elements of significance are singled out or are conceptualised as the essence of the thing being observed. Christian knows, for example, about the sharp pincers of the bull ants he has been observing and understands the pain they could potentially inflict. As Davydov (1990) notes, '*only* sensations and perceptions, sensory data, serve as the foundation and the source of all of man's knowledge about reality . . . the result of the activity of the "senses as theoreticians" are expressed in verbal form, which *carries the experience of other people*' (p. 248; emphasis added). Christian could draw upon the label and the previously established knowledge of bull ants biting to enter into a conversation with his teacher about his find in the outdoor area of the preschool.

Theoretical knowledge and thinking support children in building mental models, engaging in thought experiments and in ascertaining relational connections between many different elements within a system. Davydov (1990) argues that 'mental experimentation forms the basis of theoretical thought, which operates by *scientific* concept' (p. 249; emphasis in the original). Jacqui supported Christian's theoretical thinking through listening closely to his concerns and in relocating the bull ant; however, rather than leave his thinking at this level, she actively framed an expansive learning experience in order to build theoretical knowledge and thinking. Jacqui drew upon Christian's keen interest in the organisms in the outdoor area and framed a learning experience that could lead to an ecological understanding of the outdoor area.

> Jacqui and Christian sit together and talk about all of the creatures he has seen in the outdoor area. Christian becomes most engaged as Jacqui suggests that he take a magnifying glass into the outdoor area and a map (on a piece of paper) and mark down on the map what he sees. Christian goes into the outdoor area with his tools, seriously studying the environment. Christian's activity generates a motive for studying the environment for a number of other children, and before long there is a group of four children looking for creatures. As interest is generated, Jacqui gathers together magnifying glasses, insect capturing containers (have magnifying glass lids) and a pair of binoculars. These are used by the children. However, it is Christian who records the finds on the map.
>
> (Summary of field notes and video observations, 13 February)

A concept can represent a material object and be used to reflect on the material object. The concept enables a particular mental action to occur. To do this, a child must first be aware of the material object as a conscious mental representation. It is through this conscious reflection of the material object that the child can discover its essence. In the play-based program, Jacqui deliberately provided tools to support the children's observation of material things – the creatures to be found in the outdoor area. The tools foreground the act of looking closely at the creatures (binoculars, magnifying glasses) and the act of documenting or representing their finds on the map (piece of paper). By looking for and recording the creatures in their environment, Christian and the other children could begin to explain and describe their finds. This latter process generates opportunities in which the children can discover the essence of the creatures in their outdoor area. As Davydov (1990) states, 'mentally "drawing", "describing", etc., is none other than reproducing or constructing an object on an ideal level' (p. 250). This is an important dimension of theoretical thinking. Children learn to generate a mental representation of a material object (i.e., drawing of their insects), and through this the mentally generated object is replaced by another representation. The construction of the drawing becomes a mental model. The model is an abstraction, and this abstraction is characterised by the interrelationship between dependence and independence of factors associated with the material object. For Christian, he was representing insects in relation to where they could be found in the outdoor area. The insects and the outdoor area were transformed into a relational model of insects and habitats. On a subsequent day, Christian's theoretical learning was further developed.

> Christian takes the map he has made the day before and marked with an X, and invites Jacqui to follow him outside to look for bugs.

> JACQUI   Should we go and find the path?
> CHRISTIAN Yes.

> Christian has spent time each day looking carefully around the yard with binoculars and magnifiers but today he is trying to use the abstracted view of the yard that his map represents to locate bug treasure at point X. This is a new experience and a challenge and he seeks support from his teacher to embark on this venture.

> CHRISTIAN Can we find it . . . without the map?
> GRACE   I gave something to Christian. (*hands Christian something to encourage his treasure hunt search in the environment*)

> All four children follow Christian and the teacher
> (Field notes, 14 February)

The map represents a form of mental activity undertaken by Christian the day before. He has documented the idealised material objects – bull ants – and their system by noting their habitat. The X becomes a symbol. Davydov (1990) argues that 'Disclosure and expression in symbols of the mediated being of things, of their universality, is a transition to the *theoretical* reproduction of reality' (p. 251). The map that Christian generated focused on the relations between insect and habitat, but it could easily have been a complex ecosystem or a food chain. These latter models represent theoretical knowledge that Christian can more easily develop later because he is already building an important relational model between insects and habitats. Christian is using theoretical knowledge and thinking through the act of taking the map produced the day before, and locating the insects in their habitats. The relational model shown in figure 7.1 enables

Figure 7.1 Relational understanding of habitat and animal

Christian to work within his environment in new ways. Through this process, Christian begins to work with the abstract and the concrete. Christian plays with the idea of the particular and the general in a rudimentary way as he looks for similar habitats in other contexts. Note that a relational understanding between insect and habitat becomes established. Aidarova (1982), in her pedagogical research into theoretical thinking, has asked how can young children 'be given the idea of the universal, "key" qualities of the material, and then be taught to investigate the multifarious qualities and relationships these universal things have in reality on their own?' (p. 103). She argues that children can develop the 'ability to proceed from the general to the abstract, to the specific' through gaining 'the key enabling them to unlock the essential characteristics of the subject matter' from their teachers (p. 103). Through Jacqui framing Christian's investigations by inviting him to map his finds, Christian has used theoretical thinking and generated a relational model that can be used as a basis for expanding his current understandings of the knowledge system (e.g., habitat–animal) itself.

What is important about theoretical knowledge and theoretical thinking is the relational dimensions that are foregrounded. Davydov (1990), in drawing upon Davydova, has argued that theoretical knowledge 'always pertains to a *system of interaction*, the realm of successively connected phenomena that, in their totality, make up an organised whole' (p. 254; emphasis in the original). The unity principle that is connecting up the sensory data gathered by Christian is the relational constructs of insects and habitats. Christian's interest in the bull ant moves to an imaginary plane as he considers what bull ants eat, what other organisms eat, and how they digest the food they consume. Here he expands his relational model.

Christian's fascination with ecosystems extends and associations occur. He regularly lifts logs, collecting the slaters and millipedes under them and putting them in his bug catcher. In this encounter with Janice (assistant teacher) he seems to understand that bugs digest differently from humans.

JANICE   What do slaters eat?
CHRISTIAN Wood, leaves, everything.

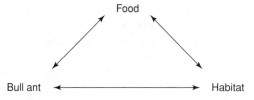

Figure 7.2 Relational understanding of habitat, food and animal

JANICE   If I ate wood, I'd get a tummy ache. Why doesn't the slater
            get one?
CHRISTIAN   It has germs in its tummy and they kick the tummy ache
            away. We don't have germs in our tummy.

When the research assistant (Avis) showed this conversation to Christian's
mother she believed that Christian's father had read him a book about this
at home.

(Field notes, 21 February)

Christian is drawing upon scientific concepts about digestion learnt at
home in order to engage in a discussion with the assistant teacher, Janice,
about what he knows within the context of the preschool centre and the
slaters he has found. The theme of eating continues as he tries to build a
relational understanding between the slater, the habitat and what the slaters
eat. Theoretical thinking enables children to expand their relational knowledge in the context of practice or concrete activity. Christian's expanded
theoretical thinking is represented in figure 7.2.

The assistant teacher has supported Christian to build a relational
model of animal, habitat and food. The play-based program operating
in Jacqui's centre enables Christian to field test his theoretical model, as is
shown below.

Christian often carries a bug catcher with him and on this day he is observed
talking to the bug as if it is a person. He seems concerned about the bug not
eating the grass he has put in to sustain it.

CHRISTIAN   Naughty boy. (*refers to bug not eating*)
AVIS   What have you put in there to help him?
CHRISTIAN   Grass, and he's not going to eat it.
AVIS   He doesn't seem to like grass
CHRISTIAN   He does eat grass.
AVIS   Does he?
CHRISTIAN   He's supposed to eat it.

AVIS   What else does he possibly eat?

CHRISTIAN   Grass, trees . . . leaves, but not trees.

AVIS   I suppose the things that are around him.

CHRISTIAN   Grass, leaves, branch, trees leaves, grass, leaves, trees, grass, trees, leaves . . . (*continues to repeat these names over and over*)

(Field notes, 27 February)

It is through the practice of interacting with his environment that Christian can grow his theoretical knowledge. Moving from the particular (slater) to the general (insect, habitat, food source) and from the general to the particular, required many experiences framed to support relational modelling by those who understood the knowledge system being used (e.g., Western science classification system) as framed by the teacher. Building a theoretical model takes time and requires many opportunities, which Jacqui's play-based program affords. This is no ordinary play-based program because Jacqui conceptually framed for Christian how to think about the animals he was regularly finding. The map was an important conceptual tool for helping Christian to build relational knowledge and supporting theoretical thinking. Once established, the theoretical model can be expanded, tested and modified according to the problem area being investigated. This type of conceptual framing builds subject matter knowledge, but in a very different way to isolated pieces of empirical knowledge that were being introduced by the teacher in the cooking and milkshake examples in chapters 1 and 2. Jacqui did not simply build a program around Christian's interests; she used the motives inherent in the activities he was participating in (see chapter 2) as the pedagogical approach and conceptually framed his activities so that he became more consciously aware of the animals, their habitat and their food. The awareness was relational, thus affording theoretical knowledge generation. Theoretical thought allows for mental modelling. Mental modelling requires imagination of a very special kind. Davydov (1990) suggests that imagination is important for universal conceptions and a powerful aspect for constructing a concept. Imagination is realised through conscious mental modelling (see chapter 10 for a fully developed discussion of imagination). In citing Shtoff, Davydov (1990) defines modelling in the following way:

A model means a mentally conceived or materially realized system that, by representing or reproducing an object of investigation, is capable of replacing it so that the study of it will yield new information about this object for us.

(p. 259–60; emphasis in the original)

Models enable children to move from the universal to the specific and from the specific to the universal. Aidarova (1982) states that

> models are used to generalise, plan and verify, by forming a model of some characteristic, children can amass an enormous amount of facts by focusing on the characteristic formalised in the model. In this way they learn to differentiate whether a particular phenomenon belongs to a given group of facts or not and why (p. 120).

Theoretical knowledge and theoretical thought enable children to think about a whole system of relational ideas or concepts. Theoretical thought is very useful to children for making sense of their world and for contributing to activities in very thoughtful ways. Vygotsky (1987a) argued that when children learn concepts, they need to learn them as part of a system, not as isolated pieces. Jacqui's play-based program enabled the relational learning of concepts within a full ecosystem in the preschool outdoor area. The children did not do mini lessons about concepts within discipline knowledge, something that is commonly associated with school timetables. Rather, Jacqui introduced learning to the children within a whole conceptual system. Learning experiences began with the whole, and through this, the children examined concepts in a relational way. Modelling resulted, but modelling was also introduced. 'Models are a form of scientific abstraction of a particular kind, in which the *essential relationships* of an object which are delineated are reinforced in visually perceptible and represented connections and relationships of material or symbolic elements' (Davydov, 1990: 261; emphasis in the original).

Aidarova (1982) suggests that

> by gradually revealing the initial, elementary model in a series of more complicated and articulated models, students get a chance to discover the interrelations between all of the problems they tackle. They construct a metaprogram of the course in terms of models. Individual topics and sections are therefore viewed not as separate, independent islets but as part of a road charted as a series of models (p. 121).

Jacqui provided a range of opportunities for Christian to model his relational understanding. Two examples follow, in which Christian uses imagination for painting and collage materials to create representations of his thinking. One extract is with Janice, the assistant teacher, the other is with Jacqui, his teacher. While the representations produced are not models per se of the relational thinking he has been undertaking, they are nevertheless thought experiments inspired by the theoretical thinking previously undertaken and captured through the medium of painting and the medium of collage. They also show how children build personal knowledge. The images created by Christian are similar in purpose (not content) to the children's work noted in research by Aidarova (1982) where older children (7–9 year olds) recorded in discovery notebooks what they were learning, next to the models they created to explain their understandings – rising from the abstract to the concrete, as they played with the general and the particular.

Observation 21 February

Christian continues to represent his earlier idea about digestion and has chosen the collage table to create an imaginary bug, such as Pacman, from a round piece of paper. He wants the character to function with a mouth that opens so it can 'burp, eat, bite and chomp'. With encouragement from assistant Janice, he cuts a design that allows the character to do this. Janice role plays with Christian's creation and he jumps with excitement when it is animated in front of his peer Cory. Christian often converses with the creatures he finds and is delighted when Janice brings this imaginary creature to life with comic voices.

JANICE Oh, wow . . . what fun . . . (*plays with the Pacman; opens its mouth*)
CORY   Excuse me . . .
JANICE He got a circle, right? And he got two dots for eyes and he cut cut cut for the mouth . . . look Cory.

(Field notes, 21 February)

Observation 27 February

Christian is at a table with food dye and brushes when he spontaneously paints and explains about a machine he has represented on paper that can suck up bull ants.
   The machine he painted represented a functional solution to managing stray bull ants that might bite and offered thought as to what might happen should they get sick.
   As he paints he explains how the bull ants find their way to the dentist.

CHRISTIAN It goes up there and it gets the ants and this is when they go to the dentist.
JACQUI   Go to the dentist?

CHRISTIAN Yeah, that's when they get sick and then they go here. (*points to a line in his picture*)

(Field notes, 27 February)

Davydov (1990) argued that even in activities that are cognitive in their mode and intention, 'human sensation *goes beyond* the limits of the appearance and immediacy of being' (p. 264; emphasis in the original). Christian organised his creative work in ways that were shaped by the concepts he was contemplating and expanding, but their expression was through the imaginary creation of bull ant sucking machines, visiting the dentist (painting) and an imaginary creature biting (collage). In both cases we witness productive imagination, as Christian foregrounds eating and biting in relation to a problem area – bull ants being in the wrong place in the preschool outdoor area. Aidarova (1982) states that 'When children construct models which reflect the basic characteristics of the material, they get a visual picture of how one model can be transformed into another' (p. 121). Christian, through his imagination, provides alternative ways of dealing with the problem area, even though it was successfully resolved by relocating the bull ant. In Jacqui's play-based program, as with many other preschool programs in European or European heritage communities, there are many opportunities for representing thinking.

Aidarova (1982) states that 'children can master modelling as a two-way, reversible operation which enables the child to proceed from the specific features of the material to general, abstract characteristics and the reverse – from the abstract to the specific' (p. 141). She has also found in her research with older children that it is also possible to formulate a problem as a model in which children examine some known facts. Through working in both ways – using and verifying models, or creating models – children learn three main functions of models – generalising, planning and verifying.

Models can be created within holistic contexts or knowledge systems because children have a sense of the whole learning situation. In Jacqui's program, the holistic context was created through noticing and supporting a problem area of a bull ant being in the wrong place. Within this meaningful situation, it was possible for Jacqui to introduce previously established scientific knowledge (i.e., Western science systems):

Jacqui has charts and insect identity sheets as resources for children in the centre who want to name the bugs they find. Christian has found a bug and believes it to be a centipede. He brings it indoors for clarification of identification. Christian looks closely at the chart and points to and names the centipede, mosquito, praying mantis and lacewing.

CHRISTIAN I think that's a centipede.
JACQUI I think that's a centipede. Yep. I'll read the word centipede. Yep, that one's a centipede. That one's a millipede. They're the ones we find around the kinder all the time.
CORY We found one. Sticks on. I think it will go through those holes.
CHRISTIAN Mosquito.
JACQUI That one's called a scorpion fly.
CHRISTIAN Praying mantis.
JACQUI Special names.
CORY Praying mantis.
JACQUI Yep.
CHRISTIAN Lacewing.

(Field notes, 27 Febrruary)

Davydov (1990) states that there are conditions for the activity of theoretical thought, one of which is the wholeness of the object under investigation. For a universal connection to be established, the learning context must work with the wholeness of the object and the interdependence of its elements. Simply naming the insects on the chart out of their ecological context would not have engaged the children or enabled theoretical thinking to take place. The children and Jacqui were studying the chart in order to identify the insects they were finding within their preschool setting, and Jacqui's conceptual framing ensured that the children were looking and thinking relationally – 'They're the ones we find around the kinder all the time'. The relational model of insect–habitat–food that was being developed could be applied across the whole range of insects being found by the children in the preschool setting. Inviting the children to represent all of the insects and all of the habitats found or could be found is not a productive activity for children to engage in and is, as Davydov (1990) states, 'beyond the potential of sensation'. However, examining a problem area – bull ant in the wrong place – and generating a theoretical model is most productive. The sense of modelling, models and theoretical thought are evident:

In principle, the view that thought is needed where our 'eyes' cannot glance, either because of external space-time obstacles (for example, the opposite side of the moon was such for a certain time), or because of the exceptionally small or large dimensions of the objects being studied (the atom or the galaxy), also amounts down to this point of view.

(Davydov, 1990: 268)

Educational programs that seek to build theoretical knowledge and thinking focus on five fundamental principles:
1 an analysis of the origins of the knowledge under investigation (rather than being presented with facts) by children acting as researchers
2 general and broad concepts are explored (rather than beginning with specific micro level ideas)
3 universal relations are needed to structure a given set of ideas
4 the relational universals are reproduced in some graphic form or model representing the material or phenomenon under study
5 teacher knowledge of these relational constructs (e.g., model) is necessary for planning and implementing the educational program.

If we were to conceptually represent what Jacqui was doing in her play-based program as a pedagogical model, we would begin by documenting the core concepts within the subject matter that Jacqui was working with. In the first part of the figure, Jacqui's knowledge system is shown. Jacqui has identified the core concepts within the knowledge system that Christian has shown an interest in. Aidarova (1982) has noted in her own pedagogical research that,

in working out a program which would make it possible to present material proceeding from abstract to specific, it was necessary to single out some fundamental concept from which all the rest, theory, and practice, would be deduced, that is, all other ideas could be presented as an extension of the more general concept (p. 106).

In Jacqui's program, she actively brings together Christian's everyday concepts and the core concepts within the deliberate framing of a map in order to support Christian in building theoretical knowledge and thought. She has knowingly drawn upon Christian's interest in observing insects to generate a motive for building theoretical knowledge through mapping the finds in the outdoor area. She has also provided tools that Christian can use for testing out the theoretical knowledge and thinking he has acquired, such as identifying the slaters on the charts or in the books, playing with some of his ideas through painting and creating with collage materials. It is through Christian building his own relational model, with Jacqui's support, that it becomes possible to single out some universal characteristics, such

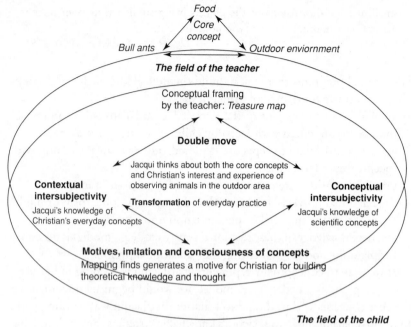

1. Jacqui is able to engage Christian in shared sustained conversations about the bull ant in relation to the core concepts of animal–habitat–food.
2. Christian is building a theoretical model that he can use beyond bull ants. He tries out some of his ideas through creative activities (bull ant sucking machine) and in identifying other insects (slaters).

Figure 7.3 Jacqui's pedagogical model for building Christian's theoretical knowledge

as habitat and organism, in order to introduce a set of specific facts – the names of the particular organisms the children have found, or some universal fact – an ecosystem. Figure 7.3 shows Jacqui's pedagogical approach and conceptual system in action.

From this practical example of Christian and Jacqui, the next section draws on the essence of those features we need to pay attention to when theorising how theoretical knowledge builds in play-based programs.

A MODEL FOR BUILDING CHILDREN'S THEORETICAL KNOWLEDGE IN PLAY-BASED PROGRAMS

An analysis of Jacqui's pedagogical approach and Christian's learning reveals that the pedagogical model built over the previous chapters were exemplified in her program. But the significance of teacher knowledge for

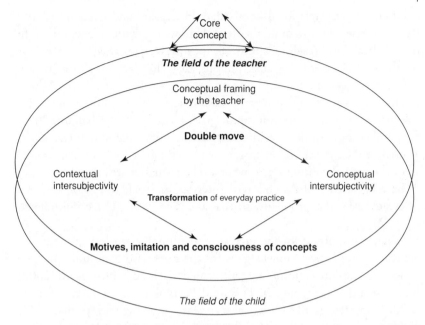

Figure 7.4 A pedagogical model for building theoretical knowledge in play-based programs

building a core concept is an additional dimension not previously featured. In this section, *core concepts* and *conceptual framing* in particular are discussed as important elements for building theoretical knowledge in play-based programs. These are shown diagrammatically in figure 7.4.

CORE CONCEPTS

Represented in the first part of the model is the identification of the core concepts that make up the relational system (e.g., animal–habitat–food). The conceptual system that it links to is subject matter knowledge (e.g., designing collages) or discipline knowledge (e.g., biology) as a valued form of societal knowledge for children to acquire in Western communities. Establishing what are the core concepts in a knowledge system is critical for giving direction for pedagogical framing in concept formation. Identifying the core concepts enables the teacher to frame learning so that it builds theoretical thinking and knowledge construction. That means the wholeness of the knowledge system, as concrete practice, must be the starting place for the child and the teacher. For Jacqui, this meant taking the problem of finding a bull ant in the wrong place as the motive for helping children establish relational knowledge. Hedegaard and Chaiklin (2005) have researched how to build theoretical knowledge with older children. In their radical–local teaching approach, they draw upon Davydov's writings on theoretical knowledge and thinking to realise Vygotsky's distinction between subject matter concepts and everyday concepts. Radical–local teaching goes one step further by taking account of children's everyday lives at home and in the community (see Hedegaard & Chaiklin, 2005, for a full account of this teaching approach). They suggest that teachers

1 analyse the subject matter area so that teaching is based on a core model of the central concept relations of a subject matter area
2 have knowledge of the children's interests and background
3 create tasks and problems, so that the core concepts are illuminated (p. 71).

What is important for the success of a cultural–historical approach for generating theoretical knowledge is for the teacher to determine the core concepts. The core concepts are represented as a model. Hedegaard (2002) has termed this a core model. This model acts as a conceptual tool for the children in Hedegaard's (2002) experimental teaching with primary aged children. For preschool aged children, the core model is created by the teacher through framing the play activity, with the support of some kind of conceptual tool, such as a map, so that the children begin to systemically see the relations between concepts. As Hedegaard (2002) has stated:

> Core models can function both as a tool for the teacher in his/her preparatory work, and as an aid to the pupils in their research activities. The main characteristic of core models is that gradually they can be extended from being a simple relationship between two basic concepts within a particular subject area, to a point where it comes to illustrate the relationship between the subject matter's central concepts. This type of model can help the teacher to formulate relevant problems for the children's exploratory activities. It can also help the children to gradually learn how to combine and sum up the various themes and concepts explored and introduced during the course of the teaching. As the assignments set by the teacher are governed by these concepts, the children, through their own research, will be able to formulate their own model which they can then develop still further and eventually use to evaluate what they are actually learning (p. 86).

Clearly, very young children are unlikely to create their own relational models; however, they can create within the system of exploration framed carefully by the teacher, representations of their thinking through the media available in the preschool environment, such as collage, drawing materials, construction materials and painting equipment. In the radical–local teaching approach, Hedegaard and Chaiklin (2005) give a nice example of pedagogical framing for primary aged children, in which the children are actively positioned to act as researchers investigating their environments.

1 Who is investigating?
2 What is being investigated?
3 What do we know, and what do we not know, about the problem area?
4 How can we formulate a model of the core relations to research?
5 What methods will we use to investigate the problem?
6 How do we evaluate our findings? (p. 73)

While this approach is most creative and engaging, it relies upon the teacher having a very clear understanding of the core model being used to frame the children's learning. Unfortunately, not all teachers believe in the importance of identifying core models (subject matter knowledge systems) as the basis of their conceptual planning. Hedegaard and Chaiklin (2005) suggest that

> many teachers are not familiar with the idea of using theoretical concepts in relation to elementary school children, and do not have experience themselves in working with theoretical concepts. They are not usually prepared to work with models of conceptual relationships, using them as tools for planning educational tasks, and helping children to investigate these tasks as a way of forming these models as tools and are used to construct explanations for the problems under investigation and formulating new questions. The teacher in the teaching experiment reported here commented once that it was sometimes difficult for her to allow the children to investigate problems, because she did not feel like a teacher if she was not telling them things. Even if the problems . . . about having relevant local knowledge and adequate subject–matter analysis of conceptual relations, were resolved, there will still be the significant problem of helping teachers to understand and use conceptual models both for planning teaching task and in teaching interactions (pp. 195–6).

CONCEPTUAL FRAMING BY THE TEACHER

In the second part of the model the conceptual framing within meaningful contexts is shown. Here, the teacher keeps in mind the core concepts (scientific concepts) while ascertaining the child's everyday concepts in relation to the intellectual area being considered. Because the teacher wants to transform the child's everyday practice through being conscious of the particular concepts being explored, it becomes important to consider how the scientific concepts may relate to the child. Determining both contexts and the thinking of the child in relation to the concepts being explored is critical. Here, a conceptual intersubjectivity is created, that is, teachers can only enter into the child's conceptual world if they find out what everyday concepts and contexts are meaningful to the child. Having the everyday concepts and the scientific concepts in mind allows for the generation of educational activity that frames the child's thinking: Jacqui created the idea of the children mapping the insects found in their preschool environment. This conceptually frames how the children think as they engage in educational activity. The children think consciously about the concepts and consider them within the relational system of knowledge they are exploring. The children and the teacher must align their thinking. Successful educational activity leads to theoretical thinking and knowledge generation. For children, thinking theoretically means they can take their models to other contexts and think and act differently.

Hedegaard (2002: 81) has shown that it is important to 'use a teaching approach that motivates the pupils to plan and participate in research activities with the object of creating a link between the pupils' own questions and the problems that are central for the subject being taught' (p. 81). The child's comment and question, 'The bull ant is in the wrong place. Where should it be?', for example, provided a useful connection to relational knowledge in biology.

> Such an approach may involve the children in an active problem formulation and exploration of central themes in the subject areas, by relating the children's own questions to the problem tackled with the subject area. If this connection is established, it will be possible to create teaching within the children's zone of proximal development (p. 81).

When teachers are conceptually and contextually in tune with the child, they are able to frame the learning activities the children participate in so that they generate a motive for expanding their play and learning. Hedegaard (2002) suggests that 'Motives and knowledge are dialectically connected because knowledge gives content to motives and motives determine knowledge appropriation' (p. 79). This theorisation of motives moves beyond that put forward by Leontiev (1978) and is more closely aligned with the original intentions of this concept introduced by Vygotsky (1987a) and discussed further by Elkonin (2005a–c) and Kravtsov (2009a) (see next chapter).

Motives have also been the subject of pedagogical research by Aidarova (1982). Aidarova (1982) introduced the idea of learning remaining eventful. In researching how children develop theoretical knowledge and thinking in relation to the Russian language, she notes, like Hedegaard (2002), that the problem formulation should be broad, such as, 'How did people first communicate with each other?' Through children acting as researchers (writing or drawing in their discovery notebooks, generating models to answer their question, evaluating and reflecting and through dramatisation of the concepts they are examining), wearing badges to denote their role (e.g., planning, formulating models, evaluating), and where these roles are rotated, that a collective orientation to the problem area is introduced, re-introduced and concluded within and across lessons. The child researchers investigating a problem area, present their research findings in a way that adds further understandings. Aidarova (1982) invited the children to create their own textbooks on how to study the Russian language. The children drew upon the findings contained within their discovery notebooks to analyse material, and decide on the essence of the content to report within the textbook they were creating. Through evaluating existing textbooks, and through writing their own, the children were able to adopt a new point of view – that of the textbook author. These pedagogical strategies generate motives for studying content knowledge within the school context and add to our understandings of how theoretical knowledge can be taught in schools.

While groundbreaking research has been undertaken with children into the building of theoretical knowledge (Aidarova, 1982; Davydov, 2008; Hedegaard, 2002; Hedegaard & Chaiklin, 2005), this work has focused on school contexts and with older children or in an afterschool setting with much older children. It is well understood that in Western communities play is a leading activity (Vygotsky, 1966) for children aged five years and younger; therefore the pedagogical work done by teachers working with this age group needs to be conceptualised quite differently from that of school aged children. While Vygotsky's (1987a) theoretical ideas on concept formation centred on the school age child, it is now evident that preschool aged children in many societies who are growing up in the 21st century are now also expected to know more about subject matter knowledge. The model shown above seeks to theorise how pedagogical approaches in play-based programs can afford concept formation in subject matter knowledges for early childhood children. The model helps foreground the significance of imagination and play for building theoretical knowledge across subject domains, such as the arts, the sciences, language and literacy and technology, not to mention other knowledges that a society values and wants its children to learn.

SUMMARY

In this chapter, the material presented in the previous chapters was brought together and a pedagogical model for building theoretical knowledge in play-based programs was introduced. In particular, the model was illustrated through examples of data where children's generate theoretical knowledge and where teachers have conceptual and contextual intersubjectivity. The model introduced in this chapter begins to make visible the highly complex work that early childhood teachers do when developing children's conceptual knowledge. However, more needs to be understood about the imaginary framing provided by the teacher or introduced and enacted by the children. In the next two chapters, imagination and children's development will be actively considered through a theoretical discussion of play from a cultural–historical perspective.

NOTE

1 *Primitive* is the term used by Vygotsky to refer to people with important cultural knowledge of their communities but who had no direct experiences of formal schooling.

Part 2
Cultural–historical theories of play and learning

8

Cultural–historical programs that afford play development

First I have a sense of the object, then I develop a relation to the object, and finally, I understand the object. I gain a social and cultural relation to the objects in my world.

(Kravtsova, 2009a)

INTRODUCTION

In this chapter a review of educational programs that specifically theorise play from a cultural–historical perspective is undertaken in order to better understand how concept formation in play can be systematically operationalised within classrooms and centres. In this chapter the programs for preschool aged children and primary aged children are reviewed, followed by an analysis of those cultural–historical conditions which afford concept formation. A more expansive discussion of play as a leading activity is considered in subsequent chapters.

This chapter begins with an analysis of the basic essence of play through an examination of the differing theoretical views on what drives play. A discussion of the fundamental differences between belief systems found within the literature on play is given in order to gain insights into cultural–historical programs that support concept formation.

MOTIVES FOR PLAY – BIOLOGICAL OR CULTURAL?

The nature and essence of play, particularly role play, has been the subject of serious study by Elkonin (2005a–e), whose research focuses primarily upon the psychological structure of mature forms of play, their origins, development and decline, and the significance of play for the future development of the child (personality). In Elkonin's analysis of play research across cultures, he argues that much of the Western literature has attributed motives in play to biological processes, while the literature in the Russian context, particularly the writings of Vygotsky (1966), has foregrounded the driving forces for engagement in play as social and cultural. This is echoed in the writings of Bodrova (2008), who also argues that Western writings on play have tended to attribute the essence of play to internal rather than external phenomena. She suggests that the fallout of this latter view is that educators in Western countries are reticent to become involved in children's play, and tend not to support the teaching of play (Bodrova, 2008).

Further, Bodrova (2008; see Johnson, Christie & Wardle, 2005, & Karpov 2005 for reviews) argues that mature forms of play are now less evident in some communities, such as the USA, when compared with the play of previous generations of children:

> Researchers from different countries agree that make-believe play of today's children is not simply different from the play of the past, but that it has declined in both quality and quantity
>
> (Bodrova, 2008, 364)

In reviewing the American literature, Bodrova (2008) suggests that children are given complete replica toys, the use of which requires little shared imagination to begin and sustain playscripts among children. She states that 'Many of today's preschoolers grow up using extremely realistic toys and as a result have a hard time with the concept of "pretend"' (p. 366). She argues for the importance of play materials that encourage children to imagine and to pretend. Göncü, Jain and Tuermer (2007) also note that in the low SES communities they researched (African American, European American, Turkish) variability in access to toys was related to economic circumstances and parents' beliefs about the value of play. They found that

> community poverty, [and] family poverty had only limited influence on US children's play. Despite their poverty, the caregivers made time and monetary provisions to provide play opportunities for the children. Although they were not provided with the kinds of play environment of the affluent families described by Haight and Miller (1993) all the U.S. children had some toys (p. 170).

In contrast to Bodrova (2008), Göncü, Jain and Tuermer (2007) noted that a perceived lack of pretence play and the associated deprivation of particular forms of representational or abstract thinking across cultures was due in part to the narrow views of the researchers in relation to what constituted play, and an incorrect belief that symbolic forms of thinking were developed only through pretend play. They cite researchers such as Sutton-Smith and Brice-Heath (1981) to illustrate other possibilities for decontextualised symbols needed in the Western world, and cite, for example, fairy tale characters in play and in Huli myth (ogre, trickster) (see Goldman, 1998, in relation to communities in the Southern Highlands Province of Papua New Guinea, who signify meaning of events, people and objects through pretend play as an interpretative activity for understanding particular symbols of Huli myth).

Comparisons between the social context of the past in relation to children's play has also been the topic of theorisation by Kravtsova (2009b). She suggests that in the Russian context, the families children live in are small when compared with the extended families of the past, in which there were many children of differing ages all playing together, taking different roles. She argues that today, when children live in smaller families, it means that there are less opportunities for multi-aged groups to work and play together. Bodrova (2008) also supports this position, and suggests that children of today have fewer play partners and less opportunities to play with more experienced play partners.

Play partners has also been the topic of research by Göncü, Jain and Tuermer (2007), who suggest that adult involvement in play reflects family values and economic circumstance. In their research they found that in low SES European American and African American communities in the USA, adults valued children's play and contributed to their children's play by acting as play partners (when chores and economic conditions allowed), while in low SES Turkish communities they researched, the play partners were mostly other children, reflecting play as a child's activity. They argued that values and beliefs around play were culturally constructed and economically embedded, a finding that has also been noted by Gaskins, Haight and Lancy's (2007) study of Euro Americans and Taiwanese communities. Gaskins, Haight and Lancy's (2007) found that even in communities who cultivate play, variability in valuing an event can be found and 'it appears that cultures have different levels of investment in play, and it is not always a privileged and unique activity in children's lives' (p. 200). Bodrova and Leong (1998) argue that with 'skilful instructional interventions' children can develop mature forms of play (p. 119), and adults need to take a major role in developing children's play.

Theories about what constitutes play activity, the motives for engagement in those kinds of activities and the place of adults within play have all changed over time. Much of the classical literature on play as summarised in most textbooks and handbooks on child psychology (see Rubin, Fein & Vandenberg, 1983) in Western communities features the surplus energy theory of play (see Schiller, 1954; Spencer, 1873; Tolman, 1932), the relaxation and recreational theories of play (Lazarus, 1883; Patrick, 1916), the practice theory of play (Groos, 1898; 1901) and the recapitulation theory of play (Gulick, 1898). Smith (2007), in reviewing much of the Western literature, argues that an evolutionary foundation for play dominated much of the literature after Darwin's evolutionary theory was published (1971 [1859]), and that researchers focused on comparisons of animal and human behaviour in their works. Smith (2007:25) argues that these studies dropped in popularity when evolutionary thinking embodied the concept of sociobiology (see Wilson, 1978) and that during 'a lull from the mid-1980s to the mid-1990s, research on play from an evolutionary perspective picked up' (e.g., Power, 2000) and emergence of cultural variations and the development of life history theory became popular (see Bock, 2002; Kaplan, Lancaster, Hill & Hurtado, 2000). Smith (2007) argues that

> An evolutionary approach embraces both universals and cultural variations in play. It would be different from a cultural deterministic view, however, in seeing human play predispositions as being influenced by our genetic inheritance, in interactions with cultural environments that themselves might vary to greater or less extents from the kinds of environments in which we evolved. A fuller rapprochement between evolutionary developmental psychology and cultural–ecological models of development is a promising task for the next decade (p. 43).

According to Elkonin (2005a), most theories of play are based on biological determinants of the motives for play activity. These classical theories have been perpetuated by the next generation of influential play theorists, such as Smilansky (1968) and Parten (1932, 1933), who have developed the concept of the biological impetus for play into theories that feature stages of play that all children go through during their development. These theories privilege a naturally evolving biological view of play. These latter play theorists have also been shown to be ethnocentric due to a belief on the part of the researchers that the absence of a particular form of pretend play represented inferiority on the part of the children and community (see Fleer, 1999; Göncü, Jain & Tuermer, 2007). Elkonin (2005a) has argued that 20th century theories of play put forward by scholars such as Freud (1959 [1908]), Piaget (1945) and Bruner et al. (1976) have also tended to foreground biological drivers for play (see Elkonin, 2005a; Kravtsov, 2008b). Other scholars who were writing in the same period, such as Vygotsky (1966), Leontiev (1944 cited in Elkonin, 2005a) and Elkonin (2005a), have provided an alternative reading to this biological view of play. These cultural–historical theorists give new insights into the nature of play for the psychological development of children, which contemporary scholars have evolved further (see Kravtsov & Kravtsova, 2009), despite the fact that many researchers were 'influenced by the dominant developmental theorists who focused almost exclusively on pretend play (e.g., Leont'ev, 1981; Piaget, 1945; Vygotsky, 1978; Göncü, Jain, Tuermer, 2007: 157)'. Some of these theories will be discussed later in this chapter.

The essence of play as a biological force in much of the Western literature is an interesting phenomenon. In order for Western heritage scholars and practitioners to appreciate the different worldview on play being put forward by contemporary cultural–historical scholars, it is important to devote some space in this section to illustrating the significance of a cultural–historical construction of motives for the play of children today through a discussion of Elkonin's (2005a) historical origin of role play.

Elkonin (2005a) sought to explicitly examine the origin, development and discontinuation of certain forms of play throughout history in order to understand the cultural nature of play for driving play activity. Through analysing the research literature on play artefacts, such as toys, and anthropological research into how societies and communities operated, particularly how children spent their time in relation to the social and economic forces at the time, he noted that the earliest societies devoted their time to simple survival activities. In those early societies, children were not given toys, but rather had access to tools or processes for food production and survival. The tools available to communities, such as digging sticks, were simple and children required no special instructions to operate them. The children participated in basic food production processes and entered adult life at a very young age (usually 10 to 12) already proficient in contributing to society.

As societies developed more sophisticated tools, scaled down versions of tools were created so that children could continue to participate in the life support process for human survival in their society. Practice or training sessions became necessary, so children used some of their time learning how to operate tools such as slings or bows and arrows. The scaled versions, with instruction and continuous practice, meant that children could, when proficient, contribute to the adult activities for human survival. These new technologies meant also that children spent time practising or being trained; hence their engagement in these forms of activities constituted an important social need for the whole community. Elkonin (2005a) cites Bogoraz-Tan (1934), where girls were given cloth dolls filled with sawdust as a fertility symbol as well as for supporting children to learn how to sew clothing, initially for the dolls, but with proficiency for making significant contributions to clothes production for the needs of the family (see also Stebnitskii, 1930, cited in Elkonin, 2005a). Elkonin (2005a) further argues that historically, string was an important technology for fishing, where nets were created using special knots and weaves. He (2005a) argued that the string games found today across different cultures of the world, such as cat's cradle, were originally designed for children to learn complicated movements and knots for the creation of technologies such as fishing nets. Elkonin (2005a) argues that the children's training and use of these kinds of scaled down artefacts were treated seriously, as the connection between them and real work were obvious. The motives for engagement with the artefacts, and therefore the time devoted to learning how to use them, was important for becoming a productive contributing member of the family and society at large.

With the further development of production within a society, and the increasing complexity of work and the resulting technologies that emerged, children's involvement in work became increasingly difficult, particularly as a division of labour began to occur within communities. Elkonin (2005a) cites Kosven (1927): initially, the tilling of the land was a family activity, with the stronger adult piercing the hardened soil with a spade; another adult followed and further loosened the soil and the children rubbed the loosened soil between their fingers, thus finalising the process of soil preparation. Later, more tools were created and scaled down versions were produced for children's use. With the advent of ploughs, which were pulled by oxen, young children could no longer participate in the preparation of the soil for planting. The increasing complexity of the work meant a division of labour resulted, after which it became difficult for children to participate in productive labour. As a result of the complexity of the technologies and the division of labour, the mastery of these more complex tools occurred much later in a child's life. Elkonin (2005a) argues that this led to the extension of childhood, and states that

> it is important to underscore that this lengthening did not occur through the addition of a new developmental period following the existing ones, but through insertion of a new period of development, causing the period

during which productive tools were mastered to be displaced to an older age (pp. 86–7).

If we are to accept Elkonin's (2005a) review of the anthropological and archaeological literature, then we can see that during society's historical evolution the child's place within society has changed as a result of new emerging social systems and more complex technologies. The child's changing position in the system of social relationships has significantly altered and created the present context in which childhood has been lengthened. The child now has a minor role to play in the production of work for survival of the family unit, and the child's relationship to scaled down artefacts has changed, even though they continue to exist within society (bows and arrows, dolls and dolls' clothes, string games, for example). Elkonin (2005) argues that during this transformation of the child's place in the system of social relationships children develop a motive towards pretending to participate in the adult world because they no longer contributed or were directly involved in it. Elkonin (2005a) states that

> Now we can formulate the most important proposition for the theory of role play; role play develops in the course of society's historical evolution as a result of changes in the child's place in the system of social relationship. It is thus social in origin as well as in nature. Its appearance is associated not with the operation of certain internal, innate, instinctive energy, but rather with well-defined social conditions of the child's life in society (p. 86).

Role play and play in general, when viewed from a cultural–historical perspective, foregrounds the social conditions that give rise to the motives for participation in play. The essence of play, the driving force for participating in play by children, when viewed from a cultural–historical perspective, is social and not biologically innate (Elkonin, 2005a). With this basic proposition in mind, we now turn to a review of contemporary play-based programs that have been designed specifically to support concept formation.

PLAY-BASED PROGRAMS THAT SUPPORT CONCEPT FORMATION

Internationally, there are few early childhood educational programs that have been developed using cultural–historical theory and which have been designed specifically to build conceptual knowledge through play. Three

examples are given to illustrate how researchers and practitioners have conceptualised and implemented cultural–historical programs that use play for
building theoretical thinking – the Golden Key Program (*Zolotoi Kluchik*)
in Russia (Kravtsov, 2009b; Kravtsov & Kravtsova, 2009; Kravtsova,
2009b; Kravtsova & Rubashkina 2009), Tools of the Mind in North
America (notably, the USA) and Developmental Teaching in the Netherlands (van Oers, 2009). They are discussed because they give insights into
the structural and conceptual dimensions for realising a cultural–historical
program in action. First, the programs are described and discussed; in the
latter section, a full analysis is presented.

GOLDEN KEY SCHOOLS

Vygotsky's (1966) theory of play, as elaborated through empirical research
by Kravtsova and Kravtsov (2009) provides a rich explanation of the
significance of play for preschool aged children's learning (Kravtsova &
Rubashkina, 2009) and is very different from that which is found in the
general European and European heritage literature (see Bodrova, 2008,
for a critique between Western and Russian theories of play). Of particular significance is the role of the adult in developing play and conceptual
knowledge through the creation of imaginary situations in the centre. In
this section, this work is considered through a discussion of Kravtsova's
theoretical and empirical work.

The development of imagination in unity with cognition has received
empirical and theoretical consideration by Kravtsova (2008a, b) and
Kravtsov (2008a) and is critical for understanding Vygotsky's cultural–
historical writing on concept formation. Concern for building concepts
within play-based programs for preschool aged children (and school aged
children) has been a topic of research in Russia by Elena Kravtsova and her
colleagues through their work in the Golden Key schools (see Kravtsov,
2008c; Kravtsova, 2008c). In drawing upon the seminal works of Vygotsky
(*Collected Works*) they have developed an approach to teaching and learning that centres on an active role of adults in children's play for fostering
higher psychological functioning, and where creativity and imagination are
integral to concept formation. Their pedagogical framing for the Golden
Key Schools brings together the educational institution and the family as a
significant and active member of the education program. They argue that
'in generally accepted models of education there is not only a separation of
teaching from upbringing, but also a one-sided domination of the values of
teaching over the values of cultivating the child's personality and emotional

well-being' (Kravtsov & Kravtsova, 2009: 203). They believe that it is very difficult to create a program for children without the unity of the family and the educational institution.

The Golden Key program in the Russian preschools and primary schools is organised around the principle of the family unit, where all adults (including all the parents of the children attending the program) are responsible for the upbringing of the children. All adults participate together with the children in the events and activities that are organised. The Golden Key Program is seen as an extension of the child's own family. Multi-age groups form the basis of the centre (*kompleks*) to unite preschool and primary aged children (3–10 years). Two educators (pair pedagogy; see below) work with each multi-aged group of 15–20 children. The outcomes of the program include

- the ability to act in the space surrounding the child; the skill to organise one's own personal space according to the goals of the activity
- orientation in time, the skill to develop, construct a sequence of actions and to plan them
- the ability to work with various materials, to use their properties and peculiarities in one's own activity
- the development of the ability to analyse one's own actions, reflect and understand oneself as the subject of these activities.

(Kravtsov & Kravtsova, 2009: 210)

These outcomes are realised over time through specifically designed events for children aged 3–6 years in tandem with their families.

In the first year of the program, the focus is on plans, schemes and models that exist in the children's lives. The children work on an axis of time travelling in a time machine and touching down at different time intervals, such as cave dwellers through to future space travel (Kravtsova, 2009c). In the second year the children learn how to orient themselves in space (Kravtsova 2009b). In the third year the focus is on materials (Kravtsova, 2009a) in different fields of art; in the fourth year the children reflect on their learning from the previous three years and explore unfamiliar cultures (Kravtsova, 2009d). These guiding conceptual themes are used to create meaning and to generate a need for engaging in problem solving, mathematical activity, literacy learning and scientific thinking.

The distinctive feature of the new educational practice is that it combines two global values which in the experience of existing educational institutions are considered to be mutually exclusive. They are the value of teaching and the goal-oriented development of children by means of education, and the value of the emotional well-being and comfort of the child. Usually either one or other value dominates and so determines the whole educational process, as well as the child's way of life in the educational institution. The main idea of the project . . . Education and mental development of children is effective only if it is closely linked with an effective development of the emotional sphere of the child.

(Kravtsov & Kravtsova, 2009: 208)

The unity of emotions and intellect is central to the Golden Key Programs and is one of the cornerstones of Vygotsky's theory (see chapter 14 for further discussion). Kravtsov and Kravtsova (2009) argue that

In pedagogical practice, the principle of unity of affect and intellect could be the theoretical pivot, which permit the union of teaching and upbringing, the private life of the child and the organised activity, family and school.

(Kravtsov & Kravtsova, 2009: 205)

In the Golden Key Program subject positioning is important for broadening the children's zone of proximal development. The principle underpinning the program is the creation of a special kind of communication (*Obshchenie*) between the teachers, the families and the children around something common to the child (as would have occurred when extended and large families lived together in small communities or villages). The concept of *Obshchenie* is central to the Golden Key schools. In the creation of *Obshchenie* within the institution, the teachers position themselves quite deliberately alongside the children (are seen as equal in status to the children), above the children (as knowing more than the children), below the children (the children guide the teacher) or with the children (primordial 'we'), or the positioning occurs through the children and the teacher acting independently of each other (they are aware of each other's activity but decide to do it alone). This subject positioning is achieved through pair pedagogy (Kravtsova, 2008d, e).

In pair pedagogy, both teachers take on different positions (as is often found within families, where both adults position themselves differently in relation to a particular context). One teacher might act above the children while the other is positioned equally with the children. In pair pedagogy the different types of positioning enable children to witness or be involved in particular kinds of communication that make explicit aspects of cognition and affect that are not possible when there is only one teacher.

Kravtsova (2008e) argues that this process broadens the children's zone of proximal development (see below). Through pair pedagogy, children's play and learning develop. Children in their multi-age groups observe elements of learning and development that are ahead of them, in the same way as a younger child observes the activities of an older sibling and become tuned into those things that are yet to come. Older children also actively support young children. The distinctive features of the Golden Key school (multi-age groupings, the iterative nature of the program) enable younger children to initially experience the program at the interpsychological level; as they grow older they begin to lead the program and work more at an intrapsychological level. Albums of children's activity (photographs, captions of activity, children's thinking are documented to be kept as records of common events, thereby creating a common history) are examined regularly by children and teachers in order to specifically note what children have done and to reflect on what they are now doing and thinking that is different from the last time a content area was explored. Through the pair pedagogy the children's learning context is broadened and they move from their zone of proximal development into a new zone of potential development. As Vygotsky argued, only something that has been experienced or observed can be imitated. Kravtsova (2008e) illustrates this nicely in her concept of the zone of potential development. Vygotsky's zone of actual development and the zone of proximal development are well understood in the literature. In short, actual development is what a child can do without adult assistance, while the zone of proximal development is what the child does with support from others. These concepts are often discussed from a pedagogical perspective rather than from an assessment perspective (see Chaiklin, 2003), that is, when viewed from an assessment perspective, they draw attention to the kinds of supports given to children as evidence for measuring the dynamic and evolving capabilities (or proximal development) of children. When viewed from a pedagogical perspective, they foreground what teachers do to support children. In a dialectical view, both are related to each other. Within the zone of proximal development, the child is willing and able to engage in the activities suggested by the adult and is actively supported through some form of pair pedagogy by the teachers.

What is less well known is Kravtsova's (2008e) theory of the zone of potential development. This zone represents the social and cultural world of the child that lies within the sphere of possible engagement, that is, it is the social and cultural activity that surrounds the child, the real social world of the child that they are a part of, in which they observe

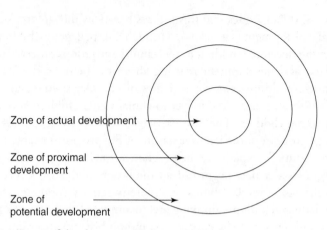

Zone of actual development

Zone of proximal
development

Zone of
potential development

Figure 8.1 Zones of development (Kravtsova, 2008e)

adults and others engaged in activities, such as designing and assembling a bookshelf. Through being in the specific contexts, motives are generated by the activities as important and meaningful experiences that they will one day be able to do themselves. In other words, engagement potential is generated for future engaged activity. The Golden Key Program deliberately seeks to broaden the zone of potential development.

In pair pedagogy, teachers are active members of children's play, sometimes leading and sometimes following, but always within situations that are meaningful to the children and their families. This is exemplified through what Kravtsova (2009b, f) calls 'events'. In Golden Key schools an event, such as 'The wolf has lost its fairy tale', is usually created by the teachers. In a pair pedagogy approach, one teacher, dressed as the wolf and asking the children to help find their fairy tale, acts below the children. The other teacher works with the children to help reconstruct the different fairy tales that a wolf might appear in, through drama, craft, letter writing, setting up problems (maps, orienteering, etc.). In this example, the children and the teachers invite back the wolf to see if their investigation has helped the wolf to find or remember which fairy tale they came from. Through this event approach, the children make the subject of the learning program their own – another important characteristic of *obshchenie*. The program content is also realised through imagination. The unity of affect and cognition are built into the teaching programs, and families continue the program at home and contribute to the program in the school where the personal life of the family is furthered.

Research evidence (see Kravtsov & Rubashkina, 2009) demonstrates that graduates from the Golden Key schools achieve cognitively at a similar level to graduates from other schools, but there is evidence that broader reflective capacities and engagement in community and social life are more highly developed. Significantly higher levels of health outcomes have been noted when compared with other school populations in Russia, and graduates also appear to be gaining more leadership positions (Kravtsova & Rubashkina, 2009).

TOOLS OF THE MIND

Tools of the Mind was originally conceptualised as a project to specifically help early childhood teachers working with children aged 3.5–7 years to use play for developing children's cognitive development, particularly in the area of literacy learning. Tools of the Mind has been designed on the principles of cultural–historical theory, but within the sociopolitical context of the USA. Bodrova and Leong, the authors of this program, have cleverly brought together cultural–historical concepts in ways that reconceptualised developmentally appropriate practice. The authors (Bodrova & Leong, 2001) focus on developing children's play expertise through the design and implementation of play plans. They draw upon the concepts of the zone of proximal development (Vygotsky, 1987a) and scaffolding (Wood, Buner & Ross, 1976) as important mediating tools for helping children move from interpsychological functioning to intrapsychological functioning. The key concepts of *orienting basis of all action* (Galperin, 1992), *external mediators* (Vygotsky, 1987a), *private speech* (Vygotsky, 1987a), *shared activity* (adapted by Bodrova & Leong, 1996) and *play as a leading activity* (Vygotsky, 1966) are used for framing the approach.

Bodrova (2008), like Kravtsova (2009b), has argued that in the past children tended to grow up in large extended families where they were likely to play in multi-aged groups. In these situations, younger children learnt from older more expert play partners, and play experts passed on their skills and knowledge to play novices. Further back in history, children tended to roam about in multi-age groups or be in one teacher schools where all age groups were together. Once again, play novices could learn knowledge and skills about being effective play partners from play experts. Bodrova (2008) suggests that 'In today's classrooms, children are almost always segregated by age and have to interact with play partners that are as inexperienced as they are. As a result, many of the play skills that children were able to learn in the past by observing and imitating their older playmates now have to be modelled and taught directly by the teachers' (Bodrova, 2008: 365). The Tools of the Mind program assumes the current socio-cultural context in the USA for age segregated classrooms and preschool centres, and works with teachers to become more active members of children's play.

Tools of the Mind focuses on initiating and sustaining an imaginary situation. To do this, children need a repertoire of themes that can be used in play. As with the Golden Key Program, which uses fairy tales and folk stories as part of its program, Tools of the Mind puts effort into generating a shared activity. Teachers take children on field trips, invite visitors to give presentations, look at videos and books; together with the children, the themes are determined based on the children's interests and those within their repertoire. In the Tools of the Mind Program, the teachers recognise that the children have regularly been presented with replica toys, so rather than imagining that Barbie is visiting the dentist, they are more likely to buy an already equipped Barbie, such as Dentist Barbie. Bodrova and Leong (2001) state that teachers in the Tools of the Mind program will 'wean children from the need for specific props by introducing games in which children think of different ways to play with ordinary objects' (pp. 17–18). The teachers will, for example, set up a brainstorming activity and find all the different ways in which a wooden block can be used and the children actively work towards giving new and varied meaning to an object. Kravtsova (2009d) has shown that when an object (e.g., Spiderman doll) has only one purpose (in this example, to be a Spiderman) then everyone wants this particular toy, because they are unable to give meaning to other objects in play, such as when a block can become Spiderman, a car or another character in the play. In the Tools of the Mind program, children gradually work towards using minimalist props, such as a piece of fabric acting as an apron, a sling or the sail of a boat.

In order to move children forward to more mature forms of play, teachers in the Tools of the Mind program help children to expand the number of roles in a theme. Bodrova and Leong (2001) argue that when children have a narrow view of roles in play, then all the children will want to be the dominant roles that they have noticed in real life, such as being the doctor or the nurse or the patient in hospital play. In this situation, children may fight over using the stethoscope or injection. During the field trips, the children's attention is drawn to what people do, not on the objects they use. This broadens the number of characters in a play theme from doctor, patient and nurse to include receptionist, radiographer, cleaner and so forth. It also enriches and deepens the play.

Bodrova and Leong (2001) argued that 'One of the most effective ways of helping children to develop mature play is to use "play plans"' (p. 18). A play plan gives a description of what the child hopes to do and achieve in their play. In particular it includes the imaginary situation, the roles and the props. For young children, it will involve the use of drawings accompanied by teacher annotations. For older children, more words are likely to feature, but drawings are still an important component of a play plan. Bodrova and Leong (2001) state that

> In some other early childhood programmes, children plan their activities aloud. However, we found that planning on paper is much more effective than planning orally. Both the children and the teacher often forgot the oral plan. The drawn/written plan is a tangible record of what the child wanted to do, that other children as well as the child and the teacher, could consult (p. 19).

According to Bodrova and Leong (2001), play plans also have other benefits: they provide a documented context through which families could learn more about what was happening in the classrooms, they could enable parents to discuss the day with children and their teachers, and they act as a record of symbolic representations and literacy skills. The play plans provided a rich context in which very young children could pretend write. Finally, the play plans provided a special time in which children and teachers could connect together.

Other features of the program included scaffolded writing and a computer generated assessment tool for helping teachers to create and use evidence for planning learning. The scaffolded writing component of the program involved the teacher development of a one-to-one association between the written word and the spoken word to help children build literacy knowledge, substituting different techniques as the year progressed and the children's competence increased. Finally, a battery of computer generated assessment techniques was developed to assist teachers empirically through determining children's ZPD in relation to literacy and with supporting decision making in relation to what kind of mediation was required to advance the children's learning. Assessment was closely tied to teaching strategies and developmental patterns.

The outcomes of the three phases of the development and evaluation of the Tools of the Mind program indicate that there were significant improvements in letter recognition, sound-to-symbol correspondence, comprehension of patterns in text, a better understanding of the symbolic function of a printed word and the capacity to separate the printed word into letters. According to Bodrova and Leong (2001), the outcomes were statistically significant when compared with their control groups. Further evaluations undertaken by Diamond, Barnett, Thomas and Munro (2007) have also confirmed these results.

DEVELOPMENTAL EDUCATION

> Developmental Education is itself both a *conceptual view* on development under instructional conditions, a type of *classroom practice*, and an evolving educational system that serves as an *infrastructure for innovation*.
> (van Oers, 2009: 216; emphasis in the original)

Developmental education is characterised as a play-based curriculum for children in their first years of school (van Oers, 2009). The generation of meaningful learning in school is an important dimension of the approach. Learning tasks are embedded within the play practices that are set up by the children and the teachers. Van Oers states that 'The purpose of education should always be to support the broad identity development of pupils as well-informed participants in sociocultural activities' (van Oers, 2009: 214–15).

Developmental education in the Netherlands has been conceptualised to include playful learning activities in the early years of school and an enquiry-based approach in the upper years. Van Oers (2009) argues that school activities are organised to create conditions for 'emancipation, identity formation and meaningful learning' (van Oers, 2009: 217). Within this context, van Oers (2009) states that teacher knowledge of subject matter is extremely important, as subject matter content 'can be introduced into the children's activities at moments when this is relevant' (van Oers, 2009: 223). To do this effectively, teachers must be accomplished in observing children and being able to identify their particular learning needs. It is only when teachers have a very good understanding of subject matter content and a detailed understanding of the children they are working with that effective learning can be organised as culturally relevant practices. Van Oers (2009) defines practices as 'culturally evolved constellations of integrated activities that aim collaboratively at the production of specific products' (van Oers, 2009: 216). Activity is viewed as a 'culturally developed, systematic, and tool-mediated way of dealing with a specific category of objects, each activity can be carried out in different ways' (van Oers, 2009: 216). An important dimension of developmental education is the freedom that is given to children as a result of the range of activities that are on offer in the play-based program and enquiry-based models. Van Oers (2009) signals that freedom of action and choice is deliberately promoted through developmental education (van Oers, 2009: 217); however, consensual meaning is featured and extended through 'virtual participants, represented by texts. Following Davydov (1983) (and specifically Bakhtin) we call this type of extended conversations *polylogue* (van Oers, 2009: 218).

The basic concepts underpinning developmental education include emancipation, practice, meaningful learning, zone of proximal development, dialogue and polylogue. Van Oers (2009) states that in developmental education emancipation is an elaboration of identity development. In drawing upon cultural–historical theory, particularly Bakhtinian theory, he states that identity

> is a polyphonous construct that is voiced by a situated person. Identity, like cognition, is a distributed phenomenon that can only exist thanks to the wealth of cultural resources that we can use for our personal enterprises. However, the potential of the individual can only be optimally developed when he or she has meaningfully appropriated the influences from others. The integration of the different voices and contents into one meaningful whole requires a critical appropriation process, in which a person not only acquires new knowledge, skills or understandings, but also critically evaluates them in the process of creating ownership and assuming personal responsibility for what is appropriated. Emancipation, then, means the development of a critical identity for participation in sociocultural practices.
>
> (van Oers, 2009: 216)

This cultural–historical collective view of identity and emancipation is very different from how those conceptions are generally defined.

Research by van Oers (2008) into developmental teaching also examines the relations between children's internal and external action in the context of early years teaching. In drawing upon Vygotsky's concept of predicate for theorising children's play in school, van Oers (2008) illustrates how 'children use predicates all the time for articulating the imaginary situation and for the elaboration of their play' (van Oers, 2008; p. 372). He also cites data from his 2008 study, where children are playing in a corner of the school buying and selling shoes. In their play they use abbreviated forms of conversation because the children have established shared meaning.

> Because of this shared attention, they assume implicitly what the other is referring to in his or her speech. There is no need to repeat this topic of

communication every time it might be relevant; rather, it is sufficient to mention those qualities that are *new to the topic under discussion*. These new qualities are called 'predicates'.

> (van Oers, 2008: 371–2; emphasis in the original)

Van Oers (2008) argues that Vygotsky, in *Thinking and Speech* (1987, chapter 7),

> tries to give a psychological explanation of the abbreviated character of thinking (or inner speech). Vygotsky notes that this abbreviation is possible when communicating people have shared attention for some common object. Because of his shared attention, they assume implicitly what the other is referring to in his or her speech . . .
>
> When we apply this idea to the child's play, we can maintain that the imaginary situation is the topic. In the case of social play (e.g., role play), the imaginary situation is the attentional topic taken as shared. The new actions or propositions of the children are the predicates that contribute to the qualities of the topic.
>
> (van Oers, 2008: 371–2)

Van Oers (2008) brings together Vygotsky's theory of meaning with Latour's work on signs in the production of knowledge, particularly the constructions of inscriptions for generating meaning. He argues that very young children use transportable inscriptions to reconstruct meaning in other contexts, but 'they can also inscribe new symbols to their inscriptions in order to focus other people's attention to specific parts of their drawing and even manipulate their attention to bring specific meanings (predicates) to their minds' (van Oers, 2008: 374). Van Oers (2008) also notes that in the shoe shop the children commenced their play arranging the shoes, the boxes and all the other shop items. This was followed by active play in the shoe shop, where classification and counting evolved. As the children expanded their playscripts, the children combined inscriptions and diagrams to help them as problems arose in their play. For instance, in trying to locate the right sized shoe for a customer from the stack of shoe boxes that had been arranged, they changed their play activity and moved into inventing but also used conventional symbols. Van Oers (2008) argues that the 'innovation of meaning often requires invention of new signs, or at least a reconstruction of old signs in order to articulate the new meanings' (van Oers, 2008: 373). The 'dialectical relationship between acting and making appropriate inscriptions' (p. 378) lead to the development of play and the evolution of the playscript. Once again, we see the dialectical relations between imagination and cognition in unity with reality. Van Oers (2008) notes in his research how '[T]he contradictions between the meanings in play (emerging from the imaginary situation) and the real actions are the main basis for children's development (see Vygotsky, 1978: 101)' (van Oers, 2008; p. 371).

Developmental education programs can now be found in approximately 10 per cent of Dutch primary schools; however, no formal evaluation of these programs for demonstrating student outcomes in comparison to other students has been undertaken.

Developmental education as discussed here is derived from the theoretical and pedagogical writings of Davydov (2008), who originated this concept for primary schools in Russia. In this work the leading activity is for learning; attention to play as a leading activity for school aged children has not been fully explored, as it has been by van Oers for the Netherlands.

Developmental education as theorised by Davydov (2008) is conceptualised as the generation of theoretical knowledge and thinking by children in primary schools through a method of ascending from the 'abstract to the concrete' (p. 16). While the concept of theoretical thinking has been the subject of discussion in previous chapters, the focus was in relation to preschool aged children.

Developmental education has been evaluated by Davydov (2008) and his colleagues, and the findings suggest that the outcomes are greater for primary aged children following this program than traditional methods in Russia. Surveys of children's development of theoretical consciousness (contentful reflection, analysis and planning, thought experiment, manifestation in active memory, imagination and thinking and overall personality development) were undertaken through a range of different tasks, and over a broad range of age groups (Grades 1–3; see summary provided by Davydov, 2008: 161–77) and advances from 1 to 2 years in theoretical thinking were noted for children in the developmental programs when compared with traditional programs.

SUMMARY

In this chapter three programs that draw upon cultural–historical theory were presented and discussed. The Golden Key Program in Russia,

Developmental Education in the Netherlands and the Tools of the Mind in North America were detailed and common outcomes were noted, even though the sociocultural contexts varied and the program designs were different. All three programs feature imagination, play and concept formation as central to their conceptualisation and operationalisation within the 3–7 age band. In addition, all programs are derived from Vygotsky's theory of play and those that followed.

Although the programs discussed in this chapter were generated in different cultural communities, they share a common theoretical approach – cultural–historical theory. While the programs are structured and conducted differently, each seeks to build theoretical knowledge and thinking through the framing of a play-based program. In these programs, the role of the teacher and the process of teaching have been thoughtfully theorised and carefully framed as active. In addition, a collective view of the learner is foregrounded.

The common features these programs share include

- cultural–historical concepts originally introduced by Vygotsky and developed further by his colleagues, students and those who followed
- a focus on 3–7 year old children or older
- the zone of proximal development for diagnosis and some form of related mediation, which feature strongly in these programs
- importantly, active consideration of the relationship between education and development as revolutionary, not evolutionary, as is common in many Western heritage communities
- child self-development, which occurs because programs connect closely with children and their families
- multi-age groupings, which are important because older children play an important role in shaping younger children's learning
- play, which is seen as an important pedagogical tool – imagination is central for play development as well as for progressing learning
- motives for play, which are viewed as having a cultural–historical origin, rather than being viewed as an innate biological driver
- the ability for teachers to take an active role in play for mediating learning
- cognition and emotions, which are viewed in unity
- play viewed as being able to mature and develop through mediation by adults.

Recognising the complexity of learning through play, as shown through the three programs discussed in this chapter, is important for understanding how Vygotsky's theory of play has evolved. The essence of a cultural–historical play-based program include

- an imaginary situation
- explicit roles and implicit rules
- *obshchenie*.

Without these three elements, the programs could not be conceptualised as play-based. These concepts are discussed further in the next chapter.

9 | Theories about play and learning

> What activity is leading in the given age period is crucially determined by the society in which the children find themselves.
>
> (Karpov, 2005: 71)

INTRODUCTION

Vygotsky's theory of play has been discussed and developed among scholars in Russia (Elkonin, 1999; Kravtsov & Kravtsova, 2009) and elsewhere (Berk, 1994; Berk & Winsler, 1995; Bodrova & Leong, 1998, 2001; Duncun & Tarulli, 2003; Gaskins, 1999, 2007; Gaskins & Göncü, 1992; Göncü, 1997, 1999; Holzman, 2009; Ugaste, 2005), which has resulted in distinctions in how play development is supported by teachers and enacted by children. Elkonin's theory of play, for instance, centres on role play, Kravtsova and Kravtsov's shows play with objects and roles within a periodisation framework. Other theories of play by Russian scholars are not reviewed here because their works have not yet been translated into English; however, an elaboration of Elkonin's and Kravtsova's theories of play provide excellent examples of contemporary cultural–historical theories of play used to support the play-based programs discussed in the previous chapter.

This chapter begins with a theoretical discussion of Elkonin's theory of play, is followed by the theory of play as outlined by Kravtsova and Kravstov, and concludes with a discussion of those who have argued against Vygotsky's theory of play.

ELKONIN'S THEORY OF PLAY

Elkonin continued and deepened Vygotsky's theory of play through discussing the development of play in relation to its origins and cultural evolution. As discussed in the previous chapter, Elkonin (1999a–e) argued that the origins of play must be viewed as both historical and sociocultural. Like Bodrova (2008), he suggested that play was not spontaneous, but rather formed as a result of the child's changing relations to society. Importantly, Elkonin's (1999a) focus of attention in his theorisation of play was on role play. He suggested that the basic unit of play was people and human relations, as represented in their activities in society.

A central problem of Elkonin's (1999a) research was the motivational dimensions of play. He argued that there are two motivational components within play – the objective field and the sense field. The object or the toy becomes to the child an 'objectivised social meaning' or *znachenie*, that is, it holds meaning because of what it represents or what its purpose is, or its design function. The object can also be imbued with a child's personal sense, in other words, the child gives meaning to the object through its actions within an imaginary situation. 'Sense invests the object, and the object acquires sense. Therein lies the role of play in the development of the child's consciousness' (Hakkaraiinen & Veresov, 1999: 9). Elkonin (1999) argued that as children acquire the techniques of play, such as the generation, generalisation and passage of meaning from one object to another, it is possible to purposefully penetrate human relations within society.

Significantly, Elkonin (1999a–e; 2005a–c) found in his research that words have a major role in play because they 'contain the experience of actions with objects in play and reveal social relations' (p. 10). Elkonin (1999a) stated that for a word to enter into the child's play it needed to 'absorb all the possible actions with the object and become a vehicle of the system of interactions with the object' (p. 56).

Elkonin (1999a) spoke about the context of objects and the contexts of roles. In the context of objects, symbolic function can be realised for the child through the objects and the sense they hold within particular imaginary situations, that is, the action with the object serves as a condition for modelling actions in society, and the child in reproducing these actions is able to examine human relations within society. In the context of roles, it is the roles adults take in society that are the focus of attention in play. The roles of adults that a child reproduces in some form of play activity serve to help the child examine the activities of humans, and therefore the general human relations found within society.

Elkonin (1999a) argued that the most expanded form of play was role play, through which 'the child creates models of human relations because of special play devices', for example, 'he assumes the role of the adult, the adult's functions and work in society; he reproduces object actions by generalising them in representational thought; he transfers meaning from one object to another; etc.' (p. 23). Elkonin (1999a) also suggested that in the context of objects, an

> object action, taken in isolation, does not have written on it the answers to questions such as: For what was it performed? What is its social meaning? Its actual motive? It is only when an object action becomes incorporated into a system of human relations that we can discover its true social naming, its purposefulness with regard to people. This sort of 'incorporation' takes place in play (p. 24).

Kravtsov (2008a, b) and Kravtsova (2008b) have drawn upon Elkonin's theory to inform their own views on play. Even so, their theory is quite different. We now turn to their conceptualisation of play.

KRAVTSOV AND KRAVTSOVA'S THEORY OF PLAY

In the Golden Key schools in Russia, the principles that support their programs deal with the unity of cognition and emotions, the foregrounding of subjectivity (unity of the personal initiative of the child and the self-consciousness of the child) and the creation of a special form of communication between children, teachers and families (*obshchenie*). As discussed earlier, in the Golden Key Programs a problem situation is generated (subjective imagination) within an imaginary situation (pedagogical event), and spontaneous or reactive responses by children are operationalised through discussions about what the children should do to solve the problem that has arisen in the imaginary situation (objective imagination). The imaginary situation is based on these three principles, and is supported by a cultural–historical theory of play developed by Elena Kravtsova and Gennady Kravtsov. In drawing upon Vygotsky's (1966) theory of play and those that followed (e.g., Elkonin, 1999a), they elaborated a theory of play that went beyond the narrowing down of mature play into the form of role play as outlined by Elkonin (1999a).

PRODUCER–DIRECTOR PLAY

Kravtsova (2008a) suggested that children engage in a symbiosis of con-current forms of play, each type influencing the other. Rather than a linear progression in play, Kravtsova argues for the deepening of a range of forms of play. For instance, an 18 month old toddler will move a block about and make noises to create an imaginary situation. The child is playing, but not taking a role inside the play. This kind of play activity is termed *producer play* or *director play*. The child gives the object meaning. The fate of the object is determined by the child – the director of the play. The child is outside the play, directing what will happen.

IMAGINARY PLAY

Another form of play that is observed among children is one in which children involve themselves in the play, such as when children take a pillow, place it on their back and crawl across the floor as a turtle. The children involve themselves in the imaginary situation. They are inside the play and they imagine themselves as something – such as a turtle.

Producer play and imaginary play are opposite to each other: in producer play the child is outside of the play looking down and directing the action of the objects, while in the imaginary play the child is inside the play imagining themselves as some object, person, animal or superhero within the imaginary situation. Kravtsova (2008a) argues that both kinds of play represent the starting point for all play.

SCENARIO ROLE PLAY

Kravtsova (2008a) further argues that in Elkonin's theory of role play, it is necessary for two play partners to have the same shared imaginary situation, such as playing the roles of patient and doctor in hospital play. What is needed here are two linked imaginary roles. Kravtsova argues that this form of play appears later in childhood because it requires a lot of energy for the formulation, maintenance and expansion of a shared imaginary situation. Kravtsov and Kravtsova call this kind of play scenario role play. In the creation of scenario play a great deal of effort is expended on playing out the rules correctly. This type of play and the metacommunicative language associated within maintaining the shared play scenario has also been noted by Western scholars such as Bretherton (1976). The positions taken in the play, as above the play directing or inside the play, playing is an important dimension of the movement between inside and outside scenario role play. Longstanding research by Bretherton (1982) has shown how children move in and out of the frame during play. The frame in her theory of play is similar to that discussed by Kravtsova's concept of moving inside and outside the play.

Importantly, it is possible to see how imaginary play and producer play help children to move inside and outside scenario role play. In scenario role play, children spend more time outside the play discussing the play than they do inside the play, playing the roles.

GAMES

As play development occurs and children engage in more mature forms of play, children can be seen to move from playing a role in an imaginary situation to being in an imaginary situation with a role. Through moving in and out of the imaginary situation, discussing how play partners should be playing, children more explicitly discuss the roles they are playing in relation to the rules within society.

Kravtsova exemplifies the first part of this equation as follows (figure 9.1):

$$\frac{\text{Role}}{\text{(Imaginary situation)}} \longrightarrow \frac{\text{Imaginary situation}}{\text{(Role)}}$$

Figure 9.1 Roles to imaginary situation

As children engage in more scenario play and their play evolves and matures, Kravtsova (2008a) suggests that rules come to dominate their play, as shown in the following equation (figure 9.2):

$$\frac{\text{Imaginary situation}}{\text{(Rules)}} \longrightarrow \frac{\text{Rules}}{\text{(Imaginary situation)}}$$

Figure 9.2 Imaginary situation to rules

We see play mature through a deepening of children's play activity from a domination of producer play, to imaginary play, to scenario play and finally to games with rules. In this latter form of play, children will spend a lot of time discussing the rules prior to playing a game. This is an important imaginative bridge from play to education. Importantly, these types of play are iterative in nature, like a spiral, maturing as each kind of play becomes more sophisticated.

PRODUCER GAME

As Kravtsova (2008a) argues, the earliest form of play – producer play – is transformed into a higher form of producer play in which more than one child becomes involved. Kravtsova (2008a) suggests that this higher order producer game should be available to school children, so that the game component of this type of play becomes hidden, and a collective consciousness about how the different objects and performers should play becomes the children's focus of attention. At this higher form of producer play, the children are still playing, but the play is not as obvious. All elements of the children's producer play can and should be linked to the learning activity. In the higher forms of producer play, children come to see themselves above the situation, and through this, are able to reflect and engage in self-assessment. In this form of play, children can participate in theatre play. Here, too, children come to see that they can take two positions or two forms of subjectiveness. In the imaginary situation, the child can be happy at play but take on the role of being sad in playing out their character. Two kinds of subjectivities appear in which, initially, the child imbues objects (optical field) with new meaning (sense field) and through this are enabled to consciously know their feelings of happiness while playing out the character who is expressing quite different emotions. In collective forms of producer play children are able to see the real objects or people (optical field) but in the imaginary situation, they imbue the objects or people with new meaning (sense field). Kravtsova (2008a) has represented this as a model (figure 9.3).

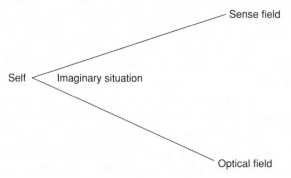

Figure 9.3 Kravtsova's model of the imaginary situation in play

While it is possible to see the essence of Vygotsky's theory of play and Elkonin's historical and theoretical view of role play within the theory of play developed by Kravtsova, it is also possible to note how their theory has evolved some of the foundational concepts in play theory. Their theory first shows play maturation that circles back to producer play, thus getting around the problem of how to move beyond stages of play when discussing play maturation. Second, their theory shows the different subject positioning that children take when engaged in the different kinds of play, and how this action helps in the development of play and in the ultimate self-development of the child. Finally, self-development occurs through engagement in different forms of play that mature over time when a collective conscious emerges as more play partners share the imaginary situation. This self-assessment also helps with the formation of the imaginative bridge from play to education.

Through their theory of play, some of the foundational problems left unsolved in Vygotsky's original theory of play have been solved and this theory of play has been successfully used within the Golden Key Program in Russia. But a cultural–historical review of play must seek to move beyond the Russian context and examine cultural interpretations and analyses. This is the subject of the next section.

PLAY AS A FORM OF CULTURAL EXPRESSION

Göncü, Jain and Tuermer (2007) argue that play is a form of cultural expression and that research should reflect local understandings and values of play, rather than be viewed as a universal construct. In a critique of Vygotsky's theory of play, Gaskins (2007) argues that objects were used in his theory to symbolically stand for other things, as 'pivots' for meaning, to help the child to separate word meaning from referents, thus allowing action to arise from ideas rather than objects. Gaskins (2007), in her study of Yucatec Mayan infants aged 18–24 months, found that the infants she observed in everyday activities in their homes only occasionally expressed symbolic relationships, and when they did it was not supported by their caregivers. She cites the example of an 18 month old Yucatec Mayan boy who used a stick to represent a horse, which he rode around the yard, laughing. Gaskins (2007) found that the caregiver took no notice of this behaviour, and after a few minutes the child put down the stick. This activity was repeated several minutes later, again with no adult encouragement or attention; eventually, the child abandoned the stick. Gaskins (2007) argues that in her study the children she observed were clearly using objects to stand for another thing, but the infants who 'spontaneously expressed these symbolic relationships . . . did not receive recognition or support from anyone present' (p. 4). This is consistent with earlier research by Gaskins and Göncü (1992), who also found that play was not valued by adults in the

Yucatec Mayan communities they studied. Gaskins (2007) states that she found difficulties with Vygotsky's theory of play in relation to children playing out everyday activities because Yucatec Mayan children did not participate in this kind of play. Rather, children aged six to 12 controlled the play of younger children, assigning them minimal roles with role-appropriate scripts. The older children performed the more complex role plays, while the younger children looked on. In addition, Gaskins (2007) found that the Mayan children devoted very little time to play, spending most of their time either legitimately participating or observing events and activities in the community and household. This is consistent with Elkonin's (2005a–c) argument that, where children contribute to the economic unit of the family or community, less involvement in play occurs or is needed. Gaskins (2007) argues that because Mayan children actually participate in household and community life, they have less need to role play these roles, while children with less opportunities to undertake authentic roles in community life are more likely to need to participate in pretend play so they can explore the rules and roles within society. This analysis also mirrors that put forward by Elkonin (2005), as discussed earlier. Gaskins (2007) states that

> How development is affected by exploring symbolic relationships, cultural roles, and emotional coping in the real world, with real consequences, as compared to exploring them in the world of play, is not clear. But the Yucatec Mayan evidence suggests that to the extent that there is a consensus between both the adults and the children that the goal is to have children engaged productively in the real world, pretend play is not a privileged place to express and explore personal and social meaning (pp. 7–8).

Unlike Elkonin (2005a), who argues for a historical reading of play within cultural communities, Gaskins (2007) comes to the conclusion that 'Rather than being "the leading edge of development" that Vygotsky proposed, play *can* serve as just a pleasant pastime' (pp. 7–8; emphasis in the original). There is a large volume of Western generated research into play that has tended to treat the play of all children as needing to be universally engaged in social pretend play, despite the diversity of economic circumstances (Göncü & Gaskins, 2005), the potential historical and technological reading of communities (see Elkonin, 2005a) and the within and across cultural differences noted (see work resulting from Rogoff's laboratory in Santa

Cruz). Göncü, Mistry and Mosier (2000) summarise this body of research and come to the following conclusion:

> The end result has been an overlap between Western researchers' concep-
> tualizations of play and the play of children from the communities, often
> generating misrepresentations of non-Western children's activities as lacking
> if they did not have the pretend features of Western children's play. Indeed,
> some scholars have developed intervention programs to teach non-Western
> or low-income children how to play according to norms, so that their devel-
> opment would benefit from this activity just as does Western middle class
> children's development (p. 323).

Göncü, Jain and Tuermer (2007) argue that much of the Western research literature on play has tended to position 'low-income and non-Western children's play as inadequate from a Western middle-class perspective' (p. 165), and suggest that researchers need to pay attention to economic factors, the value of play held by the community and the communicative structures of participants being researched, as they influence the occurrence of play. In their review of the play literature they note three factors that have influenced the cultural validity of research into play. They make the point that previous experimental research tended to see unfamiliar adults take children from familiar contexts and invite them to play in 'experimental settings or laboratories', which revealed more about the children's ability to deal with unfamiliarity than with their engagement in symbolic play. Previous research examined play in the absence of documenting or considering the analysis the economic circumstances of the community (as was argued earlier by Elkonin, 2005a) and how that may influence the kinds of play available to children. Göncü, Jain and Tuermer (2005) also suggested that researchers tend to look for particular categories of play (based on previous research into Western middle-class families) and did not look for, or notice, other ways of playing. In their research Göncü, Jain and Tuermer (2007) found a new category of play for low SES African American children that focused on rhythm, rhyme and movement. They state that 'Without entertaining the possibility that low-income children may have play kinds that may not have been identified in Western theory and research, previous work yielded potentially ethnocentric information' (p. 157).

Göncü, Jain and Tuermer (2007) state that in their analysis of their study of low SES African American, European American and Turkish communities that

Representational play is not limited to pretense, as other play forms such as teasing also involve representations. Therefore, in assessing the development of symbolic functioning we must carefully consider different forms of representation (p. 176).

Göncü, Jain and Tuermer (2007) point to something important here in relation to the play activities of children growing up in the 21st century across a broad range of cultures, including remote communities with large populations of indigenous families who have access to an extensive range of symbols and hence symbolic functioning, including digital television, internet, interactive games technologies (e.g., Wii, robotic toys, Pokemon) and other integrative and interactive technologies realised through the platform of digital handheld devices with Bluetooth, such as mobile smart phones or iPod Touch devices. The latter of these technologies enable exchanges between children that go beyond sound bites, video images or apps to the creation of avatars and their activities in second life. Schultze and Rennecker (2007) call these latter technologies and play spaces synthetic worlds. They argue that in these play contexts, players use these synthetic worlds as extensions to their own real world. In *Second Life*, for instance, players consciously play out the rules of everyday life through actively engaging in the rules of second life, even protesting at the taxes that were imposed on players by the designers (Linden Labs) at one point in the evolution of the game. It is possible to see how Vygotsky's theory of play, when used to examine the psychological development of players, foregrounds the consciousness of concepts enacted in everyday life. Contrary to those critiques of Vygotsky's theory of play undertaken by scholars interested in examining play across cultures (see Gaskins, 2007; Göncü & Gaskins, 2007), these cultural expressions of play through synthetic worlds appear to support and validate the reach of Vygotsky's theory from when it was first conceptualised to technologies not even imagined during Vygotsky's lifetime. If we are to fully appreciate the cultural nature of play afforded through these new technologies, further analysis of these new forms of play activity are needed.

SUMMARY

In this chapter, the contemporary theories of play that have drawn upon Vygotsky's (1966) original theory of play were discussed and critiqued. It was proposed that cultural differences in play require consideration in relation to country-specific needs. The culturally specific ways of constructing knowledge, of framing teaching or upbringing and the resultant institutional practices that are valued within a particular society should be foregrounded in play research. A brief discussion of synthetic worlds in relation to play was given in order to illuminate the importance of the need for a more expansive view of play theory for the 21st century. In the next chapter, the concept of imagination is discussed explicitly, as this appears to be an important component in bringing together play and cognition.

10 | The imaginative act as conceptual play

> The development of a creative individual, one who strives for the future, is enabled by creative imagination embodied in the present.
> (Vygotsky, 2004: 88)

INTRODUCTION

In the previous chapters it was shown that imagination in play is particularly important for building children's theoretical thinking, and that all educational programs (including those focused on discipline knowledge) need to develop imaginative thinking in unity with cognitive development. As discussed previously, play and conceptual knowledge should not be viewed in competition with each other, but rather they should be conceptualised as mutually constituting each other. In this chapter, this unity between play, cognitive development and imagination is theorised further.

This chapter discusses imagination from a cultural–historical perspective, and as such, readers used to working with Cartesian logic will note two counterintuitive ideas about imagination. The first counterintuitive point taken up in this chapter challenges the belief that imagination should be centred on the arts. Vygotsky (2004: 87) held the view that 'science, like art, permits application of the creative imagination'. His theoretical works show clearly that those 'who attempt to master the process of scientific and technological creativity are relying on the creative imagination to the same extent as in the area of artistic creation' (p. 87). Imagination will be considered here in relation to all discipline areas. Imagination as a cultural–historical construct will be foregrounded.

A second counterintuitive premise underpinning this chapter is the cultural and social nature of imagination, rather than the position that imagination is an innate biologically determined characteristic of children and adults. The essence of a cultural–historical perspective on imagination moves the theoretical lens from the individual to the dialectical relations between collective imagining and individual imagining. Bodrova (2008) reminds us that 'Vygotsky disagreed with those who viewed rich imagination as an innate characteristic of young children gradually replaced by their conforming to the reality principle' (Bodrova, 2008: 363).

Imagination and creativity, as put forward by Vygotsky (1987c, 2004), will feature in this chapter; in the last part of the chapter, the ideas will be discussed in relation to concept development. This chapter begins with a cultural–historical discussion of imagination.

WHAT IS IMAGINATION?

Previously, many Western scholars thought that imagination was separate from realistic thinking and viewed it as a subconscious act. It was also claimed that creative imagination had no relationship with reality, but rather generated affective connections, such as satisfaction. Researchers thought that imagination was different from realistic thinking because the latter could be verbalised and communicated within a social context and directed to reality, while imagination, thought to be non-verbal in character, used images and symbols, and was essentially embedded within fantasy and therefore not communicable (Vygotsky, 2004).

While imagination has traditionally been viewed as an individual activity, disassociated from reality, this perspective makes it very difficult for educators to take an active pedagogical role in developing imagination. It is also difficult to theorise the nature of imagination in relation to concept formation. When a cultural–historical view of imagination is draw upon, it is possible to move from the traditional belief of an internal, subconscious and biological process to a conscious and social act, in which mediation becomes important. Vygotsky (2004) argued that 'imagination is not just an idle mental amusement, not merely an activity without consequences in reality, but rather a function essential to life' (p. 13). Imagination becomes the means for broadening a person's experience. Vygotsky (2004) suggests that humans imagine what they cannot see, conceptualise what they hear from others and think about what they have not yet experienced, that is, a person

> is not limited to the narrow circle and narrow boundaries of his own experience but can venture far beyond these boundaries, assimilating, with the help of his imagination someone else's historical or social experience (p. 17).

Imagination can also be conceptualised historically. Vygotsky (2004: 25) stated that 'Every act of imagination has a very long history'. The creation of new ideas and inventions requires a particular form of imagination that is culturally and socially located. Vygotsky (2004: 30) put forward the view that 'Creation is a historical, cumulative process where every succeeding manifestation was determined by the preceding one'. These imaginings of inventors or 'even a genius, is also a product of his time and his environment. His creations arise from needs that were created before him and rest on capacities that also exist outside of him' (p. 30). Imaginative creations arise when the material and psychological conditions that are necessary for its formation are available. The need for greater food production, for instance, arises as communities grow in size, and through this change in societal circumstances, new technologies, such as tools for cultivating the soil, are invented (see chapter 7 on the history of role play). Material access, such as wood, stone or metal, determine the nature of particular technological inventions. Cultural and social histories build and inventions are incrementally generated. A contemporary example of needs and structural conditions can be seen in the culturally specific invention of clotheslines. The expansive Hill's Hoist washing line (rotating clothes line, which looks like the metal frame of a large outdoor umbrella) in Australia, where horizontal space is plentiful, is very different from the creation of a pole washing line projected out of windows from high-rise buildings (looks like a mast angled at 45 degrees to the building) in Singapore, where vertical space is utilised.

Discussion now turns from the use of cultural and historical contexts for understanding imagination to a discussion of those psychological conditions that frame the construct of imagination.

IMAGINATION AS A NEW PSYCHOLOGICAL FORMATION

IMAGINATION AS A CONSCIOUS ACT

Imagination is first and foremost a conscious act. But, as discussed earlier, this conscious act of imagination is not biologically determined. As Vygotsky (1987c) found, 'Imagination is a new formation which is not present in the consciousness of the very young child, is totally absent in animals and represents specifically human form of conscious activity' (p. 8).

A cultural–historical perspective foregrounds the relations between the child and the child's activity in the social world and examines how these activities shape or determine opportunities for new psychological formations. Imagination as a new psychological formation in the preschool years occurs through play because play is a leading activity at that time. According to Bodrova (2008), Vygotsky (1987c) argued that

> role-playing in an imaginary situation requires children to carry out two types of actions simultaneously – external and internal. In play, these internal actions – 'operations on the meanings' – are still dependent on the external operations on the objects. However, the very emergence of the internal actions signals the beginning of a child's transition from the earlier forms of thought processes – sensory–motor and visual–representational – to more advanced abstract thought.
>
> (Bodrova, 2008: 361)

These more advanced forms signal that the child can imbue objects with meaning, but at the same time change the meaning of an object through imagination, that is, imagination becomes a conscious act by the child. As discussed earlier, a child can move from the objective field to the sense field in relation to external objects within an imaginary situation (see chapter 7; Kravstova, 2008a). Through this, the new psychological formation of imagination is born. This is evident because

> a more profound penetration of reality demands that consciousness attains a freer relationship to the elements of that reality, that consciousness departs from the external and apparent aspects of reality that is given directly in perception. The result is that the processes through which the cognition of reality is achieved become more complex and richer.
>
> (Vygotsky, 1987c: 349)

Further, when constructive imagination is considered, such as when children use wooden blocks or use sand at the beach, 'the creative activity of consciousness associated with technical-constructive or building activity, we see consistently that real inventive imagination is among the basic functions underlying this activity' (Vygotsky, 1987c: 346–7). The child acts consciously in relation to these constructive materials and exhibits inventive imagination.

Significantly, because imagination is a conscious act, imagination becomes a directed and goal-driven activity. In order to understand the complexity of imagination as a new psychological formation, it is necessary to examine more closely the relations between imagination and reality.

IMAGINATION AND REALITY

Vygotsky (2004) argued that imagination plays a dual role in that 'it can lead a person either toward or away from reality' (p. 37). When, say, imaginative play takes the form of role play, a movement towards reality can be seen, as children explore the rules of society that govern the roles and activities of its people (Elkonin, 2005). When children imbue objects with new meanings and change their sense, children move away from reality. Yet a child can perform role play, using objects that represent something different from what they see (e.g., when a stick becomes a horse). Here, the dialectical nature of imagination is most evident because of the dual role imagination plays in moving towards and away from reality. Vygotsky argued that the dual role of imagination was also evident in the work of well-known inventors and scholars:

> natural science is impossible without imagination. [Isaac] Newton used imagination to see into the future, and [Georges] Cuvier into the past. The great hypotheses that give rise to great theories are the offspring of imagination (1987c: 37)

and that

> by observing the forms of imagination that are linked with creativity, that is, the forms of imagination that are directed toward reality, we find that the boundary between realistic thinking and imagination is erased. Imagination is a necessary, integral aspect of realistic thinking (1987c: 349).

Through the process of foregrounding the duality of reality and imagination it becomes possible to see the unity of imagination with realistic thinking about reality. This dialectical position lies in strong contrast to Cartesian logic, which separates the mind and body and which has traditionally viewed imagination as occurring in the mind, reinforcing the view that imagination is innate and biologically driven. Significantly, educators interested in developing imagination must work with imagination in unity with thinking, while at the same time recognising the child's activity as a dual and dynamic process that moves to, from and between reality and imagination. The complexity of this unity is highlighted by Vygotsky (1987c) where he notes a contradiction:

> There is a contradiction inherent in the problem as it actually exists. No accurate cognition of reality is possible without a certain element of imagination, a certain flight from the immediate, concrete, solitary impression in which the reality is presented in the elementary acts of consciousness. The processes of invention or artistic creativity demand a substantial participation by both realistic thinking and imagination. The two act as a unity (p. 349).

This unity is foregrounded when educators create imaginary situations (see chapter 8, Golden Key schools), or when children initiate or engage in imaginary play (see chapter 1, medicating Humpty Dumpty). At more advanced levels of thinking, the images or imaginary thinking formed by a child are not reproduced in reality. In essence, 'Each step in the child's achievement of a more profound penetration of reality is linked with his continued liberation from the earlier, more primitive forms of cognition' (Vygotsky, 1987c: 249). In order to engage in higher forms of cognition and imagination, 'consciousness departs from the external and apparent aspects of reality that is given directly in perception'. The cognition of reality and the development of imagination become richer and more complex. As Vygotsky (1987c) suggests:

> The essential feature of imagination is that consciousness departs from reality. Imagination is a comparatively autonomous activity of consciousness in which there is a departure from any immediate cognition of reality (p. 349).

In Vygotsky's theorisation of imagination and reality, two things can be noted. First, imagination moves a child away from reality to give higher forms of cognition. Second, when children act upon reality with imagination they generate a form of constructive imagination or a form of creativity. Discussion now turns to creativity through the concept of collective and individual creativity.

COLLECTIVE AND INDIVIDUAL CREATIVITY AND IMAGINATION

In a cultural–historical reading of creativity and imagination, it is important to acknowledge the collective and the individual construction of creativity. In collective creativity all individual acts of creativity are clustered together as a product of a generic created humanity. Much of today's artefacts, systems and processes were originally created by unknown inventors. Vygotsky (2004) drew the conclusion that creativity should be thought of as the rule rather than the exception. Collective creativity generated over centuries are enshrined in the living processes and artefacts that society uses today, and continues to be shaped in relation to new needs and materials. Wertsch gives an interesting example in the history of the creation of pole vaulting technology to illustrate this point.

> When pole vaulting was still an event whose goal was to leap horizontally across streams and during its first years as an event in the modern Olympics, vaulters used heavy and inflexible hickory, ash, or spruce poles. Bamboo poles, which were lighter, hence allowing competitors to reach greater speeds in approaching the vaulting box, were introduced in the 1900 Olympic Games. The greater affordance of bamboo poles – and by implication the constraints of earlier wooden poles – were quickly recognised, and bamboo poles quickly came to be universally adopted.
>
> (Wertsch, 1998: 41)

Wertsch (1998) noted that after World War II, when steel and aluminium alloy became more readily available, pole construction changed again. Then, in the 1960s, fibreglass poles were invented, which afforded even better results. These examples illustrate the collective invention of technologies to support a particular need – to win pole vaulting competitions.

In contrast, individual creativity read from a cultural–historical perspective is conceptualised quite differently. It has already been discussed in the preceding sections of the book how children engage in imitation, how they involve themselves in role play and how they seek out through play to understand the rules and objects within society. Vygotsky (2004) argues that, through play, children never simply reproduce reality.

> A child's play is not simply a reproduction of what he has experienced, but a creative reworking of the impressions he has acquired. He combines them and uses them to construct a new reality, one that conforms to his own needs and desires (pp. 11–12).

In other words, the child has some agency in creativity. In many Western communities, the individual nature of creativity, rather than collective creativity, has tended to be foregrounded. This individualism has also been directed to history, but in a way that splits the individual from the collective

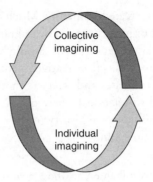

Figure 10.1 Collective and individual imagining

community and ignores the collective contribution to creation. Wertsch (1998), in discussing the work of Frye (1957), notes that there is now a practice in many Western communities of focusing only on the 'individual's contribution rather than on the conventions (i.e., cultural tools) employed'. Wertsch (1998) argues that this relatively recent phenomenon has arisen due to

> the assimilation of literature into private enterprise in the 'copyright age'. In the copyright age, we have such a strong tendency *to focus on the unique contribution of the individual* that we overlook what Frye saw as the fundamental shaping force of conventions employed as a kind of tool in the creative act (p. 18; emphasis added).

In some societies there is a belief that every psychological act in itself is thought to be sufficiently distinct to afford individual ownership for its creation. Wertsch (1998) suggests that inventions and creations should be considered as 'a moment of action rather than a separate process or entity that exists somehow in isolation' (p. 23). What is noticeable here is that creation and imagination are attributed to the individual, that they focus only on one dimension of what is essentially a dialectical process between collective creativity and individual creativity. A cultural–historical view, rather than an individualistic view, positions technologies and other creations as dynamic historical events that are ever changing. Consequently, creativity must be viewed as a dynamic interplay between individual and collective creativity, a relation that is shown in the circles of figure 10.1.

HOW DO IMAGINATION AND CREATIVITY DEVELOP?

As discussed above, a cultural–historical perspective considers imagination to be a new psychological formation. The development of imagination proceeds in a dialectical way, where the importance of children's prior experience, the disassociation and reassociation process involved in the imaginative act and the crystallisation process of imagination into a material form come into play during their development. These potential pedagogical processes are discussed in turn.

THE IMPORTANCE OF EXPERIENCE

Imagination is something that is generated by the child. The child draws upon their previous experience to bring together different elements of these collective experiences into a new creation. This new creation is not something that reproduces what already exists, or something that has been observed or seen. Rather, imagination enables the child to combine the old elements in new ways to produce a new structure, and this forms the basis of creativity. The imaginative–creative dimensions of activity are totally dependent upon the richness and diversity of the child's previous experience. This experience provides the working material for imagination and for creative activity. Vygotsky (2004) argues that 'The richer a person's experience, the richer is the material his imagination has access to' (pp. 14–15). This mutual dependence between experience and imagination acts as a double or reciprocal action, that is, 'imagination is based on experience' and 'experience itself is based on imagination' (p. 17).

DISASSOCIATION AND REASSOCIATION

Vygotsky (2004) argued that in order for imagination to create something new, the process must begin with a holistic scenario in which a process of disassociation and reassociation must occur, that is, a child must first break apart those natural elements of a holistic object, process or system. During this disassociation process, along with other disassociation processes of holistic systems, the child can then combine disassociated elements in new ways. A child can bring together disassociated elements from a range of holistic objects, systems or processes and combine them to form a new creation. In order to do this, not only does it matter that the child has a depth of rich prior experience, but the child also needs to be able to make realignments in disassociated elements in novel ways to solve problems or fulfil a need. Importantly, the child must make decisions about what to include and what to ignore for both the disassociation and the association process. Vygotsky (2004), who pointed out that 'imagination is the combination of individual images, their unification into a system, the construction of a complex picture' (p. 28), gives the following example to illustrate this process:

> Before generating the image of Natasha in *War and Peace*, Tolstoy had to separate out the individual traits of two of his female relatives. If he had not done this, we would not have been able to combine them, 'to grind them up together', to create the image of Natasha. It is this isola-tion of individual traits and neglect of others that we call disassociation. This process is extremely important in all human mental development; it is the foundation of abstract thinking, the basis of concept formation (pp. 25–6).

This disassociation and reassociation process as a basis for concept forma-tion is highly significant (see next section).

IMAGINATION BECOMES REALITY

Vygotsky (2004) believed that when something completely new is imag-ined and created, it becomes externally embodied. It takes on a material form or crystallised imagination as an object that can exist in the mate-rial world. As a new object, concept or system within reality, it is able to affect other things, and through this process 'imagination becomes reality' (p. 20).

When imagination and creativity are conceptualised as developing through a process of building prior experience, disassociation and asso-ciation, and through the crystallisation of imagination into something new that is able to influence the material world, then pedagogical practice must support the development of this new psychological formation in the child. This is shown in figure 10.2.

In the next section, imagination as a new psychological formation is discussed in relation to the kinds of pedagogy that support imagination in unity with cognition for generating concept formation for early childhood and primary aged children.

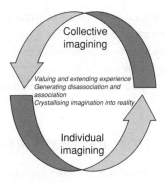

Figure 10.2 Imagination and creativity

PEDAGOGICAL PRACTICE FOR SUPPORTING THE DEVELOPMENT OF IMAGINATION

In this section empirical material discussed in the first part of this book is reintroduced to illustrate how imagination becomes a new psychological formation in young children. In particular, the features of valuing and extending experience, generating disassociation and reassociation and crystallising imagination as reality are examined in relation to pedagogy. As potential pedagogical features they are introduced within the context of the empirical material in order to show how imagination and creativity can be developed in young children. This section seeks to show the dynamic nature of imagination and creativity in relation to pedagogy, as this captures the spirit of a cultural–historical reading of cognition and play – as an imaginative act.

VALUING AND EXTENDING EXPERIENCE

In the example given in chapter 7, a group of preschool children were finding insects in their preschool outdoor area. One particular child, Christian, had a great deal of prior experience with insects and a keen interest in learning about his natural world. His mother, a scientist, had fostered this keen interest, and Jacqui, his preschool teacher, had framed the children's spontaneous interactions with their environment by introducing the idea of a map in order to build relational understandings and generate theoretical thinking. Theoretical thinking – an important educational goal for programs that draw on cultural–historical theory – commenced with connecting with the children's personal world and interest. In this example, one child's interest was the focus of attention; however, the child's prior and expansive interest in exploring the natural environment had oriented all the other children to this same activity (Elkonin, 2008). The teacher and the children were working in conceptual unity because conceptual and contextual intersubjectivity had been established by the teacher (see chapter 7).

IMAGINATION BECOMES REALITY

In order for the children to be able to conceptually participate in this new experience, they needed to have an image of a map in their mind and to imagine themselves, the creatures they were finding and the preschool outdoor environment (food sources) as part of this map. Only then could the children document their finds onto the blank piece of paper that the teacher had labelled as a map. Consequently, the children could use the theoretical model of an ecosystem to support their interactions with the material world. These two imaginative processes are discussed in turn.

THEORETICAL MODEL OF ECOSYSTEM

The teacher drew upon a form of imagination that was directed towards the children's reality – their environment, their motive to gather and examine the insects within that environment. The children's imagination was a necessary and integral part of thinking differently about the creatures in their environment, as a relational construct of habitat, food sources and organism. Imagination helped the children move from a spontaneous everyday interaction with their environment to thinking theoretically, from which the children and the teacher could collectively generate core concepts and create a core model for organism, habitat and food sources (see figure 7.2). The idea of a map supported the children's use of imagination for thinking theoretically. Imagination helped to conceptually bring together everyday and scientific concepts about the organisms the children were finding. In consciously considering the scientific concepts, the children moved beyond the immediate concrete everyday context. As Vygotsky (1987c: 349) states, 'The essential feature of imagination is that consciousness departs from reality'. It is when consciousness departs from reality or the child's embedded context that children can take their newly acquired theoretical model and use it in new contexts. The theoretical model of the ecosystem is used in the material world, just as a spade works physically with the soil. In other words, the imagined ecological model becomes reality.

A MAP AS A CONCEPTUAL TOOL

The example of mapping an ecosystem also illustrates not only how imagination provides children with the ability to understand the idea of a map and to build a map in relation to reality but that the map and the theoretical model are also crystallised into reality and thereafter influence the real world. The map is an invention, a new creation, something that takes on a reality of its own. It is initially imagined by the child as a piece of paper; through building the map in relation to reality, the child turns the piece of paper (imaginary map) into a reality, a tool to be used to build theoretical knowledge. Through this, imagination becomes reality for the child. It is not a complete representation, but a creative representation of reality for the child. This example shows how the links between realistic thinking and imagination become merged. As noted by Vygotsky (1987c):

> Moreover, by observing the forms of imagination that are linked with creativity, that is, the forms of imagination that are directed toward reality, we find that the boundary between realistic thinking and imagination is erased. Imagination is a necessary integral aspect of realistic thinking (p. 349).

DISASSOCIATION AND REASSOCIATION

The new psychological structure of imagination forms because the theoretical models introduced by the teacher (through the experience of mapping) and used by the children to document and analyse their environment connect all the separate processes (mapping) and parts (elements of the ecosystem), and in this way cultural concepts (scientific knowledge) contribute towards the enriching of new psychological functions (imagination), which changes children's behaviour (capacity to use theoretical knowledge) (Vygotsky, 1929).

In this example (elaborated in chapter 7), the teacher and assistant teacher worked together with the children in many different ways – alongside them, above them, below them and as equals – in the process of orienting children to their environment (see subject positioning in chapter 8; Kravtsova, 2008d–f). The children were supported by the teacher to pay attention to particular insects, in relation to the habitat, and to ignore others – active support for disassociation. The teacher worked with the children in active exploration in order to support them with not just the process of disassociation but also with reassociation. This

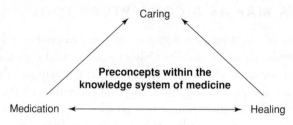

Figure 10.3 Building theoretical knowledge

guided support, different to children working alone, illustrates in action the pedagogical practices needed for developing imagination.

The historical nature of disassociation and reassociation in imagination is also foregrounded in this example. The teacher, as the keeper of collective imagining of the historical knowledge of science, and the child, as novice to this learning, actively engage in individual imagining. The history of scientific knowledge development is foregrounded through the teacher's interactions with the children – what to pay attention to and what to ignore when searching the environment. The children, through active experience with the teacher (see chapter 7), go beyond causal association and use relational thinking (theoretical knowledge), thus actively experiencing scientific processes and scientific modelling.

INDIVIDUAL IMAGINING WITHIN THE HISTORICAL COLLECTIVE

The play vignette of Humpty Dumpty being medicated that was introduced in chapter 1, also shows the potential for imagination laying a foundation for building the core concept of a knowledge system in society, that of medicine, that is, the relational preconcepts of medication, healing and caring. This is shown as a relational model in figure 10.3.

The example is considered to be a preconcept because the history of the development of the knowledge system of healing and the knowledge system of medication as constructed from a medical paradigm were not examined through these children's play (see chapters 1 and 2). Davydov (2008) has argued that the history of the development of a concept in a particular knowledge system needs to be embedded within the pedagogical process of building theoretical knowledge. In the example given in chapter 1, it is unlikely that we would see children building a theoretical model about medicine without some form of adult support. Karpov (2005) has argued against this position in relation to discovery learning, because knowledge of this kind takes centuries to build and only occurs through a slow process of incremental discoveries. In the example of Jacqui introducing a map to the children during their explorations of the outdoor area, the children were connecting with historically formed scientific knowledge. The teacher's role was critical for this orientation and for building a theoretical model for a concept of an ecosystem. But in the Humpty Dumpty play example, the children played without adult support, follow-up or intervention. As already argued, the historical development of a concept must be examined by children (but not as history lesson) in order to successfully build a concept because concepts are embedded within a system of concepts that have been generated over time as a particular form of knowledge, such as science.

The preconcepts represented in figure 10.3 do have the potential for building concepts in play, but the teacher must be involved in some way if the children are to connect with historical forms of knowledge and be oriented sufficiently to disassociate, reassociate and begin to build a theoretical model of medicine. For young children, imagination helps make children's previous experiences and their motives visible to the teacher so that the teacher can connect conceptually and contextually with the children. Figure 10.3 outlines the cognition that can be deliberately foregrounded by the teacher in play for those children who were medicating Humpty Dumpty in their play. The teacher not only connects conceptually and contextually with the children but also analyses their play for possibilities for active concept formation; figure 10.3 is an example of the kind of conceptual mapping that could be undertaken by teachers when they bring together the historical knowledge traditions (collective imagining) valued in society, with the child's world made visible in play (individual imagining). This is not a surprising pedagogical direction, as researchers in Russia interested in cognition in play have shown. Bodrova (2008), in reviewing cultural–historically framed studies in which play development was researched in the early childhood and early school periods, has shown that when adults actively support play development 'not only the quantity and quality of play improves, but so do many other competencies – language, cognitive, social and emotional [leading to] the development of early academic skills' (p. 367).

Bodrova (2008) has argued that a 'Vygotskian approach suggests that the young child can master necessary prerequisites of academic skills through engagement in mature make-believe play' (p. 257). However, as discussed previously, Hedegaard and Chaiklin (2005) found in their research that the teachers in their study were not accustomed to examining what might be the core concepts within the curriculum, despite the fact that they are actively teaching concepts. The relational model in figure 10.3 is illustrative of how a teacher can analyse children's play and determine what might be the relational links they need to build in order that children engage not only in the imaginative process of disassociation but also in reassociation so that they build their own concept or theoretical model. Teachers interested in drawing upon play as a leading activity for building core concepts can use this modelling processes for analysis and for curriculum planning. Once teachers have a stock of core concepts from which they have identified the relational elements needed for building concepts in play, it is possible for teachers to use these for systematically analysing play or creating opportunities in play for building concepts. But clearly, the teachers need to be able to enter into the children's imaginative world and connect conceptually with them.

Significantly 'new developmental accomplishments do become apparent in play far earlier that they do in other activities' (Bodrova, 2008: 360). Logically, then, Bodrova's (2008) research can support the view that in developing concept formation it is important for teachers to actively consider the nature of the history of discipline knowledge as a collective imagining and to determine its relationship with children's individual imagining during play. While this finding gives evidence for utilising play for concept formation, the pedagogical practices that currently dominate Western communities must be significantly better theorised if teachers are to effectively use play for conceptual development.

THE IMAGINATIVE ACT AS CONCEPTUAL PLAY

The examples given in this chapter (and discussed in detail previously) illustrate how imagination serves children to think consciously about something and to work imaginatively to solve problems and generate potential solutions. The imaginary situation generated by the teacher lifts children into a conceptual space above reality, but this imagining is also dialectically related to reality, which is demonstrated as children design and make their creations. Children work consciously rather than act subconsciously, and in these imaginary situations the teacher is able to connect conceptually with the children. Bakhurst (2008), in discussing Vygotsky's (1987a) writings on thinking and speech, states that

Vygotsky's view of the relation of mind and meaning leads him to a sophisticated successor to the notion of 'doubled experience.' Mental phenomena take as their objects meaningful states of affairs in the world or representations thereof and any mental state can itself become the object of another: my thought can become the object of attention, reasoning, memory, volition, and so forth. Any being capable of such reflexive mental acts is conscious. With this, consciousness is fundamentally related to meaning and Vygotsky concludes that 'consciousness as a whole has a semantic [*smyslovoe*] structure' (1933b: 137 [SS I: 165]). We might say that a conscious being occupies the space of meanings (pp. 55–6).

The theoretical discussion in this chapter serves to illustrate the dialectical nature of imagination and cognition (doubled experience), and begins to point to the multiple pathways for its development (in unity with reality). Imagination, when used consciously by children, helps them to rise above reality, to descend to reality, to document reality and to play with reality in ways that afford scientific concept formation. This imaginative act can be seen as a model (figure 10.4) that builds upon previous models shown in this book, models that have been incrementally built. The model is representative of how play can be used for concept formation. The theorisation given in this book is embodied in this model and named as a new theory, *conceptual play*. Because this book uses dialectical logic, the model of conceptual play should be viewed as dynamic and active, as an imaginative act. Hence, the new theory must be conceptualised and named dialectically as both an imaginative act and as conceptual play.

Imagination as the generation of an imaginary situation by the teacher (imaginary framing) now also becomes an important conscious act on the part of the children (as discussed in this chapter), a situation in which adults and children can rise above reality, descent to reality, connect with reality and play with reality. In this theoretical model, it is possible for the imaginary situation to also be created by the child, but as a deliberate pedagogy for concept formation this can only be achieved if the teacher has conceptual and contextual intersubjectivity, that is to say, if the teacher has an understanding of the everyday concepts and contexts that the child has gained through home and community experience, thus foregrounding the importance of the child's personal world in the context of family and community.

The imaginative act allows for a consciousness of concepts on the part of the child as well as the teacher, for the building of shared knowledge and for the generation of a common experience between teacher and

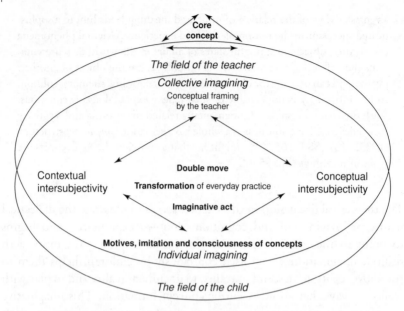

Figure 10.4 The imaginative act as conceptual play: a dialectical pedagogical model for building theoretical knowledge in play-based programs

children (achieved through contextual and conceptual intersubjectivity). The concept of an 'event' in the Golden Key schools is also illustrative of this shared experience for generating an imaginative act.

This model, which has been designed for teachers of children whose leading activity is play, represents a dialectical relation between the student and the teacher. It becomes a pedagogical bridge for teachers when supporting children from play as a leading activity to learning as a leading activity. Foregrounded in this model is concept formation. This pedagogical model sits alongside those discussed in previous chapters, such as the Golden Key Program, Tools of the Mind and Developmental Teaching.

SUMMARY

In this chapter imagination was theorised in relation to concept formation. In particular, it demonstrated how imagination is a necessary part of helping children to rise above reality, to engage with reality and to play with reality. It is through imagination that abstract thinking is possible and theoretical thinking can be achieved. Imagination in play helps children to consciously consider actions and concepts, and through this process, self-development is possible. It was also shown how imagination supports children to make conscious the relations between external and internal functioning.

A cultural–historical reading of imagination, as presented in this chapter, provides a useful way forward for the early childhood profession for realising concept formation in play-based programs. A dialectical model that captures the relationship between all the concepts discussed in this and previous chapters in this book was given in order to build upon the theoretical and empirical material provided earlier and to create a new theory of play. Dialectical logic was used for explaining the model of conceptual play as an imaginative act.

For teachers to successfully use a dialectical model of play, it becomes important that a dialectical view of development in play, and child development generally, be considered. The last part of this book turns to an analysis of existing theories of child development that guide early childhood education.

Part 3

Learning and development as cultural practice

11 | Views on child development matter

We already know that the child's chronological age cannot serve as a reliable criterion for establishing the actual level of his development.

(Vygotsky, 1998: 199)

INTRODUCTION

Karpov (2005), in noting Hetherington and McIntyre's (1975) 'expansive review of development' (p. 2), suggests that dissatisfaction among scholars and practitioners has resulted from a longstanding reductionist research tradition. In contrast to this research orientation, he argues that

> The kernel of any theory of child development is the description of *the determinant of development* (that is, the major factor that leads to development) and the explanation of *the mechanism of development* (that is, the analysis of how the suggested determinant of development leads to development) (p. 2; emphasis in the original).

He also notes that different theoretical perspectives on learning (e.g., Piaget, Erikson, Freud) focus on only one aspect of the whole child, such as cognition or moral development. Even expanded developmental models (e.g., Kohlberg's use of Piaget's theory of cognition) 'have not resulted in a holistic view of child development because they do not describe interrelationships of different aspects of child development' (p. 8). This problem has also been identified by Kravtsova (2008c). Not only has Vygotsky (1998) studied the complexity of the many dimensions of development but his research also foregrounded the dialectical relations between the social situation and the biological child and the changing nature of the child's relationship to the material and social world (see Kravtsova, 2008c). This revolutionary view of development provides a theoretically rich framework for undertaking research with children in the 21st century.

This chapter seeks to examine child development through a critique of the existing dominant views of child development that underpin early childhood education in most Western communities. Data from a cultural–historical study of child development will be used to illustrate key concepts important for critiquing views on child development. Subsequent chapters will look more closely at the empirical material introduced in this chapter, and will examine more closely Vygotsky's theory of child development and those who have further elaborated his theory. The book will conclude with a cultural–historical view of child development, pedagogy and play that is directly relevant for early childhood education.

DEVELOPMENT AS A NATURALLY EVOLVING PROCESS

CONCEPTUALISING PERIODISATION

Vygotsky (1998) provides a powerful critique of child development, arguing that the schemes that have been proposed to divide up childhood can be organised into three areas. The first and most relevant to the study of early childhood education is the organisation of childhood in relation to some stepwise (not directly or biologically connected) process, such as education; preschool age, primary school age and secondary school age can be considered examples of this type of periodisation. The categorisation of childhood is related to the process of teaching, and childhood development follows pedagogical principles. Another example relates to the periods of children's play as reproducing the history of humankind where a biogenetic theory informs the categorisation of childhood periods. This second kind of categorisation has dominated traditional psychology. This view of development focuses on the identification of a single trait for dividing up childhood development, such as the emergence of the first teeth, second teeth and wisdom teeth. This approach to dividing up childhood development is also evident in Steiner education. Dentition becomes the criterion for making judgements about children's general development. Dividing up childhood in this way is visible and always accessible for informing judgements, and it is viewed as being objective. Vygotsky (1998) argued against this form of categorisation of childhood development when he suggested that although an objective trait is used – teeth – it is a subjective and inadequate process for establishing periodisation. Using only one criterion for making judgements is narrow and is unlikely to signal what matters at another age period. Growing your first set of teeth, for example, does have a significant bearing on what can be eaten. Moving from first teeth to second teeth has no bearing at all on what children can eat, and the markers of second teeth do not signify of themselves anything important for development. As Vygotsky (1998) notes:

> The breaking through of teeth at the boundary between infancy and early childhood can be used as an indicative trait for the general development of the child, but the replacement of teeth at approximately seven years of age and the appearance of wisdom teeth cannot be compared in its significance for general development to the first appearance of teeth (p. 188).

According to Vygotsky (1998) the use of single traits for establishing periodisation does not take into account the 'reorganisation of the process itself of development' (p. 188), and single traits do not treat seriously the complexity of children's development. Further, Vygotsky argued that examining easily identifiable traits focused attention on the study of externally visible features, and did not take account of the internal essence of a process that contributed to the emergence of the visible traits. Studying what underpins these clusters of visible traits in order to determine them is a very different process to simply identifying a single trait and using it as a criterion for breaking up periods of childhood development:

> With respect to the problem of dividing childhood into periods, this means we must reject attempts of symptomatic classification of age levels and move on, as other sciences have done in their time, to classification based on the internal essence of the process being studied (1998: 198).

Dividing up childhood development into ages has been a common practice in Western education. In bringing together the single trait for classification – age – and the stepwise process for periodisation – education – differently common and taken for granted approaches in education can be viewed. It is, for instance, 'normal' for children of the same age to be placed into the same year level and the same classroom in most Western and European heritage schools. Rogoff (2003) presents the case that it was in the late 1800s that age became a criterion for ordering life and for framing development:

> With the rise of industrialization and efforts to systemize human services
> such as education and medical care, age became a measure of development
> and a criterion for sorting people. Specialized institutions were designed
> around age groups. Developmental psychology and pediatrics began at this
> time, along with old-age institutions and age-graded schools (p. 8).

The criteria used to divide up child development are clearly a strong force
in how a society views development and what kinds of institutions and
practices that emerge. Age as a criterion for dividing up development
focuses attention on the externally visible biological traits of childhood,
and does little for the framing of thinking about development in other
ways. It is like holding up two fingers and asking for three bananas when
shopping. The shop attendant will focus on the visual cues and sell you
two bananas, even though it is in the salesperson's interest to sell you three
items. The visible trait dominates and distracts us from determining the
essence of child development.

In some parts of West Africa the principle underpinning child development is social rather than age-related, as noted by Nsamenang and
Lamb (1998) in their study of Nso children in the Bamenda Granfields of
Cameroon, West Africa (211 men and 178 women who were parents or
grandparents of children under the age of 10 years):

> children are progressively assigned different roles at different life stages
> depending on their perceived level of social competence rather than on their
> biological maturation (p. 252).

This finding is not surprising when we examine how people, historically,
'rarely knew their age, and students advanced in their education as they
learn' (Rogoff, 2003: 8). As noted by Rogoff (2003):

> Children's groups around the world generally include a mix of
> ages . . . Grouping children by age is unusual around the world. It requires
> adequate numbers of children in a small territory to ensure availability of
> several children of the same age (Konner, 1975). It also seems to be prompted
> by the growth of bureaucracies and reductions in family size.
>
> (Rogoff, 2003: 125)

Age as a criterion for child development is generally unquestioned, and
it is difficult for people from Western communities to imagine a time in
society when age didn't dominate, as noted by Rogoff (2003):

Both expert and popular writing in the United States rarely referred to specific ages... Over the past century and a half, the concept of age and associated practices relying on age-grading have come to play a central, though often unnoticed role in ordering lives in some cultural communities (p. 8).

Gesell (1933) also sought to construct periods of childhood in relation to the rhythm and tempo of the child at particular ages, as though there was a flowing stream of development. He presents a naturally evolving process, in which nothing new arises in development, but rather the rhythm and tempo associated with a particular age change. Vygotsky (1998) was highly critical of this view of development because in this conception of development 'nothing new arises in development, no qualitative changes occur, and only what is given from the very beginning grows and develops' (p. 189). Rather, Vygotsky (1998) argued that

development is not confined to the scheme, 'more–less', but is characterised primarily and specifically by the presence of qualitative neoformations that are subject to their own rhythm and require a special measure each time (p. 189).

The third category Vygotsky (1998) identified for understanding the periodisation of child development related to the methodological difficulties associated with studying development. He suggested that theorists such as Gesell primarily studied external traits of child development and did not seek to examine the internal essence of the process. These studies were limited because they did not take account of the complexity and wholeness of human development, and therefore provided little useful information for guiding theoretical work into child development.

THEORIES OF CHILD DEVELOPMENT

Vygotsky (1998) argued that all theories of child development could be reduced to two major conceptions of child development. First, 'development is nothing other than realisation, modification, and combination of deposits. Nothing new develops here – only a growth, branching, and regrouping of those factors that were already present at the very beginning' (Vygotsky, 1998: 190). The second perspective views 'development as a continuous process of self-propulsion characterised primarily by the continuous appearance and formation of the new which did not exist at

previous stages' (Vygotsky, 1998: 190). This view of child development –
as a naturally evolving process (Vygotsky called this an evolutionary view
of development) – has become entrenched in the theorisation and research
practices of many who work with children in the birth-to-eight age span
(see Dahlberg, Pence & Moss, 1999). An example to illustrate the longevity
of a naturally evolving view of child development can be seen in the growth
charts produced in 1977 by the US National Center for Health Statistics
(NCHS) and used throughout the world as a result of their adoption by the
World Health Organisation (WHO). The development of these growth
charts was originally based on data obtained from babies who came from
middle-class white families in Ohio. These babies were unusually heavy
because they were bottle fed, a common practice 33 years ago in many
US communities. These data were not updated until 2006 (see growth
charts below in figure 11.1; Coghlan, 2007: 6). Coghlan (2007) states
that 'Now research is beginning to confirm what many mothers have long
suspected – that the most commonly used growth charts, based on babies
fed high-protein formula milk, wrongly classify lean but healthy babies
as underweight. What's more, by encouraging mothers to overfeed their
babies, the charts may be setting perfectly healthy children on the path
to obesity' (p. 6). Through the adoption of the 1977 NCHS data as the
standard by the WHO, these charts have proliferated throughout communities, culturally diverse communities, where breast feeding, not bottle
feeding, is the norm. Coghlan (2007) suggests that 'Many new mothers
come to dread the arcane growth charts produced by the baby clinics to
assess whether their new arrival is being under or overfed' (p. 6). The US
Center for Disease Control and Prevention (CDC) undertook the task of
generating the baseline data in 2000 for the redevelopment of the growth
charts, and thereby created a new standard.

These kinds of charts not only establish generic standards, but also generate particular expectations by clinicians. Vygotsky (1998) argued that an
evolving perspective of development highlights a linear path, where deviat-
ing from 'the normal path' can be considered as 'diseases of development'
(p. 191). Clinicians used the data on the growth charts to advise families
about the relative health and nutrition of their babies. Data obtained in
one community with particular societal expectations, such as bottle feeding infants, creates different developmental opportunities to what may be
found in another community, where practices and beliefs may be quite
different. Once norms are established, such as the growth charts, the data
that were used to develop the tool are no longer easily questioned. The
growth chart is not used just in relation to what data produced the norms

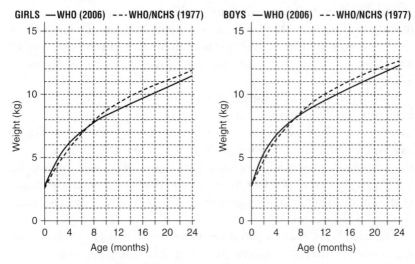

GIRLS —WHO (2006) ---WHO/NCHS (1977)   BOYS —WHO (2006) ---WHO/NCHS (1977)

Figure 11.1 Comparison of growth charts from 1977 to 2006 (adapted from Coghlan, 2007: 6)

for measuring physical development (data from Ohio middle-class white bottle fed infants). When the growth chart is used to weigh babies from other cultural communities or at a different period of time, then questions need to be asked about the measurement tool. The growth chart becomes disembedded from the cultural context that produced it and an objective instrument that takes on a life of its own as a measurement tool. The new measurement tool helps clinicians make judgements and to give advice to families about their babies. What underpins this practice is a particular view of children's development. It is child development that follows a linear progression and has been normalised and validated to generate a particular standard. The tool has been created based on a belief that child development is a naturally evolving process.

Growth charts produce expectations of how much a baby should weigh at a particular age. This view of development can also be seen in relation to expectations of children's behaviours. When, for instance, children should be able to walk has been grounded in a physiological expectation and a sense of folk wisdom. An example of expectations around when a child should begin walking follows. These data are drawn from a study undertaken by Fleer; the study design and findings are published in Fleer and Hedegaard (in press).

In this study, families were videotaped at different times in the day across a range of contexts over a period of 18 months. The family that is introduced here (Peninsula family) to illustrate constructions of child development lives in a low SES community in Australia. The family has six members: a mother, a father and four children. The youngest, Louise, was 18 months old at the commencement of the study, and 36 months at its conclusion.

In the Peninsula family, the children return from school (Andrew), from kindergarten (Nick) and from childcare (JJ) to enjoy a snack provided by the researcher. The dog Millie interacts with each member of the family and the research team. During their eating of the snack, the children simultaneously interact with the researchers, each other, their parents, the DVD playing in the corner of the room and other artefacts in the room. In this simultaneously highly interactive context, the family discusses their views on development.

Embedded understandings of development are initiated by Nathan (four years) when he states that Louise (16 months) cannot yet stand up.

ANDREW   She, she can't stand up.
RESEARCHER No. Do you think she'll be able to stand up soon?
ANDREW   Soon.
RESEARCHER Soon.
ANDREW   She can't stand up.

(*the mother refutes this claim while passing out drinks to her children and observing Louise crawling on the floor*)

MUM No, she does stand up. (*baby crawls along floor, mother interacts with baby, other children also participate*)
MUM Yeah, no, even . . . I mean, even *her* (*Mum points to Louise*)
JJ   (*yelling at mother as she speaks to researcher*) Mumma, Mumma, Mumma.
MUM I mean, at one stage – at *one* stage we had a few people *say* she was 13 months old – at the time when we were in Railway Crescent at Newton [suburb pseudonym]. (*looks at JJ*) Do you want a drink? (*Mum nods*)

The video continues to capture the images of Louise crawling across the floor and pulling herself up on the sofa. As this occurs, the mother talks about how other people have questioned Louise's apparent late development. The age related perspective of child development is actively contested by the mother, who states:

MUM At one stage there, um, we had a few people saying oh, she's a bit under*developed* at *13* months old – cause she wasn't *walking* and . . . or, she wasn't *up* walking or *up* standing or any . . . or *crawling* or anything but . . . (*Louise is on her side*) I mean she's starting to *get* up and stand, she's starting to crawl and roll around and everything.

(*Louise rolls onto stomach and starts crawling*)

RESEARCHER (*speaking over Mum*) Absolutely. Yeah, yeah.

MUM But I mean they all *get* up and learn at their own level or *ability* you know.

(*Louise has crawled to lounge chair and uses her right arm to lift herself up*)

MUM And that's one thing I *try* to tell Amanda [the social worker] . . .

(*Louise brings her left arm up and rests her hand on top of her other hand, looks from direction of camera to Mum and back to camera*)

RESEARCHER Yeah.

MUM Our protection worker when she used to come over. Just to *see* how things are going. I said to *her* I said *look* they all learn at their own ability.

RESEARCHER Yeah.

MUM They *don't* all *learn* . . .

RESEARCHER No.

MUM . . . you know, in exactly the same way, at the *same* . . . the same level. I mean they *get* up and walk when they're ready to walk. (*Louise looks v/camera, mouth open and smiles*) I mean she *won't* be far off it.

RESEARCHER No.

(*Louise rests head on her left arm while hands on lounge chair; Louise smiles*)

MUM She's starting to *pull* herself up.

Contrary to Vygotsky's (1998) claim, chronological age remains an important criterion for determining behaviour in the Peninsula family. The mother specifically mentions that at 13 months Louise was not walking. At 18 months she was pulling herself up (shown above) and at two years she was walking, bouncing a ball, climbing up a slide and sliding down unassisted (see chapter 12). The social worker who visited the Peninsula family made specific mention of Louise's slow development – that she should have been walking by a particular age. The social worker looked for, and expected, particular behaviours; when they are not forthcoming concern was expressed about the individual. In this case, the social worker expressed concern about Louise's overall development. The external visual trait of walking at a particular age was used as the criterion for making judgements about Lousie's overall development. This represents an evolving natural view of child development (see figure 11.2).

Growth and developmental milestones that are standardised, such as NCHS or the classic 'developmental profiles' by Allen and Morotz (1989),

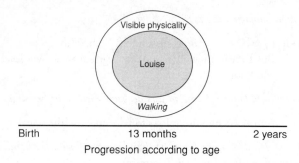

Figure 11.2 A naturally evolving view of child development

provide a powerful normalising effect that generate discourses in communities that position some children and their families into a negative light. Had a different set of milestones been generated for physical development, or a different theory of child development been drawn upon, the Peninsula family would not be feeling external pressure for Louise to walk. The mother, in refuting these milestones, is fighting against having Louise labelled as being a failure in her physical development.

Expectations associated with externally visible milestones that are judged in relation to age leave little scope for making different judgements about Louise's development. If she is late in walking, then there are problems with her development, noted by Vygotsky (1998) as 'diseases of development'. Views of child development clearly matter, as they determine the judgements made by the social worker and other professionals who work with young children and their families. Clearly, a different view of child development would have produced a very different set of expectations and interactions between the social worker and the mother.

SUMMARY

In this chapter Vygotsky's (1998) critique of child development was outlined. The dominant views of child development within the professions were given and the relevance of Vygotsky's original review of child development was shown. Empirical data were presented to illustrate how views on child development shape relations and practices between professionals and families and their children. In the next chapter a different view of development is discussed and Vygotsky's revolutionary view of development is detailed.

12 | A revolutionary view of child development

[T]he development of the child is a dialectical process in which a transition from one state to another is accomplished not along an evolutionary, but along a revolutionary path.

(Vygotsky, 1998: 193)

INTRODUCTION

One of Vygotsky's (1998) many contributions to theorising learning and development centred on the view that child development should be 'a single process of self-development' (p. 189): he articulated a theory that focused on a holistic model of development that included the dialectical relations between psychological, biological and cultural dimensions as noted through motives, cognition and the social situation of development. Vygotsky presents a revolutionary view of child development in *Child Psychology*, the fifth volume of his collected works, and although his theory requires further interpretation (see Kravtsova, 2005; Veresov, 2006), it represents a conceptualisation that has inspired many to research and theorise in new ways (Karpov, 2005). Karpov (2005) states that 'Unfortunately, he [Vygotsky] presented this model in an abbreviated and schematic fashion, which makes it difficult to understand' (p. 41).

In order to understand the complexity of Vygotsky's theory of child development it is important to go beyond isolating and explaining single concepts – such as the zone of proximal development – as this approach gives a limited reading of his theory. Karpov (2005) states that

> Many reviewers present Vygotsky's theory as a set of separate ideas (such as the idea of mediation, psychological tools, higher mental processes, zones

of proximal development, scientific concepts, etc.) without showing (or even understanding) that these ideas are interrelated as basic components of Vygotsky's holistic theory (p. 12).

This is specifically mentioned here because Vygotsky's concept of child development as presented in this chapter must be read within the context of the previous chapter (Vygotsky's and my own critique of the Western context) and the previous section of the book, which elaborates a number of concepts that will be drawn upon for this chapter in order to discuss a revolutionary view of child development.

In this chapter the interrelated concepts of stable periods, crises and neoformations will be discussed and elaborated on from a Vygotskian perspective and from the perspective of contemporary scholars interested in a new view of child development. Discussion of Vygotsky's theory of child development begins through an elaboration of stable periods and crises.

STABLE PERIODS AND CRISES

In Vygotsky's theorisation of child development he suggests that what is most obvious about children's development is its slow and evolving incremental movement, or lytic flow (often translated as 'stable periods'). He argues that children's development appears to be smooth and unremarkable, and writes that 'change that is accomplished by insignificant "molecular" attainments' (p. 190) appears to take several years, without abrupt shifts or alterations to the child's personality. Vygotsky states that 'They appear outside and are accessible to direct observation only as a conclusion of long-term processes of latent development' (p. 190). Vygotsky suggested that when these stable periods are considered chronologically, they make up much of children's childhood development. In this theorisation, 'development proceeds as if underground, great alterations in his personality are evident if a child is compared at the beginning and at the end of a stable period' (p. 191). Vygotsky (1998) notes that

> Stable age periods have been studied significantly more fully than those that are characterized by another type of development – crises. The latter are disclosed purely empirically and thus far have not been brought into the system, have not been included in the general division of child development into periods. Many authors even doubt that there is any internal need for their existence. They are more inclined to take them as 'diseases' of

development because of its deviation from the normal path. Almost none of the bourgeois investigators could theoretically realize their actual significance. For this reason, our attempt to systematize them and interpret them theoretically and include them in the general pattern of child development must be considered as almost the first such attempt (p. 191).

Kravtsova (2006) has taken these original theoretical ideas proposed by Vygotsky (1998) and has developed them further. In her theorisation of child development, lytic flow (or latent/stable, as it has also been named) and crisis (or critical age, as it has also been termed), is represented as a diagram (see figure 12.1). In this example of age periods, she shows the crisis evident for the one year old infant as being closely linked with the primordial we (see chapter 8) and the child's growing consciousness of their everyday social and material worlds. The infant under one year of age encounters the world directly through the carer's orientation and narration as the baby is held and moved around in the adult's arms. The infant is oriented to those things that are important (e.g., pointing out relatives as they walk past in a community context) and common practice within particular families and communities (e.g., observing cars, cooking, or looking intently at flowers). The infant experiences the world in unity with the adult, and hence does not distinguish themselves as separate from their carers – conceptualised as primordial we (or 'great we', as named by Vygotsky, 1998). As noted by Vygotsky (1998),

> for the infant, the centre of every object situation is another person who changes its significance and sense and, second, that the relation to the object and the relation to the person have not yet been separated in the infant (p. 235).

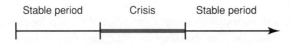

Figure 12.1 Age periods (adapted from Kravtsova, 2006: 11)

Learning during this stable period slowly changes the nature of the interactions, the child's relationship to all those around them and to the physical world. Vygotsky states that 'Because the infant himself does not walk and cannot move an object closer to himself or father away, he must act through others' (p. 248). The infant begins to gesture and make sounds that direct attention towards the objects they desire. In Vygotsky's (1987) opinion, empirical research shows that when an object of desire is out of reach, infants will only gesture their wishes for the object if the adult and the object are within the infant's field of view. The infant, in unity with the adult (primordial we), will work together to gain the desired object. Infants who communicate their intention to be closer to an object of desire display a new type of self-awareness (object is viewed as separate from the infant), and can in some instances create a tension, such as when, for example, the infant wants to engage with a fast moving car or many other dangerous objects in the infant's environment, but the adult does not allow this. According to Vygotsky, these crises appear at particular points in a child's development and their essence is marked by the acquisition of new psychological formations, such as speech (the early childhood child realises that autonomous language – child's made up sounds or words – cannot always be understood by an adult, and that a common language is needed for effective communication), and imagination (that words can free a child from their visible field or context, and abstraction becomes possible [see Vygotsky (1998) *Collected Works*, volume 5, for details of the child's other new psychological formations and how self-awareness emerges in relation to the periods one, three, seven, 12 and the teenage years]). The concept of crisis is simplistically represented in figure 12.1 as the zone between the two stable periods. But the complexity of the relations between stable periods and crises requires further elaboration.

In order to understand these relational concepts of stable periods and crises within Vygotsky's theory of child development, the concepts of leading activity and of neoformations need to be examined. The latter will be discussed further on in this chapter.

THE CONCEPT OF LEADING ACTIVITY

This concept, introduced (but not defined) earlier, was first mentioned in Vygotsky's (1966) original writing on play, and was elaborated by D.B. Elkonin (2005a–c) in relation to a cultural–historical view of play (play as a leading activity) and also by Davydov (2008) in relation to learning (learning as a leading activity). The term 'leading activity' was 'introduced into wide usage by A.N. Leontiev' (Kravtsova, 2006: 8); the concept is seminal for understanding Vygotsky's theory of child development, but only in the context of understanding how one leading activity changes into another leading activity (see Kravtsova, 2006 on neoformations, discussed further below).

Leading activity as a general concept 'defines the specific nature of a child's development at a given age' or period in the child's development (Kravtsova, 2006: 8). Kravtsova (2006) argues that a 'child's transition from one chronological stage to another is marked by a change in leading activity' (p. 8), which in turn create the conditions for generating mental development within that period, that is, the leading activity refers to the visible activity or behaviours of an individual in the social world and to the psychological criteria for participation in these activities, particularly the motives (see chapter 2) that are generated through this dialectical process. While the psychological criteria for engagement in the social and material world can be foregrounded, consideration must also be given to how the activities themselves generate the motives and psychological criteria. Engagement in the social and material world forms the motivation for the leading activity. Kravtsova (2006) suggests that 'any attempt to define the motive of a particular leading activity, to determine the psychological component of the activity encounters serious difficulties' (p. 8). In much of the Western literature on play, as shown previously, there is a belief that 'children's desire to play is what generates the motive for engaging in play'. This simplistic and skewed view of play has been empirically and theoretically refuted by scholars in Russia or of Russian descent (see Bodrova, 2008; Kravtsova, 2008a b c; see also chapter 7). A full discussion of the dialectics between motives and play activity can be found in chapter 2.

Davydov (2008) has introduced the concept of learning as a leading activity for school aged children, Vygotsky (1966) has conceptualised play as a leading activity for preschool aged children and Kravtsov (2008b, d) has coined the term 'communication as a leading activity for infants'. These conceptualisations draw attention to how one leading activity changes into another leading activity. Kravtsova (2006) critiques the distinctions that are drawn by Davydov (2008) for play as a leading activity being replaced by learning as a leading activity when she says that

> The assertion by V.V. Davydov that educational activity replaces play when the latter has been exhausted is contradicted by the fact that in real life both young school-age children and adolescents, not to mention adults, take pleasure in play. Therefore, there is no justification for talking about the disappearance of play. At the same time, educational activity, which becomes the leading activity during early school age, in Davydov's opinion, can initially take a collectively distributed form that very little resembles education and is much more reminiscent of play (p. 9).

Empirical evidence for this proposition can also be found in the Western literature on the transitions from childhood to adulthood (Nairn & Higgins, 2009). The conception that the transition between childhood and adulthood can be represented as neatly linear has been problematised within the youth sociological literature (e.g., Ball, Maguire & Macrae, 2000; Higgins & Nairn, 2006; Maguire, Ball & Macrae, 2001; Nairn, Higgins & Ormond, 2007; Wyn & Dwyer, 1999; 2000). Nairn and Higgins' (2009) claim that the events that have been traditionally associated with the transition from childhood to adulthood 'are no longer accumulatively achieved in linear fashion, but are processes to be managed, often concurrently and on a contingent basis' (p. 31). Markers of this movement include leaving education, gaining employment, independent living, engaging in intimate adult relationships and having children. Nairn and Higgins (2009) argue that young people need to make choices about 'a multiplicity of possible future directions where once, for the grandparents and even the parents of these young people, relatively few choices existed' (p. 31).

Evidence for these claims can be found in an investigation by Nairn and Higgins (2009) of 93 young people's work identities and movements from childhood to adulthood. Participants were drawn from three sites across New Zealand; they were interviewed in their final year of high school and once again when they embarked upon their postschool lives. Thirteen participants acted as peer researchers who interviewed one or two peers. Participants also produced identity portfolios. Nairn and Higgins (2009) found that in their final year of school (17–18 years) a distinct border between adulthood and childhood was drawn by teachers and that students felt they were babied. They cite the following example from a postschool interview of a youth called Laura: 'We were still sort of babied and yeah, weren't really treated like adults' (p. 33). In contrast Nairn and Higgins (2009) found that in the world of work, youth were given major responsibilities and treated as adults, but because of how they had been positioned at school, they felt that their age was an impediment to feeling and acting like an adult. In the worksite they acted as children and as adults. They cite the following interview data of a transitioning youth that reflected on their work context for their claims:

And I've got people under me, well I've got the school age kids and that's alright, they do as I tell them to. But there's a new girl and she's just come from, she's just finished her degree at Uni and I find it so hard, yeah, I don't like telling them what do to, but yeah (p. 33).

Nairn and Higgins (2009) suggest that the youth struggle with the adult–child borders and perceive themselves as being treated as an adult and as a child. As Kravtsova (2006) states, 'on the one hand, his new relationship with the adult [is] built on the basis of the lytic-period formation, and on the other, they already contain features of the formation of the new critical period' (Kravtsova, 2006: 14). In the example cited above, 'this role required her [Laura] to act as an adult but she had more experience in contexts where she was expected to act as a child, subordinate to parents and teachers' (p. 33). Importantly, Nairn and Higgins (2009) found that age was a criterion named by many of the youth interviewed. In this example of Laura, Nairn and Higgins (2009) argue that 'She framed her interpretations of her progression at work in terms of her age, which she saw as a potential barrier, and her boss whom she saw as relatively unusual for challenging other adults' perceptions of appropriate ages for particular roles' (p. 33). They cite the following interview data:

> He [boss] stuck up for me about my Manager's certificate coz the head office thought I was too young to be doing it and they have paid for it and yeah, I don't know, I guess I'm just lucky that I got the job really (post-school interview) (p. 33).

Nairn and Higgins (2009) argue that the identity is shaped by the concept of age determining what may be done, what is possible and what someone can do. Nairn and Higgins (2009) state that

> Laura's account of her identity work constitutes an important challenge to any conceptualisation of human development as somehow a linear movement from one stage to the next . . . Laura's words demonstrate what we think is a more appropriate conceptualisation of the child–adult border, a fuzzy zone rather than a distinct line, one that young people move backwards and forwards across as they constitute themselves, and are constituted by others, as children and adults, sometimes simultaneously (p. 34).

Specifically, in Nairn and Higgins' (2009) conception of child–adult borders, they note the following in young peoples' identity work:

> The term 'child–adult border' is intended to encapsulate how young people in their teenage years move backwards and forwards between identities associated with childhood and adulthood – a movement shaped by their context and the social relationships in which they are enmeshed (p. 30).

Figure 12.2 The person's changing relations to their social world, which generates a new kind of self-awareness or consciousness (adapted from Kravtsova, 2006: 11).

What becomes evident in the findings of Nairn and Higgins (2009) is a new awareness, on the part of the adolescent, of needing to be an adult in the world of work, despite how uncomfortable this might feel. For some this represents a crisis when the person's relationship to their social world changes as they move from the school world to the postschool context (see representation of this in figure 12.2). Kravtsova (2006), in discussing Vygotsky's theory of child development, states that the 'crisis formation is associated with the emergence of *new self-awareness*' (p. 11; emphasis in the original).

Laura's changing context – from school to work – created a crisis for her. However, at work, through communication with her boss, where he positioned her as an adult with responsibilities, he progressively supported her in her transition to work. As Kravtsova (2005) notes, the child achieves the transition through the support of others.

A further example of the significance of Vygotsky's relational concepts of crisis and stable periods and Kravtsova's explanation in relation to a new self-awareness can be seen in the research of Hedegaard (2009). In her investigations of kindergarten children in Denmark she notes 'how differences in practices between school and kindergarten contribute to the creation of a developmental crisis' (p. 66). She cites the example of Jens, a five year old child attending a local kindergarten (Hedegaard 1992):

> The pedagogue asks Jens to go with her and another child to a small room, where they usually read. She wants to read for them. Jens runs away from her and places himself next to the observer in the common room.
> Jens says he has to write a letter. The observer shows him how to write JENS and invites him to write underneath her writing. He starts the task, but writes JES, and then inserts an N when the observer shows him how to write an N by drawing two straight lines and combining them with a diagonal line.

The pedagogue asks Jens again to come into the reading room and join her and Christina. Jens folds his paper with his name on it; he wants to take it home and give it to his daddy. The observer enters together with Jens. The pedagogue puts her arm around Jens while reading a fairy tale.

JENS My dad will be angry.

(*the pedagogue continues to read without listening to Jens*)

JENS Did you hear? My dad will be angry if you read that book. (*jumps up and runs around in the small room*)

The pedagogue wants to put her arm around him again. He becomes wild when she touches him and runs out of the room. The pedagogue runs after him. They come back and, reluctantly, Jens sits down next to Christina so that the pedagogue cannot put her arm around him. The observer asks Jens to listen so that afterwards he can explain to her what Anita, the pedagogue, is reading. The pedagogue has chosen a new book that is about whales and is rather technical.

ANITA (*directed at the observer*) This is not such a successful choice for a storybook. (*she continues reading; Jens is very concentrated; she points at a picture*) This is a baby.

JENS That is not how a baby looks.

PEDAGOGUE Yes, whales!

JENS Not baby whales. (*Jens corrects the pedagogue to show that he knows they are talking about whales*)

In the analysis of this transcript by Hedegaard (2009) she indicates that from the child's perspective Jens wishes to be treated as a schoolchild. He is oriented towards school learning, so having a pedagogue read fairy tales with her arm around him in a cosy manner is unacceptable to Jens. He shows through his interactions that he is interested in technical books, in learning to write his name and in other school activities. Hedegaard (2009) argues that Jens is 'influenced by values at home, such as his father's, and this could be why Jens told the pedagogue his dad would not appreciate the "childish" book that she first chose as a reading text' (p. 67). The pedagogue on the other hand wishes to engage Jens in a storyreading session and to build a warm relationship with him by putting her arm around him. Hedegaard (2009) states that this is common practice within kindergartens in Denmark.

The conflict noted by Hedegaard (2009) is in relation to Jens' changing relationship to the kindergarten context. Jens no longer wants to play and build close relationships with the pedagogue, rather he wishes to participate in school activities and school learning. Jens does not want to be treated as a small child, but rather as a schoolchild. The findings of Hedegaard (2009) are consistent with those of Nairn and Higgins (2009), where Laura's self-awareness changed in relation to the new work context – but there it was a fuzzy, backward and forward process of being an adult and being a child in the workplace. For Jens it was in relation to kindergarten and being treated in a childish manner by the pedagogue, and for Laura it was about being babied at school and on entering the workforce, where she found it difficult to be an adult when most of her experiences were about being treated as a child. Both these studies highlight a crisis or transition point, and both demonstrate that the child–youth had a new self-awareness about their relationship to the original (Jens) or new (Laura's workplace) context. Further, both examples illustrate how age as a single criterion was being used by the teachers or pedagogue to determine how to interact with the child–youth. But both Jens and Laura found this problematic. Vygotsky (1998) argued that

> In a very short time, the child changes completely in the basic traits of his personality. Development takes on a stormy impetuous, and sometimes catastrophic character that resembles a revolutionary source of events in both rate of the changes that are occurring and in the sense of the alternations that are made (p. 191).

In line with the findings of Nairn and Higgins (2009), Vygotsky points out that there are no boundaries between stable periods and crises. 'The crisis appears imperceptibly – it is difficult to determine its onset and termination' (p. 191). The second feature noted by Vygotsky (1998) during critical periods is a general drop in interest, productivity and success that is 'accompanied by more or less short conflicts with those around him. The child's internal life is sometimes connected with painful and excruciating experiences and with internal conflicts' (p. 191), as was noted for both Laura and Jens. Vygotsky (1998) notes that 'Dissimilar in different children, they bring about a very mixed and diverse picture of variants of the critical age' (p. 192). It is now possible to understand Vygotsky's (1998) construction of child development as a revolutionary process, as mentioned at the beginning of this chapter:

> Critical periods alternate with stable periods and are turning points in development, once again confirming that *the development of the child is a dialectical process in which a transitions from one state to another is accomplished not along an evolutionary, but along a revolutionary path* (p. 193; emphasis added).

In returning to the empirical example of Louise (see chapter 11), note that although concern was expressed by the professional about Louise's late development in learning to walk, no motive for walking had been generated for her. If Vygotsky's theory, thus far explained, is used, it would have to be said that she was in a stable period. Louise's development as a revolutionary process can be better understood if the family context is examined:

> Louise is part of a family that is living on or below the poverty line. The family receives government assistance for housing and is totally dependent on government funds for living. The family must walk 10 kilometres each day to go to childcare, preschool and school. The family cannot afford to buy a car, and the road system is set up for cars rather than public transport, making travel by bus extremely difficult. As a result, the family must rise early each morning in order to prepare for the one hour walk to, and one hour trip from childcare, preschool and school. It would be a liability to the efficient management of this walk if Louise were to toddle along with the older children.
>
> The routine in Louise's family is, for the adults and the older children, to rise and dress ready for the 10 kilometre walk. At the last moment in the morning, Louise is woken and taken from her enclosed cot and placed in the stroller, which is parked in the hallway near the front door. Final arrangements, such as lunches, are made by the mother, while Louise drinks a bottle of milk in the stroller and the older children assemble at the doorway. The walk is repeated on the return trip in the late afternoon. Louise is usually placed in the highchair as dinner is prepared, is held while the adults perform late afternoon chores or supervised outside while the older children play with their bikes or with balls, etc. Louise is often placed in the highchair when the children are outside, or held and moved about as the carer moves about doing things inside or outside the house. In this context, there is no need or opportunity for Louise to walk. She is able to observe all the activity from the vantage point of the stroller, the highchair or the arms one of the adults – who are usually highly mobile – thus affording a dynamic view of all the action occurring within the Peninsula family (summary of field notes, Louise at 16 months, period 1, visits 1–4).

When viewed within this family context, Louise's development demonstrates that she is within a stable period and no critical moment is evident. This is demonstrated in figure 12.3.

In support of Kravtsova's (2006; 2008e, f) position, it is possible to note that Louise's relations with her family can be conceptualised as a primordial we perspective. The adults continue to hold Louise in their arms, to move her about the family and use tools such as a highchair or stroller to support

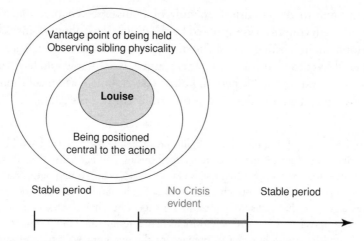

Figure 12.3 The stable period – Louise positioned through the primordial we

this subject positioning. Louise is able to access her environment centrally through being placed within a mobile household, in which the siblings will move to her, around her and always within her field of vision; if they do not, their absence will be brief. As such, there is no need for Louise to walk and no motive for walking is generated. Within the first observation period, which commenced at 16 months of age, there was no crisis evident for Louise and development continued underground as a stable period.

Three months later, a different kind of observation is noted. The summer period begins along with a two month holiday period. Christmas gifts to the children – a swing and slide set, new balls and a totem tennis set – and six weeks in which to use them (summer school holiday) have created a new kind of context for Louise from that described above. In the first observation it was noted that her father continued to be focused on Louise's inability to walk:

> Louise is seated on a swing. She is holding on to the metal bars that support the swing as her father gently moves the swing back and forth. The father explains to the researchers, who have not visited the house for three months, 'She won't go and walk by herself'. The father takes Louise from the swing and places her on her feet. He continues to hold one hand and walks with Louise saying, 'She will walk around everywhere doing this'. Louise looks to the researchers and smiles as they show appreciation of her walking. The father then explains that if he lets go of her hand, Louise immediately sits down and won't continue to walk
>
> (Observation period 2, visit 1)

Louise is very keen to be able to slide though. During visit 3, she is now able to walk in the direction of the slide, even though she is unable to climb the ladder:

> Louise slowly toddles over to the ladder of the slide. She attempts to lift one leg onto the rung of the ladder – she makes eye contact with an adult who is close by. The adult is visiting the family and notices Louise's repeated attempts to step onto the ladder. The adult lifts Louise to the top of the side. He then supports her body all the way down the slide. He steps back. Louise walks around from the slide to the ladder and again attempts to step onto the rung. After two attempts she looks to the adult, who steps forward and lifts her to the top of the slide and, once again, supports her down the slide. This process continues, with the adult each time giving less support on the slide. Eventually, the adult invites the father to observe Louise going down the slide without adult support, saying 'She can now do it on her own'.
>
> (Observation period 2, visit 3)

This experience with the visiting adult gives Louise the skill to be able to slide unaided down the ladder. By visit 5, Louise can climb the rungs of the ladder and, although unsteady, slides down the slide by herself:

> Louise has climbed to the top of the slide. She is seated on the slide holding onto the rails at the top. She calls to her mother. Her mother is inside and responds with a call, but does not come out to Louise. Louise pushes herself from the top of the slide, sliding down awkwardly, jolting from side to side. She arrives at the bottom of the slide and drops to the ground, knocking herself back as she falls. She rubs her back with her hand and cries. Both Nick and JJ look to her as she cries. JJ takes an inner tube from a bicycle and wraps it around Louise's neck. She is annoyed and instantly removes it.
>
> (Observation period 2, visit 5)

In Louise's household, physical movement is a dominant activity for all the children (discussed further later), and this is exemplified through being able to master the physical coordination, strength and balance needed for successfully using the new toys. The slide and swing set has created not only the conditions for the visible activity and behaviours noted in the observations but also the psychological criteria for participation in the activities themselves, particularly the motives generated through the introduction of the new toys, and the time and weather conditions for supporting new activity within the Peninsula family (that Louise observes daily). This example of Louise's development shows how the psychological criteria for engagement in the social and material world and the visible physical behaviours are dialectically related and must be foregrounded in any discussion of childhood development. The example also illustrates more than simply understanding context or how context influences development – particularly when conceptualised in deficit – it also shows the relationship between motives and visible behaviours while considering biological and cultural dimensions of development. This empirical example illustrates the dynamic nature of Vygotsky's holistic and revolutionary theory of child development.

Activity theory, as discussed by Karpov (2005) as an explanation for leading activity in child development, is not sufficient for understanding the complexity of the psychological processes noted here. Louise has developed physically, not just strength, but also balance and coordination of her upper body through being held constantly, placed in a highchair or in a stroller to travel 10 kilometres a day around the school, preschool and childcare route. Her biology is important here. Had she been a two month old baby without the strength or balance to stay sitting on the swing or slide when placed there by family members, it would have been unlikely that she would have generated the motives for doing as the others were doing on the new equipment. It is the relationship between her biology and her context that has generated new psychological conditions for Louise. Activity theory invites us to pay attention to the activity generating the new motives. This is an important contribution, but it is not the only factor at play in the form of motivation that has been generated for Louise. As noted earlier, no motive for learning to walk had arisen prior to the swing and slide set arriving – as she was positioned centrally within her world through strollers, highchairs, being held by an extremely mobile parent, and active children who continued to run into her field of view. This example of Louise's development refutes Karpov's claim that 'The neo-Vygotskians, however, refused to accept Vygotsky's (1984/1998) idea of the role of physiological maturation in the development of new motives in children' (p. 76).

What is noted (see figure 12.4) is the emergence of a period of new self-awareness for Louise. She observes her brothers using the new equipment. Her growing strength, along with the motive that has been generated towards the swings and slides through being physically placed on the slide or through physically being placed on the seat of the swing, have changed the relationship that Louise now has with her environment and with her family. She now indicates that she wishes to be on the slide or the swing. Her constant motive for this activity is not matched by

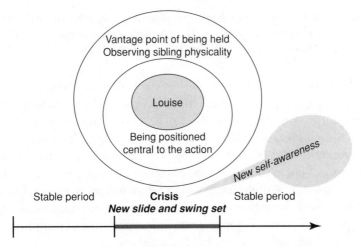

Figure 12.4 An important moment in Louise's development – the new swing and slide set generates a motive for physicality

the parents' desire to spend all their time holding her on the slide or on the swing. Her siblings do not have the strength to lift her and place her on the equipment, but they will join her on the equipment. A new social relationship has emerged. According to Vygotsky (1998) this would constitute an important moment in Louise's development.

The slide and swing set changed the concrete conditions of Louise's everyday world and thus generated an important moment in Louise's development. This in itself shows why variability in development arises. This example of Louise also shows the importance of the dialectical relationship between the concrete world and the child's psychological development – motives and self-awareness. The importance of the new leading activity is illustrative of a specific child and family developmental trajectory. Karpov (2005) states that 'the notion of leading activity explains the reasons for children's transition from one period to the next' (p. 76). The example of Louise cannot be understood as only a theorisation of a leading activity because her goal for being on the swing and slide could only be achieved through the action of walking. There was no prior need for walking. Rather, a new self-awareness arose due to the introduction of the swing and slide set, which created a new psychological state for Louise. The significance of psychological development is an important contribution that has been theorised by Vygotsky (1998) and further elaborated by Kravtsova (2006). As Vygotsky (1998) stated:

> But neither the presence nor the absence of some specific external conditions, but internal logic of the process of development itself is responsible for the critical, disruptive periods in the life of the child (p. 192).

In order to understand how the new psychological conditions for Louise develop, the concept of neoformations (Vygotsky, 1998; Karpov, 2005) or new formations (Kravtsov, 2008b) or novel formations (Kravtsova, 2005) must be examined. This concept was originally conceptualised by Vygotsky (1998) but has received very little research attention since (Kravtsova, 2006). Vygotsky (1998) has discussed neoformations as a transitional character, as subordinate within future neoformations, as latent or as underground development for the creation of a new formation within stable periods. Because Vygotsky wrote little explanation of neoformations, expanded quotations are given and discussed below:

> Progressive development of the child's personality, the continuous construction of the new, which has been so prominent in all stable ages, is seemingly attenuated or temporarily suspended. Processes of dying off and closure, the disintegration and breakdown of what had been formed at preceding states and distinguished the child of a given age more to the forefront. During the critical periods the child does not much acquire as he loses some of what he had acquired earlier. The onset of these age levels is not marked by the appearance of new interests of the child, of new aspiration, new types of activity, new forms of internalisation. The child entering a period of crisis is more apt to be characterized by the opposite traits: he loses interests that only yesterday guided all his activity and took the great part of his time and attention but now seemingly die off; and forms of external relations and internal life developed earlier are neglected. L.N. Tolstoy graphically and precisely called one such critical period of child development the desert of adolescence.
>
> (Vygotsky, 1998: 192)

Kravtsova (2006) argues that Vygotsky emphasised two types of new psychological formation, formations that emerged during the critical periods or crises and those that occurred during the stable periods:

> The most essential content of development at the critical ages consists of the appearance of neoformations which, as concrete research shows, are unique and specific to a high degree. Their main difference from neoformations of stable ages is that they have a transitional character. This means that in the future, they will not be preserved in the form in which they appear at the

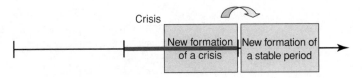

Figure 12.5 New formations within periods
(adapted from Kravtsova, 2006: 13)

critical period and will not enter as a requisite component into the integral structure of the future personality. They die off, seemingly being absorbed by the neoformations of the subsequent, stable age and being included in their composition as subordinate factors that do not have an independent existence, being dissolved and transformed in them to such an extent that without special and penetrating analysis, it is frequently impossible to detect the presence of this transformed formation of the critical period in the acquisition of the succeeding stable age. As such the neoforms of the crises die off together with the onset of the following age, but they continue to exist in a latent form within it, not living an independent life, but only participating in the underground development which leads to the spasmodic appearance of new formations during the stable ages, as we have seen.

(Vygotsky, 1998: 194–5)

Figure 12.5 shows the new formations.

In order to fully appreciate Vygotsky's theory of child development, the nature of the interactions between adults and children in the context of new psychological formations must be reintroduced into the discussion. As Kravtsova (2005) so clearly states,

The ability of the child to build and perform the leading activity by him/herself leads to the change of relationship between the child and the adult. At the previous stages of a stable period the adult gradually helped the child to perform and develop the leading activity, but when the child learns to accomplish it by him/herself his/her attitude towards the adult changes a lot. The child, say, overgrows the old relationships with adult. Thus, one can conclude that the leading activity built upon the novel formation and not vice versa, as many representatives of the activity theory claim.

(Kravtsova, 2005: 23)

The child's outgrown relations and interactions are clearly visible in the example of Jens and that of Laura. In Laura's final year of high school, she was positioned as a child, not as an adult. Here we see how the relationships

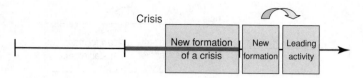

Figure 12.6 Leading activity and new formation
(Kravtsova, 2006: 15)

between adult–child no longer work for Laura's awareness of her pending entrance into the workforce.

> The inclusion of the novel formation of the stable period into real life leads to emergence of new activity, that obtains the status of leading activity, and the novel formation of stable period becomes the foundation and the main criterion of this activity.
>
> (Kravtsova, 2005: 23)

Kravtsova (2006: 15) states that 'the leading activity is built on the basis of the new formation'; this theorisation is shown in figure 12.6.

Kravtsova (2005) writes about the double self-consciousness within age periods:

> So we can say that during one age period the changes in self-consciousness occur twice . . . The first change is connected to the emergence of the child's new attitude towards him/herself as a result of the crisis. In the other case the changes are connected with his/her ability to accomplish the leading activity and be aware of him/herself as its subject.
>
> (Kravtsova, 2005: 24)

In the examples of Laura and Jens, it is possible to see how a child moves from one leading activity to another. It is not simply the activity, but rather the new self-awareness that occurs for the child, that is, a child's double self-consciousness, as created initially through the crisis (transition to work, wanting to be a school child) and the communications with the adult (boss, researcher or pedagogue) in the process of everyday life activities (transitioning to work, story reading session). Kravtsova (2006) argues that the 'new psychological formations reflect the consciousness and self-awareness of the subject' (p. 16), and through this we learn that 'the conditions [of] this activity's development are also the conditions for the child's full mental development at different ages' (Kravtsova, 2006: 8). As such, the problem of movement from one leading activity to another is resolved:

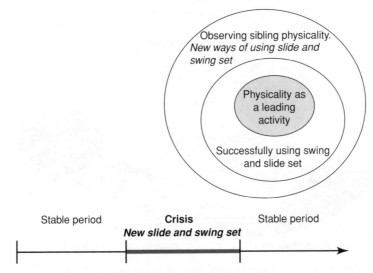

Figure 12.7 A cultural–historical view of child development

We can conclude that psychological age novel formations not only charac-
terize the particular features of certain period, but allow [for the solving of]
many fundamental problems of psychological science. This approach allows
[for the solving of] the question of criteria of the leading activities by means
of the novel formation of stable period, thus, it becomes evident how the
transition from one leading activity to another is performed.

(Kravtsova, 2005: 24)

According to Vygotsky, development in the stable periods takes small
incremental steps, often not noticeable to those around the child. In the
example of Louise, her self-awareness of her inability to go down the slide
was noticed: the swing and slide set changed the material conditions for
Louise. This situation was resolved through the help of an adult. Louise,
who is embedded within the practices of the family, where physicality is a
dominant activity, was able to develop a new self-awareness of herself as a
successful participant in using the swing and slide set. This example illustrates how everyday life, and the developmental opportunities it affords,
also creates the conditions for children's development.

The social situation of development will not only be community defined
and culturally determined, but, as was shown through the empirical example of Louise, it will also be family specific. In figure 12.7, Louise's development is represented in relation to Kravtsova's model and theorisation,
with Louise becoming the subject of her own activity – physically being
able to use the swing and slide set. In figure 12.8 a more generic model

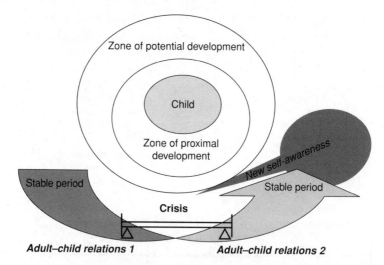

Figure 12.8 Changes in material conditions afford opportunities for development

of development is shown in order to capture the complexity of the adults' relationships with a child in the context of the child's changing relations to the social and material world.

Vygotsky (1998, volume 5) discusses the changes in development in terms of central lines of development and peripheral lines of development. What is deemed central and what peripheral will be determined by the social situation in which the child is located:

> The process of development that are more or less directly connected with the basic neoformation we shall call *central lines of development* at the given age and all other partial processes and changes occurring at the given age, we shall call *peripheral lines of development*. It is understood that processes that are central lines of development at one age become peripheral lines of development at the following age and conversely, peripheral lines of development of one age are brought to the forefront and become central lines at another age since their meaning and relative significance in the total structure of development changes and their relation to the central neoformation changes. Thus, the transition from one stage to another, the whole structure of the age is reconstructed. Each age has a unique and singular structure specific to it (p. 197; emphasis in the original).

In the example of Louise, walking was a peripheral line of development until the swing and slide set arrived. Walking then became a central line of development, and over time Louise mastered this and the climbing of the slide ladder; walking becoming peripheral once more. Karpov (2005) has stated that transitional characteristics are dependent upon the cultural community in which the child lives or, as noted by Hedegaard (2009), the institutional contexts that a particular society has created for its citizens (preschool, school, clubs, etc.) (see chapter 13). These transitional points as community constructed and culturally defined draw attention to the variability in the child's changing relationship to their own personal reality and social relations. As such, it is important to examine Vygotsky's concept of the social situation of development:

> The social situation of development represents the initial moment for all dynamic changes that occur in development during the given period. It determines wholly and completely the forms and the path along which the child will acquire ever newer personality characteristics, drawing them from the social reality as from the basic source of development, the path along which the social becomes the individual
>
> (Vygotsky, 1998: 198)

Hedegaard (2009) remarks that as children participate in institutional practices, it is important to note what kinds of activities dominate these institutions. Similarly, we need to be mindful of the kinds of crises children experience when they transition between institutions. Hedegaard (2009: 72) argues that as children transition, they experience new demands. 'These forms of practice initiate but also restrict children's activities and thereby become conditions of their development' (p. 72). In much the same way, the disparity between a child's motives and the institution's motives may be due to biological changes or changes in children's competencies. Karpov (2005: 43), in explaining Vygotsky's theory of the social situation of development states that

> As the result of the adults' mediation in the context of the present social situation of development, the child develops new mental processes and new motives (the development of which is also influenced by physiological maturation). 'These neoformations that arise toward the end of a given age lead to a reconstruction of the whole structure of the child's consciousness and in this way change the whole system of relations to external reality and to himself. . . [which] . . . means that the social situation of development. . . must also change' (Vygotsky, 1984/1998, p. 199). The change of the social situation of development manifests the child's transition to the next period of development. In Vygotsky's (Vygotsky, 1984 [1998])

Table 12.1 *Periodisation*

Fundamental concepts	Age periods (in year bands)					
	0	1	3	7	10	14
Central psychological new formation		Primordial we	Speech	Imagination	Attention	Self-reflection
Social situation of development		Non-verbal communication	Emotionalisation of objects	Imagination in action	Collective theorising	Theory of practice
Central psychological function		Sensory motor	Perception	Emotions	Memory	Thinking
Leading activities		Relating, communicating	Experience with things	Play	Learning	Relating, communicating

Source: Kravtsov, 2008b, 2009a, b

words, the forces moving the child's development at one age or another inevitably lead to rejection and disruption of the base of development of the whole age, with internal necessity determining the annulment of the social situation of development, the termination of the given period of development, and a transition to the following, or higher age level (p. 199).

Postmodern perspectives on child development (see Alloway, 1997; Cannella & Viruru, 2004) would find the complexity of views on development as the new norm sitting comfortably within the post-post paradigm that has emerged in recent times (see Lather, 2007). However, as has been noted by contemporary theorists working in early childhood education (see Blaise, 2009), professionals in the field are in need of some guidance on childhood development. This is particularly important for guiding professionals in thinking about the nature of their interactions when considering transition points and planning learning experiences for children. How, for instance, professionals interact with an infant (e.g., Louise) needs to be conceptualised differently from how they interact with youth (e.g., Laura) (see chapters 13 and 14).

A revolutionary view of child development considers the concept of complexity and theorises how crises appear within the child's developmental trajectory at particular age periods. Crises are, for instance, connected to the logic of the child's leading activity (e.g., play as a leading activity, learning as a leading activity), to the appearance of new psychological formations (speech, imagination, attention, self-reflection), to the central psychological functioning of the person (perception, emotions, memory, thinking) and to the child's social situation of development (non-verbal communication, emotionalisation of objects, imagination in action in play, collective theorising). These interrelated concepts are summarised below in table 12.1 (Kravtsov, 2008b, 2009a, b). Here, it can be seen how the complexity of a revolutionary view of development can be framed within a periodisation table.

SUMMARY

In this chapter Vygotsky's (1998) theory of child development as a concept of self-development has been closely looked at. Contemporary writers have been drawn on, such as Elena Kravtsova, who have elaborated Vygotsky's original theory and who have solved the problem of progression from one leading activity to another. Through the examples of research and empirical data presented in this chapter, the complexity of critical periods and stable periods in relation to specific individuals – Laura, Jens and Louise – has been shown. Though the research of Hedegaard (2009) our attention has also been drawn to child development in relation to society and institutions. In the next chapter how institutions influence children's development and how they generate possibilities that early childhood professionals need to pay attention to when framing their interactions and when conceptualising and implementing their educational programs will be examined.

13 | Children's development as participation in everyday practices

How do people participate in sociocultural activity and how does their participation change from [them] being relatively peripheral participants (cf. Lave & Wenger, 1991), observing and carrying out secondary roles, to assuming various responsible roles in the management or transformation of such activities?

(Rogoff, 1998: 695)

INTRODUCTION

In the previous two chapters an examination was conducted of Vygotsky's theory of child development as elaborated through a critique of this area and through a discussion of contemporary theoretical writings of scholars drawing upon cultural–historical theory. In those chapters a revolutionary view of child development that illustrates key concepts through empirical data of an infant–toddler called Louise was considered. In this chapter those ideas are built upon, and further empirical data from Louise's family are presented in order to broaden the conception of child development to include children's participation in everyday practices across institutions. The chapter begins with a discussion of Hedegaard's (2009) theory of child development because she has been instrumental in elaborating Vygotsky's original writings to include institutional practices as part of this view of child development.

CHILD DEVELOPMENT AS CHILDREN'S ACTIVITY IN EVERYDAY PRACTICE

Hedegaard (2009) has researched the construction of childhood and development within the framework of the institution, the society and the individual. Her work draws extensively upon Vygotsky's (1998) seminal theory of child development discussed in the previous chapter. In line with Vygotsky's work on a dialectical approach to development, and the social situation of development, Hedegaard (2009) takes a step further than Vygotsky by relating society and community to the concept of institutional practice. She has conceptualised child development through considering the societal conditions that form cultural practices in institutions, which in turn shape those activities that children participate in. She focuses on the relationship between children's activities as participants in different institutions. Like Vygotsky, she has conceptualised development not as a process within the child, but rather as taking place as children participate in practices within their own cultural community.

Hedegaard (2009) has drawn attention to the significance of children's participation in different institutional contexts for shaping their development, and discusses how practices in these institutions create sociocultural pathways for children. In gaining understandings of how children participate in different institutions, it is possible to gain greater insights into children's changing relations with reality. Vygotsky's concept of the social situation of development is extended through Hedegaard's theorisation of institutional practices in relation to children's activity as they negotiate the practice transitions within and across institutions. Hedegaard (2009), inspired by Vygotsky (1998), identifies crises in children's lives, which she believes provide the dynamics for development. She argues that when children enter a new institutional context where expectations and practices are unfamiliar, children experience demands that can result in a crisis in their new social situation. She outlines three main perspectives (see figure 13.1):

- the *societal perspectives*, which give conditions for institutional practice through political material conditions and through traditions that can be found in the dominating value positions in a society
- the *institutional perspectives*, with their different practices such as the ones we find in home and school
- the *person's perspectives* (the child, the mother, the father or the teacher), which are reflected in the person's motives and personal values.

These are shown in figure 13.1 below.

In Hedegaard's model (figure 13.1) the societal perspective depicts the conditions for institutional practice as political material conditions, cultural traditions and values. In many schools, for example, there will be a teacher, a certain number of children (that number depending upon the regulations set by a society) and particular kinds of materials available for the children

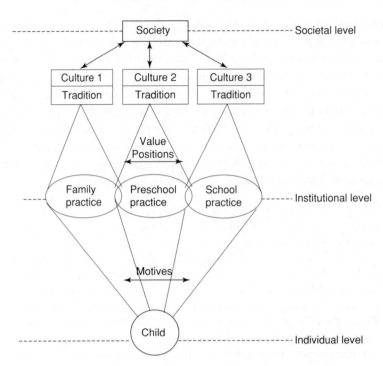

Figure 13.1 A model of children's learning and development through participation in institutional practice (adapted from Hedegaard, 2009, p. 73)

to use. There are also specific procedures for participating in preschool practice, as well as a set of values about what are deemed appropriate practices for children's learning activity.

The institutional practices in her model depict family practice, preschool practice and school practice. In principle these institutional practices can also refer to practices in afterschool care settings or clubs, at work, in church, scouting groups and so forth. These are places and spaces, organised within a society, that have their own procedures, rules and traditions for daily practices.

The person's perspective, as shown in the model, is reflected in a child's activities in the different institutions the child attends. The play activities that the child creates for themselves and with others within a child care centre, for example, would be viewed as the child's perspective in this model.

In drawing upon Vygotsky's (1998) concept of the child's social situation of development (see chapter 12) in the context of Hedegaard's model of child development across institutions (see figure 13.1), it becomes possible to gain a broader view of the potential reach a theory of child development must have. The case study of Louise from the Peninsula family is drawn on in order to illustrate the importance of considering the societal and institutional dimensions of a theory of child development. In the empirical material that follows, the example of eating in the Peninsula family is looked at and this family practice in relation to the practices within the childcare centre that Louise and JJ attend is considered. In this first example, what eating means for JJ (who is two years five months at the time of the observations) at home, and then in childcare are looked at.

Eating at home: It is 6.00 pm and the Peninsula family are preparing their evening meal. The father cooks a meat and pasta dish. He then retreats from the kitchen and the mother serves up the meal into four bowls. Louise, who is 16 months, is seated in a highchair. She is given a bowl and spoon. Andrew who is five, Nick who is four and JJ who is three, all sit at the table. The mother leaves the kitchen and the children begin eating. Andrew makes long and very loud howling noises. He moves about the table between the children's bowls, squirting tomato sauce into the bowl of anyone who wants the sauce. Nick takes his food and moves into the lounge room and continues to eat, while watching TV. JJ eats a small portion of his food and then walks around the house while eating. Louise is left in the kitchen alone, strapped into her highchair. She eats for a short period, and then makes soft sounds, as though indicating she would like to be let out of the highchair. The parents occasionally appear in the kitchen for brief periods, but are generally busy with their own activities elsewhere in the house. During this time the children also move in and out of the kitchen area.

(Summary of video observation, period 1, visit 3)

Eating in the childcare centre: All the children at seated at tables waiting for their lunch meal to be served. JJ is sitting under an easel in close proximity to the lunch tables. He moves backwards and forwards beneath the easel. The teacher goes over to JJ and takes his hand and physically moves him to the table. He is compliant. He sits for a short moment, and then raises his body in a standing up position, shuffling his chair five metres from the tables, and back to the table when asked by the teacher. The food arrives and he sits facing the table, with his feet lying across the table next to his lunch bowl. He is asked to take his feet off the table by his teacher. He does so.

(Summary of video observation, period 1, visit 5)

There are few demands placed upon the children in the Peninsula family at meal times when they are at home. They are free to move about while eating. Although the family meal begins in the kitchen at a table, there is no expectation that the children need to or will stay there or to be seated while eating. This is the family practice for the children. However, when the children attend an early childhood centre or school the practices and expectations are very different. The children are expected to sit and wait for their meals at the table, to stay seated and to sit in a particular manner while eating. While the family does not demand this of them, the institutions they attend do make these demands. At home the children experience a kind of geographical grazing: they are able to effectively and easily combine eating with other activities, to physically manage eating their meals while walking, talking and attending to other activities. While they do drop a small amount of food, they expertly manage their food and their other activities. In the institutional settings, they meet new demands – waiting, sitting still and fixed point eating. This is very different from geographical grazing, and this creates a development opportunity for the children. When we examine the institutions that children participate in we learn about different opportunities for learning and development that are generated across families. This is a cultural–historical view of development, in which children's interaction with their social and physical world as mediated by the family or the institutions the child attends, determines the developmental trajectory. Development is not viewed as being located within the individual child in relation to how old they are, but rather a revolutionary approach that foregrounds the relationship between the child and their social and physical world, as well as their changing relationship to it. This is represented in table 13.1 (Fleer, 2008a).

In order to contextualise family meals within the Peninsula family, it is important to know more about the physicality of their family (as alluded to in chapter 12 in the discussion of Louise's physical development). Continual movement in the Peninsula family is a common practice. It can be seen in the family members' movements illustrated in figure 13.2. Louise was not mobile at the time of this observation. Figure 13.2 only shows the movement from room to room, rather than the movement within each room, which was a continual flow of activity from person to person, from furniture (standing on, next to or over) to furniture and changes in children's directions as they moved around the available floor space within particular rooms. This level of detail was difficult to show in the figure.

Movement is a continual phenomenon within the Peninsula family. The example given above also illustrates the mobile context that makes up JJ and Louise's social situation. If we return to the example in chapter 12 of Louise not walking, we can see in figure 13.2 that this mobile context makes

Table 13.1 *Development related to everyday practices across institutions*

Family practice	Child care centre practice	Transitions between institutions
Geographical grazing	**Fixed point eating**	**New demands**
Meal times begin in the kitchen, but usually turn into a mobile activity (except for Louise who is in a highchair).	Meals occur at fixed times and in fixed locations, and movement from the table/eating area is actively discouraged.	*Transitions generate new possibilities for development*
No demands on the children at meal times.	JJ being encouraged to join the others at the table for lunch	*JJ sits at the table, but also moves away from the table. He is encouraged to sit at the table with his feet under the table.*
The family meal is served.		

a mockery of the advice given by the social worker to the mother about Louise's apparent late development in walking. Because the social worker was using a theory of child development that focused on the single trait of age, she did not look beyond the child and consider the social situation of development within the family institution. The societal demands for walking that this social worker embraced were completely at odds with Louise's psychological resources (rather than biological only), as she was highly tuned to mobility (observing this as the family practice). The social worker was unable to see that Louise's relationship to her family meant she had access to everything she wished for at 16 months, and had no need to walk: either the family came to her or she was held or placed centrally to all the action (see chapter 11). It should also be noted that because the context framed movement as a dominant family practice in which all the older siblings were extremely good at moving about – as they danced around each other, navigating through the continual movement, balancing their meals and eating as they walked – in Louise's developmental

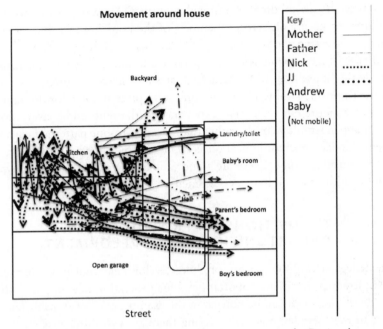

Figure 13.2 The geography of movement between rooms in the Peninsula household (by person)
(Fleer & Hedegaard, forthcoming)

trajectory it is more likely that she will be highly mobile once a motive for walking is generated.

Theorising development as participation in everyday practices across institutions means that it becomes important to understand the different practices that a child experiences. To fully appreciate movement as a family practice, the reasons for this physicality must also be examined. As such, communication practices between family members need to be looked at more broadly. In the Peninsula family conversations take place across walls – both inside and outside. Listening in across walls is common, so the children are keenly aware of what is happening in each room. Any slight change or incident, or the introduction of something of interest, immediately brought children from all corners of the house back to the point of interest. Listening in across walls is facilitated by the continued movement of all members of the household between rooms. With the exception of the dog (who occasionally sat on the sofa), the adults and children rarely sit down, but rather appear to be moving between rooms and around each other, like a dance.

Through the children's continued movement, it was possible for the children to keenly observe all members of the household (including visitors) while eating and replenishing their drinks (with support from adults) from the fridge, viewing television, playing outdoors and generating games inside the household. Movement facilitates and supports communication in the Peninsula family. This communication pattern noted for this family appears to represent a collective experience, with events and conversations that happen simultaneously, rather than in a one-to-one pattern of engagement. Collective communication is facilitated by ongoing movement in the Peninsula family. These are important family practices that provide opportunities for children's development.

TRANSITIONS AS PROVIDING NEW OPPORTUNITIES FOR DEVELOPMENT

In Hedegaard's (2009) theory of child development transitions between institutions provides an important site for generating new opportunities for development. It can be noticed in the example of the Peninsula family that in the everyday practice of eating there are vast differences between the practice traditions of the family and the practice traditions of the childcare centre. From the child's perspective, meals at home place no demands upon the members of the family. They are provided with food at a central point and they elect to eat it across the house, as this fits within the organic mobile nature of the family practices generally observed within the Peninsula family. From the perspective of JJ at the childcare centre, he experiences major demands from the staff in relation to the centre practice for sitting still to eat a meal. The centre practice replicates middle class practices found within many Western societies where eating meals together in one location (fixed point) is the norm. JJ's behaviour does not fit with what the centre staff expect and demand of him. They gently move him to the table, encourage him to sit with his feet on the floor rather than on the table and invite him to stay at the table rather than move away from it. This coaching to sit still to eat a meal is a practice that not only supports the eating routines that the centre expects all its children to observe but also reflects the general pattern of group control of children in centres and schools as a practice tradition for sitting still for extended periods.

Hedegaard (2009) has argued that a 'diversity of traditions and values for a good life is central for outlining a cultural–historical approach to development and important for the conceptualisation of children's development through their participation in a variety of institutional practices'

(p. 66). In this example, the childcare centre's view of a good life included all of the children sitting together at tables to eat their meals. As Hedegaard (2009) notes, child development must be conceptualised as being anchored in societal values and what institutions value as 'the good life'. Making visible what is often not programmed – meal times as a cultural practice – helps early childhood professionals better understand not just the taken for granted practice traditions but also what demands these practice traditions place upon some children as they enter the institution.

Child development has been conceptualised in this chapter as being shaped by participation in everyday practices across the institutions that a child attends – family, childcare and school. The different demands, expectations, and activities that a child experiences across these institutions shape their motives and create new possibilities for development. This view of child development builds upon Vygotsky's revolutionary theory of child development, giving it a contemporary context for explaining not only how development changes incrementally during more stable periods but also how everyday life forms the basis for child development, creating small critical moments. A child's participation across institutions as a theory of child development explains the multiple developmental trajectories observed in children and gives early childhood professionals a new perspective and theory of child development. As noted so eloquently by Hedegaard (2009):

> The general conceptions of developmental trajectories have to be integrated with the child's concrete activities and social relations in institutional practices. Only through this integration will it be possible to understand how differentiation in child development proceeds (p. 75).

SUMMARY

This chapter has drawn attention to the need to think beyond a narrow reading of development as a naturally evolving process contained within the child and to consider a broader view of development as related to the everyday practices of children as they experience life across institutions. A cultural–historical perspective on development that foregrounds the social situation of development within a dialectical framework of the child's perspective, the family's perspective and the childcare–schools perspective offers a genuine step forward for early childhood educators.

14 A cultural–historical view of play, learning and development

> Methodological difficulties that result from an antidialectical and dualistic concept of child development are a fateful obstacle that prevents it from being considered as a single process of self development.
>
> (Vygotsky, 1998: 189)

INTRODUCTION

This chapter begins with a discussion of the dominant assessment practices found in many Western early childhood learning communities, and shows how they are aligned to a dualistic conception of child development. It also seeks to elaborate a cultural–historical view of how to measure learning and development and introduces the concepts of *potentive assessment* and *the assessable moment* as examples of how to conceptualise development, learning and pedagogy together.

The second part of this chapter brings together the major themes introduced in this book – pedagogy, play, concept formation and child development. Through reuniting these concepts in this final chapter the significance of the concept of *obshchenie* for realising a dialectical conception of development and learning is shown, and through this to illustrate the importance of Vygotsky's conception of a single process of self-development, where one stitch (concept) in the fabric (conceptual system) can only ever be understood within the context of the whole tapestry that represents the child's life.

VIEWS ON DEVELOPMENT SHAPE
EXPECTATIONS – ASSESSMENT

How professionals conceptualise child development shapes what they expect for children's learning and development. Hedegaard (2009) discusses how some theorists have developed 'content free conceptions of developmental stages', and argues that this begs the question: Development of what? Learning theories do vary in their conceptualisation of development, and this, Hedegaard (2009) argues, characterises the nature of the leading questions that are being asked about what is being developed (p. 17). Who decides upon these expectations (what should be developed) and what instruments does a society invent and use for measuring learning and development? In a thought provoking article by Peers (2009) where he critiques the Australian Early Development Index (AEDI), the population instrument currently being used within Australia, and the Early Development Index (EDI), the instrument being used in Canada, to determine how communities are faring in health, social and physical development, and learning, he states that

> In believing they [governments and neoliberal researchers] can determine causes and effects about right and wrong characteristics of children, neoliberal scientists and policymakers commit the fatal mistake of imagining a power to choose the composition and nature of the community. But this flaw is obscured by the shiny promise of a statistical 'holy grail' that could miraculously rid the world of ill-health, crime and poverty. It is imperative that the AEDI be understood as loaded with political values and that its claims to a scientific value-neutral 'truth' be recognized as good marketing (p. 6).

A close inspection of this instrument shows that it has been based upon a naturally evolving view of child development (see chapter 11); the results of this population instrument are therefore unlikely to be helpful to teachers for informing cultural–historical understandings about children's development in the early childhood period. A cultural–historical view of pedagogy and child development demands a cultural–historical view of assessment and measurement of learning and development.

Traditionally, early childhood teachers have drawn upon the longstanding approach known as *child study*. A close examination of the tools for child study used by early childhood professionals for framing how they measure child progression show that most tools are based upon a maturational view of child development (Fleer & Richardson, 2003). In addition, many sociological analyses have shown that the focus has been on the

> individual child who, irrespective of context, follows a standard of biological stages. Despite frequent talk about a holistic perspective... the child is frequently reduced to separate and measurable categories, such as social development, intellectual development, motor development. Consequently, processes which are very complex and interrelated in everyday life are isolated from one another and viewed dichotomously, instead of viewing them as intrinsically interrelated functions that all work together in the production of change.
>
> (Dahlberg, Moss & Pence, 1999: 46)

In contrast, a cultural–historical perspective would view the measurement of development quite differently, as noted by Kozulin (1998):

> Vygotsky argued that the task of assessment must identify not only those cognitive processes of the child that are fully developed, but also those that are in a state of being developed at the time of assessment. This development, according to Vygotsky, depends on a cooperative interaction between the child and the adult, who represents the culture and assists the child in acquiring the necessary symbolic tools of learning (p. 96).

As discussed in chapter 9 (figure 9.1), Kravtsova has shown through her subject positioning (e.g., taking a position of above, below, equal, primordial we) and through the zones of actual, proximal and potential development how it is possible to conceptualise this type of interaction in practice. Vygotsky's theoretical work in relation to the zones of proximal and actual development have also been used for theorising assessment practices to draw attention to assessment for the future (see Fleer, 2006), through the concept of potentive assessment and proximal assessment. Potentive assessment is retheorised in this book to take account of the expansive work of Kravstova on actual, proximal and potential zones of development (see chapter 9). Proximal assessment seeks to capture the whole dynamic interactions associated with a performance as it is enacted by a child, a group of children or as adults interacting with children (or vice versa), and through the wholeness of this performance, the assessor makes judgements about individuals or groups of children in the context of their interactions and in the wholeness of their cooperative task. In research undertaken by Fleer and Richardson (2003) into assessment practices within early childhood centres, for example, they give an example of a group of five children aged

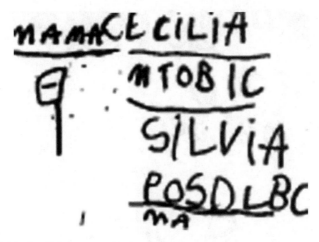

Figure 14.1 Cecelia's letter to the Aussie Postie
(Fleer & Richardson, 2003, p. 48)

between three and five years who are working together to write a letter to
the Aussie Postie (a character created by the teacher to collect their letters).
Each child is seated around a table writing a letter to the Postie on either
their own piece of paper (Cecelia [figure 14.1], Freya [figure 14.2] and Eliza
[figure 14.3]), or are working together on a single piece of paper (Grace
and Zoe [figure 14.4]). However, their activity is constructed jointly, as
they each support each other in sounding out and writing the word 'postie'.
Four of the five children have written POSD (Postie). Cecelia has written
letterbox (LTB) and Freya has written mailbox (MALB), each indicating
that they are drafting their letters in relation to the words familiar to them
in their own family context – letterbox or mailbox. The children also add
to their letters the words they already know how to spell and write, such as
Mama, or their own names. Eliza, who is three, just writes her name, but
actively observes the others. She performs the writing through recording
on the paper the word she knows how to write – her name. Traditional
assessment practices would assess these samples as individual efforts, yet
the work was created collectively through jointly sounding out words. This
is exemplified further when the cooperative writing of Grace and Zoe is
examined. Zoe is already a competent reader who regularly writes when
she is at the centre, where she has established a friendship with Grace.
When Zoe is present at the centre, Grace always works closely with her
and together they write more complex texts, including short stories and
personal messages. When Zoe is absent from the centre, Grace's writing

Figure 14.2 Freya's letter to the Aussie Postie
(Fleer & Richardson, 2003, p. 49)

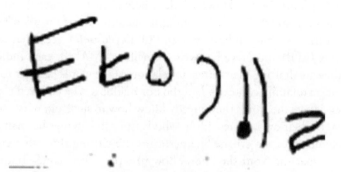

Figures 14.3 Eliza's letter to the Aussie Postie
(Fleer & Richardson, 2003, p. 49)

efforts only feature the names of family members (e.g., Mama) or her own name. In this situation, when asked by the teacher about the quantity and variety of the written work produced, Grace replied, 'But that's when I'm with Zoe [I write more]'. Recognising the significance of the relationship

Figures 14.4 Zoe and Grace's letter to the Aussie Postie
(Fleer & Richardson, 2003, p. 48)

between Grace and Zoe, so subtly alluded to in Grace's aforementioned writing sample, enables us to more fully understand how Zoe works with Grace in her zone of proximal development and how that enables her to perform at a much higher level. Recognising this capacity in Grace is important for making a valid judgement of her proximal development. This collective view of assessment practices, in which the whole interactional context between children and adults is used for framing assessment, is what constitutes proximal assessment. In this dynamic assessment context, it is possible to document proximal performance, as made visible through the carefully organised interactions between children and staff, and through the children themselves. In these situations, it is not just the wholeness of the performance that is important but also the support received that allows individuals to engage in the collective task or performance.

In the example of Eliza, it can be noted that she is clearly imitating (as defined by Vygotsky; see chapter 2) the writing actions of the older children. She is socially primed by this collective experience to pay attention to the approach adopted by the children (e.g., sounding out words to record the letters that represent those sounds) and to be placed within a literate context, even though she is unable to write a letter to the Aussie Postie. Eliza imitates these socially meaningful actions through writing her name as her letter to the Aussie Postie. She is part of the collective, surrounded by experiences that, in the future, she will be able to participate in as a more active and competent member.

Zoe's social forms of behaviour are in advance of her cognitive development. This kind of social participation is also important to assess as it is the precursor to active and full membership of a learning community. This kind of potentive assessment enables educators to note children's engagement in imitation and motives within holistic contexts, that is, educators need to document the increasing connection children have with historically established knowledge and behaviour that a community values, such as learning to read and write. As has been discussed in previous chapters, these concepts are important signals to teachers for building conceptual and contextual intersubjectivity with children.

The outcomes of potentive assessment also enables the early childhood professional to organise learning situations that project children into future learning context (primordial we), where they observe or gain insights into the learning that is still to come. Potentive assessment is a conception that will help teachers in their observation and planning for children's learning.

Proximal assessment involves not only assessing the children's proximal capacities as enacted through interactions with more highly performing others but also making judgements about when, in everyday practices, assessments should be made about children's actual and proximal zones of development. The timing of these assessments is significant, as teachers must make judgements at times when children can best show their capabilities. This kind of teacher judgement is termed the *assessable moment*, and mirrors the established and well-known idea of the 'teachable moment' (see Fleer, 2006). These concepts are important because they represent a just in time moment for furthering learning (teachable moment) and a just in time moment for measuring or observing the proximal, actual and potentive development of children (assessable moment).

Teachers working with cultural–historical theory need to ensure that the adoption of this theoretical orientation is applied consistently across assessment practices, philosophical views on pedagogy (and therefore teacher–child interactions) and views on development. It makes, for example, very little sense to espouse a postmodern view of pedagogy while keeping records of children's development within the fields of cognitive, social, emotional and physical development – assessment categories heavily critiqued by sociologists and post-post theorists, as noted above. A cultural–historical conception of assessment (actual assessment, proximal assessment and potential assessment) must be dialectically related to the cultural–historical conceptions teachers hold about development (chapters 11–13) and learning (chapters 1–9). Yet this theoretical robustness is not always understood or valued.

Even in professional communities where new approaches to pedagogy are adopted, many early childhood professionals continue to be expected to keep detailed developmental records of children's learning and development. Assessment documentation has traditionally followed a biologically deterministic developmental pathway and protocols in which the teacher observer is distant and uninvolved, and where the assessment practices are about individuals, not groups of children interacting together. These approaches have been extensively critiqued (Dahlberg, Moss & Pence, 1999) and therefore will not be elaborated further here, but what many of these critiques neglect to examine is how difficult it is for early childhood professionals to move from an understanding of child development as framed maturationally (see chapter 11) to a cultural–historical reading of child development (see chapters 12 and 13) (Fleer & Richardson, 2003, 2004a, b; Fleer & Robbins, 2004a, b). This challenge must be acknowledged and respected, and a series of supports offered in the transition to a cultural–historical conceptualisation of children, childhood and child development (see Fleer, Hedegaard & Tudge, 2009).

In a series of studies undertaken to examine how early childhood professionals move from an incremental biologically determined model of child development to a cultural–historical view of development and learning, it was noted that many problems arise (Fleer & Richardson, 2003, 2004a, b). For instance, when early childhood educators were asked to consider a new approach to assessing and programming for young children their initial response was cautious. 'From the moment I started to speak [about using a cultural–historical approach to staff] I realised that it was going to be a challenge' (diary entry, 2 May 2002). The teachers' initial response was: 'What could be so wrong with present methods of programming and what would require such a change in direction?' (post diary reflections, 2 January 2003). The child development models mostly used by early childhood professionals in these studies (Fleer & Richardson, 2003, 2004a, b; Fleer & Robbins, 2004a, b) centred on thinking about learning, and therefore assessment, as an individual construction and an individual measurement. Considering children as a relational group in teachers' approaches to assessment was highly contested by teachers, as noted in their diary entries:

D— [staff member] made an interesting observation as we [staff members] talked this through. She said that she had thought that starting a program with a jointly constructed group concept map had appealed to her until she had interviewed individual children about their understanding about 'living and non-living'. . . She had found that the children often gave very different responses individually to those they offered in the group context. Why was this? Perhaps, she thought, they were influenced by each other's responses and this then had a cascading effect in that one response could elicit a whole range of others that may not have occurred on an individual basis. This, she felt, could mean that individual understanding was lost as the group took over. I suggested that this could be viewed as a good thing because the ideas generated by the group could spark a different and broader set of responses than those offered by the individual and these ideas could then belong to the group, or 'community of learners', and provide rich material for investigation. D. disagreed feeling that she didn't feel confident that she would then understand what each individual child really understood. Does this indicate a resistance to the notion of group learning? Are we still very much influenced by the pursuit of individual outcomes?

(Diary entry, 2 May 2002)

In changing theoretical lenses the teachers seem to struggle with changing their observations that focus on individuals to observing children in a collective and dynamic context. The community conditioning in 'observing and planning for individual learning' (Fleer & Robbins, 2004a, b) makes it difficult for teachers to notice and value the way groups of children construct ideas and progress learning together (as noted above with Zoe and Grace). D— showed great resistance to the idea of a group of children developing a concept together. She felt this somehow contaminated the children's individual thinking and she would not be able to determine their pure uninfluenced thoughts. Viewing learning as owned by individuals and residing in the heads of individuals is a powerful force against looking differently or being accepting of children's group participation.

In discussing research methods, Wertsch (1998) suggests that 'individualism assumes that cultural, institutional and historical settings can be explained by appealing to properties of individuals' (p. 179). This fundamental conceptual block, displayed by D—, lies at the heart of the difference between an incremental developmental model (chapter 10) and a cultural–historical perspective on assessment. Kozulin (1998) suggests that an 'individual lives not so much in the world of his or her experience as in a world perched at the top of all of previous history' (p. 10). The cultural–historical context in which the teachers are currently located has firmly echoed an individualistic orientation. Terms such as 'developmentally appropriate practice', 'planning for individual needs', following 'children's interests' and finding the 'child's voice' are part of established discourses in early childhood education in many European heritage communities (see Anning, Cullen & Fleer, 2009) and predominantly reflect a biologically deterministic view of child development. Actively putting this perspective to the side and reimagining early childhood education and assessment as a collectively constructed and dynamic enterprise is difficult.

In a follow-up study designed to examine how teachers' observation and assessment practices (observational data collected on 25 children over a full teaching year made by six staff) changed after being introduced to cultural–historical theory, it was noted that teachers' recorded observations changed to reveal much richer and more informative data sets for understanding children and the dynamics of their learning environment (Fleer & Richardson, 2009). It was also found that the observations made later in the year were not only qualitatively different but also provided a broader and richer landscape of the learning occurring in the centre. Teacher observations at the beginning of the year followed the tradition of recording objective statements, such as 'K— recognises the numbers 3 7 5 8 2. He is unable to represent quantity with dots when asked verbally' (27 March 2001). The observations made later in the year took on quite a different form, for example:

> 'Z— came and told me she knew my T-shirt said "princess". I asked her how she knew that. Z— replied 'Easy (and covered the ess). This part says Prince, because Kerrie wrote it for Grace once, and this says "ss" so I put them together and it says princess'. I replied 'That's very clever Z—'. Z— said, 'And it also has a crown so I knew I was right' (25 October 2001).

After 12 months the teachers were more informed and practised in using cultural–historical theory. Their observations included
- the voice of the collective, rather than simply the individual
- reciprocity of interactions between peers
- the teacher's interaction as part of the observation (they were no longer invisible).

Importantly, these studies found that it took approximately 12 months of active professional learning and reconceptualisation before teachers were comfortable with observing, assessing and planning from a cultural–historical perspective. These examples also illustrate how the work of teachers changes when a different theory of child development is used to inform their work and when new conceptions of observation and measurement of children's performances are acquired. As Edwards (2000) reminds us:

> research is not simply a product that can be applied universally to solve the problems of practice. If it is to enhance practice, research has to be able to inform both the interpretations and responses of practitioners. It needs to become embedded in the practical knowledge of the community of practitioners and inform practitioners' ways of seeing and being as they work with clients. At the same time it needs to be sensitive to the existing values and expertise, that is cultural capital, that practitioners already bring to bear on their professional decision-making (pp. 185–6).

A theoretical alignment of pedagogical practices, the conceptions of child development held and the assessment practices adopted is necessary when realising a new theory into practice. While professionals new to the field can be introduced to cultural–historical theory when they are at university, realising it into practice is difficult for them if they enter a profession steeped in a maturational view of child development, pedagogy and assessment practices (see Fleer & Robbins, 2004a, b). As Vygotsky (1997a) reminds us, 'It is easier to assimilate a thousand new facts in any field than to assimilate a new point of view of a few already known facts' (p. 2).

In the next section of this final chapter, the new conceptions of pedagogy, child development and learning, introduced throughout the chapters of this book, are brought together. Through this it is hoped that a new point of view of a few already known facts about childhood learning, development and longstanding pedagogical views on play will be realised.

PLAY, LEARNING AND DEVELOPMENT

If the working models introduced incrementally throughout this book are summarised, it can be seen that a new conception of learning and development for early education emerges. In this final part of the book, a model for a new theory of play – *conceptual play* – is generated, as this brings together the empirical material outlined in this book. This term best names the pedagogical need that has been generated through the changing political landscape of early childhood education outlined in chapter 1, where it was noted that a greater focus on conceptual development has recently emerged. This section begins by summarising three important contexts for understanding children's development within conceptual play:

societal and institutional conditions, the introduction of the pedagogical event and critical moments in everyday practice. At the end of this section the pedagogical model of conceptual play is introduced, together with the features that have in previous chapters been carefully argued and presented. This model is then aligned with the cultural–historical view of development discussed in the previous chapters, generating a dialectical view of play, learning and development.

SOCIETAL AND INSTITUTIONAL CONDITIONS FOR SHAPING LEARNING AND DEVELOPMENT

The salient feature of a cultural–historial theory of child development is to understand the conditions that are created for children's development in everyday life. In table 14.1, Hedegaard (2008) suggests that in order to determine the conditions that a child experiences in everyday life, it is important to consider first what are the societal conditions that shape what might be possible, such as laws and legislation in, for example, greenhouse gas emissions or tree heritage orders within a community, as these determine what might happen within an individual institution. At the institutional level, these laws might govern early childhood education in a particular centre, through planting more trees in the outdoor area or not removing a tree from the grounds, but erecting a protective fence. The particular activity setting that the children experience, such as playing in the outdoor area, which has restricted space but with visibility of wildlife, creates a social situation around observing nature and, potentially, generates a teaching program that is directed towards caring for the environment. At the individual level (person) the activity that the child engages in could be represented as studying insects and generating a map of the finds (see chapter 7). Here, the biology of the children influences what they might draw on the map, as their growing physical skills enable certain levels of representation. Teachers observing children in their centres would find Hedegaard's (2009) analysis framework useful, as the content of this table mirrors the child development model introduced in chapter 13.

The demands that are created through these different levels – society, institution, activity setting, individual – create possibilities for children's development. Hedegaard's (2008) theorisation of development in this way shows clearly how demands create the conditions and therefore determine the range of developmental pathways (see chapter 13). The new demands placed upon children in preschools (and of course in homes) is

Table 14.1 *Levels of analysis*

Structure	Process	Conditions/dynamics
Society	Tradition	Societal needs – political and economic
Institution	Practice	Values/motive objects
Activity setting	Social situation	Motivation
Person	Activity	Motives/engagement/intentions
Biology		

(Hedegaard, 2008b: 17; adapted by Hedegaard; personal communications).

central to Hedegaard's model of children's development. In this concept-ualisation of child development, the child's changing relations to real-ity, as a new self-awareness emerges, as children meet new demands, is foregrounded.

CRITICAL MOMENTS IN EVERYDAY PRACTICE

It is impossible to discuss child development within a pedagogical frame-work without also discussing how this development is made visible to teachers during children's play and everyday life. Critical moments in a child's everyday practice are equally important (see chapter 12), as when Louise encountered a new swing and slide set. An understanding of these critical moments by a teacher means that the teaching and learning situa-tion must be viewed in the context of all the institutions a child participates in (see chapter 13). This was also noted by Kravtsova in relation to the Golden Key Programs in Russia (see chapter 8), where the significance of the collaboration between the family and the centre or school is fore-grounded. Through these collaborations it is possible for teachers to be more in tune with the critical moments of children's development in the home and community context, thus deepening contextual and conceptual intersubjectivity. Teachers can then notice the changing reality that chil-dren experience at home (see chapter 2), as when Jens no longer wanted to read picture books but wanted to be treated like a schoolchild. Jens was oriented to school learning. This new self-awareness can be made visible through play-based programs (see chapter 9), as children express their existing and changing everyday experiences (contexts) and concepts through shared playful events with other children. Children's relations to reality, for instance, was noted (see chapter 2); here, the sighted and visually impaired children each had different kinds of reference point in their play for signalling what mattered in the rules for driving a train (how it felt, or where you sat).

GENERATING A PEDAGOGICAL EVENT

The nature of the support given through the pedagogical process (subject positioning; see chapter 9) when actively building theoretical knowledge (see chapter 7) is dialectically related to the new pedagogical demands generated by the teacher. The zones of development signify the close relations between the child's psychological resources in the context of the new demands, as well as the nature of the pedagogical relationship and interaction enacted by the teacher (e.g., subject positioning) to help them deal with the new demands. This highlights the significance of the teacher determining (assessment) what are the particular child's psychological resources for dealing with the new demands (actual, proximal and potentive assessment).

Determining the nature of this dialectical relation requires conceptual and contextual intersubjectivity (see chapter 6); to achieve this, some form of embedded observation and analysis on the teacher's part is needed (i.e., assessable moment). Ongoing assessment of the child's psychological resources and contexts enables the teacher to engage effectively in a double move process. Hedegaard's concept of the double move (see chapter 1) enables the teacher to have in mind not only the resources the child brings but also the concepts that the teacher wishes to deliberately introduce. The double move can be initiated through a pedagogical event. Teachers in the Golden Key Programs in Russia (see chapter 7) introduce an event as the catalyst for the pedagogical journey the teachers want to embark upon with the children and their families. When teachers have established contextual and conceptual intersubjectivity with children, it is possible to determine the pedagogical event that best connects with the group of children, while at the same time pedagogically framing how the play activities will proceed towards greater understanding of the concepts deemed important by the community in which the child lives. This was also noted earlier (see chapter 6), where the pedagogical event that was designed by the teacher was a map to record all of the finds (insects) in the outdoor area in order to develop theoretical knowledge about habitat, organism and food. The pedagogical event conceptually framed how the children played and interacted within the outdoor area. In the double move approach, teachers hold in their mind the children's psychological resources, the contextual dimensions of children's everyday lives and experiences (everyday concepts), and the concepts they want children to learn (scientific concepts).

INSTITUTIONAL PRACTICES AND CRITICAL MOMENTS GENERATE DEMANDS

Institutional and societal demands are broad. Society would expect, for instance, children going to school to learn to read. At an institutional level, children may be expected to sit and listen to the teacher and put up their hand if they wish to make a contribution to the discussion. Many institutional expectations are often taken for granted, as assumed practice, and therefore potentially invisible. The difference between what is expected at preschool or school and what is enacted at home maybe vastly different, as was noted in the Peninsula family. In the Peninsula family there was rapid and constant movement at home (geography of movement) and at school, where most activities involve the children sitting, movement was minimised. Eating routines were also very different, reflected in grazing in different locations at home versus fixed point eating at childcare and school. Even though these differences place great demands upon children, they are often invisible to teachers. At the individual level, children experiencing this disparity are acutely aware of the new social situation they find themselves in and the changing reality they now encounter. These examples (see chapters 12 and 13) show how developmental pathways vary among children and highlight how critical moments in development can be quite specific for individuals.

The child's changing reality can also be created by the teacher through the introduction of a pedagogical event. Through a pedagogical event the teacher creates an imaginary situation for the children. The teacher conceptually frames how play may take place within the centre when play is deliberately used for conceptual development (see chapter 7).

The teacher draws upon collective and individual imagining (see chapter 10) so that children are introduced to, or construct for themselves (make their own), the tools that the particular society uses and values. In rising from the abstract to the concrete (see chapters 7 and 8), the child draws from the concrete context everyday concepts, such as when Christian examined the bull ants in the bushy outdoor area of the centre. It was possible for Christian to rise from the abstract to the concrete because the teacher had conceptually framed his interactions in the environment by inviting him to map the organisms, habitat and food source available. In this way collective imagining between Christian, the teacher (holder of knowledge traditions in Western science) and the other children who participated was possible. Through this playful context, the children used the binoculars and magnifying glasses to investigate their environment in quite new ways, which enabled them to build their theoretical knowledge. The problem situation (bull ants in the wrong place) and the teacher's conceptual framing (introducing a map) created a contextually and conceptually relevant experience for Christian and the other children. They could bring into their imagination the idea of a map, that is, the children could see a piece of paper (optical field), but they imagined they were generating a map (sense field). Through working together to record their finds, they turned the imagined map into a tool for further and future activity. Through this, Christian was able to move from the general to the particular, and from the particular to the general. This was less evident in another example (see chapters 1 and 2), in which the children engaged in narrative knowledge, to reenact the Humpty Dumpty nursery rhyme. They used the materials provided by the teacher (where no conceptual framing was given) to create a new storyline of medicating Humpty Dumpty. The objects (Humpty Dumpty, a spoon and a pump action bottle of coloured water) within the children's optical field were transformed into a game of medicating Humpty Dumpty, expanding their collective imagining, even though the building of theoretical knowledge was limited. Through collective and individual imagining the child contributes to the association and disassociation of elements found within their cultural community, making possible their own unique contribution to imagining and creating new cultural tools and practices.

A DIALECTICAL MODEL
OF CONCEPTUAL PLAY

When societal and institutional conditions are brought together, critical moments in everyday practice and pedagogical events with the models incrementally introduced throughout the first part of the book (motives, consciousness, imitation, double move, collective and individual imagining, core concepts), it is possible to realise a new theory of play – conceptual play. Conceptual play can be symbolised as a model (see figure 14.5) to include societal and institutional conditions, critical moments in everyday practice and pedagogical events.

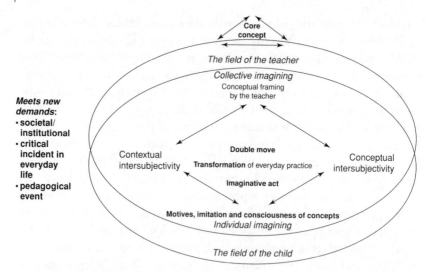

Figure 14.5 A dialectical model of conceptual play for early childhood education

Conceptual play concentrates specifically on building theoretical knowledge (see chapter 7) so that children learn scientific or academic concepts (see chapter 1) during play. The teacher's role is active through analysing existing play activity (assessable moment) or critical moments in children's development (zones of proximal or potential development) and through using these opportunities to conceptually frame the play so that conceptual development is foregrounded and children think consciously about the concepts being privileged.

In conceptual play, the teacher can also introduce a pedagogical event for generating an object–motive for consciously working with concepts in play, thus affording conceptual development. Through the teacher generating an imaginary situation, children can engage in an imaginative act, thus allowing them to consciously play with everyday concepts and scientific concepts.

In the literature, there are many different views on what constitutes play espoused but there are no consistent definitions of play. What is clear is that there is no theory of play that specifically focuses on concept development (discipline knowledge or curriculum content knowledge). Conceptual play as defined in this book seeks to provide a theory and a pedagogical model for teachers who want to deliberately use play for supporting conceptual development of preschool aged children so that theoretical knowledge is generated.

A model of conceptual play (figure 14.5) can only be effectively used by teachers when it is located within a cultural–historical theory of child development (see chapters 12 and 13; see also below) (but including the demands introduced above) in figure 14.6.

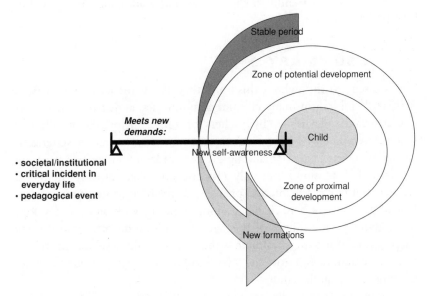

Figure 14.6 A cultural–historical view of play, learning and development

Conceptual play foregrounds cognition, but does so only in unity with emotions and with imagination. It is recognised that cognition does not sit in isolation, and that any pedagogical model must take account of a person's emotional construction of their world, as noted by Gonzalez Rey (2008):

> This emotional sense is a consequence of the complex encounter of already subjectively configured individual needs and the emotions that appear during the subject's ongoing interactions. For example when entering a new social situation, a person feels different emotions related to previous needs resulting from his/her prior experiences (p. 261).

It is the role of the adults who work with young children to understand the demands – those that are generated simply by being a member of an institution, those that a child meets during their everyday life at home and in the community and those that are created specifically through the generation of a pedagogical event. When a teachers bring together their pedagogical model of conceptual play with their dialectical model of child development, they create the conditions for children to make learning their own, rather than something to be done to the child and for the child to do for the teacher. It is when a teacher has conceptual and contextual intersubjectivity that children can engage and work conceptually within play-based programs.

SUMMARY

It was discussed throughout this book that play is the leading activity of preschool children in many cultural communities, and that in these particular societies play is used by teachers for supporting preschool children's social development. However, governments – and education systems as agents of society – are demanding greater academic outcomes for young children. This tension is not only a practical problem for early childhood teachers but is also a theoretical problem, as the basic assumption or value base of government here challenges long standing work on child development about what children of this age are ready to do or should do (see chapter 10). What is central here is the view of child development that is held, what should be learnt and what kind of pedagogy is needed to meet these new societal demands.

This political context has created a new self-awareness of early childhood teachers as they grapple with their new role to foster academic knowledge, as was noted about the Nordic countries, the Netherlands and Australia (see chapter 1). In drawing upon cultural–historical theory it has been possible to demonstrate that the old theories of child development cannot achieve this new political imperative, and therefore the old theories guiding pedagogical practice are no longer relevant for early childhood education in current times. Teacher perceptions of their role as active or passive agents within the preschool context was discussed in chapter 3, and it was found that the dominant theories of child development and pedagogy in Western communities did not allow teachers to work conceptually with children. It was also shown that highly skilled early childhood professionals can, and already do, create the contexts that can bring about concept formation in play-based programs, but the existing pedagogical and child development theories promoted make it difficult to achieve higher forms of cognition.

This book makes visible the theoretical problem and the conceptual challenge that has arisen for early childhood educators and those who work closely with young children and their families. Through theoretical analysis, a review of relevant literature and empirical evidence, this book puts forward a cultural–historical model of pedagogy, play, learning and development. The model of conceptual play introduced in this book provides one approach that early childhood professionals can use to generate higher forms of conceptual learning within play-based programs. The conceptual model of play created within a cultural–historical framework of child development has been developed in direct response to the contemporary challenge facing early childhood educators. In undertaking the work of this book, I have sought to reposition early childhood professionals to reclaim their expertise as pedagogical experts, rather than being seen as one variable within the political landscape for improving the life chances of young children from low socioeconomic communities.

Glossary

Cartesian Cartesian is a theoretical perspective attributed to French philosopher René Descartes, in which dualisms dominate thinking. The most highly featured dualism in this philosophy is the split between the mind and the body: the mind is seen to be rational and the body as a mechanical physical form. Cartesian dualisms often cited include good–bad, boy–girl, black–white, soft science–hard science and working with your hands–working with your mind.

Conceptual intersubjectivity When a teacher has gained knowledge of the everyday concepts of children.

Contextual intersubjectivity When a teacher has gained knowledge of the everyday practices of children across a range of contexts (e.g., home, centre).

Dialectic(al) According to *The Penguin Dictionary of Psychology* (see Reber & Reber, 2001), dialectics is a theoretical stance in which conflict and change underpin life. Although there are many nuances surrounding this term, ancient and more recent dialectical approaches (those of Heraclitus, and later, Hegel and Marx, for example) foregrounded the concept of contradiction. In Hegel's writings on dialectics, every action produces a counter action, which is followed by the integration of the opposites. It is not possible to consider the idea of a 'student' without also considering the idea of a 'teacher' and their successful integration results in learning.

Double move Hedegaard's concept enables the teacher to have in mind not only the resources the child brings but also the concepts that the teacher wishes to deliberately introduce.

Everyday concepts Everyday concepts, also referred to as spontaneous concepts, refer to the everyday tacit knowledge that children use but do not necessarily think consciously about. It is usually located within a practice context of some kind.

Imitation Vygotsky (1987) introduced the psychological concept of imitation. The everyday use of the term *imitation* usually means to engage in an act of copying. When the term is used in a psychological sense, it refers to a child socially and mentally noticing a particular activity within a meaningful social context and being able to do the same activity with some conscious awareness.

Maturational or naturally evolving view of development A view of child development in which children's progression in development is conceptualised as biologically determined. Ages and stages or milestones are markers of maturational view of development. In the context of early childhood education, a maturational view of development usually foregrounds the social–emotional, language, physical development.

Motives *Motives* as a term has been defined in different ways. Leontiev argued that a motive can exist as material or tangible or can be within a person's imagination as an ideal. Activity is driven by something existing objectively in the world, even if the original conditions which formed the motive are no longer visible or tangible. Others have suggested that this view of motives does not take account of the child's perspective. Elkonin, in returning to Vygotsky's original theorisation of activity, foregrounds the importance of the dialectical relations between the child and the object through the social. His theorisation of motives makes visible the child's perspective within the child–social–object relations, and is helpful for gaining a deeper understanding of children's lived world and their relation to it.

Pedagogical framing in play In an educational context, pedagogical framing occurs when the teacher actively introduces a learning experience or transforms an existing learning experience so that the children and the teacher think about the context in the same way (in conceptual unity).

Psychological intersubjectivity When a teacher has gained knowledge of both the concepts and everyday practices of children across a range of contexts (e.g. home, centre), the child and the teacher can enact cognitive practices together.

Scientific concepts Scientific concepts does not simply mean concepts in science, but rather it captures the mature concepts captured within disciplines, such as the arts, history, mathematics, literacy and so forth. It has also been termed *academic concepts* or *school concepts*. Scientific concepts are usually disembedded from practice.

Sustained shared thinking Introduced by Siraj-Blatchford and Sylva, sustained shared thinking involves a balance between teacher initiated and child initiated group work and play activities in early childhood programs, where there is a mutual understanding of the other and where learning is achieved through a process of reflexive co-construction. Children and teachers are involved in worthwhile content that is instructive.

References

Aidarova, L. (1982). *Child Development and Education*. Moscow: Progress Publishers.

Ailwood, J. (2003). Governing early childhood education through play, *Contemporary Issues in Early Childhood*, 4(3): 286–98.

Allen, K.E. & Marotz, L. (1989). *Developmental Profiles. Birth to six*. New York: Delmar.

Alloway, N. (1997). Early childhood education encounters the postmodern: What do we know? What can we count as 'true'?, *Australian Journal of Early Childhood*, 22(2): 1–5.

Alton-Lee, A. (2003). *Quality Teaching for Diverse Students in Schooling: Best evidence synthesis*. Wellington: Ministry of Education.

Anning, A., Cullen, J. & Fleer, M. (eds) (2009). *Early Childhood Education: Society and culture* (2nd edn). London: Sage.

Appleton, K. (2006). Science pedagogical content knowledge and elementary school teachers. In K. Appleton (ed.), *Elementary Science Teacher Education. International perspectives on contemporary issues and practice*, pp. 31–54. Mahwah: Lawrence Erlbaum.

Ball, S., Maguire, M. & Macrae, S. (2000). *Choice, pathways and transition post-16: New youth, new economies in the global city*. London: Routledge Falmer.

Bateson, G. (1976). A theory of play and fantasy. In J.S. Bruner, A. Jolly and K. Sylva (eds). *Play – Its Role in Development and Evolution*, New York: Basic Books, pp. 119–29.

Beatty, J.J. (1990). *Observing Development of the Young Child* (2nd edn). New York: Merrill.

Belfield, C., Nores, M., Barnett, W.S. & Schweinhart, L. (2005). Updating the benefit-cost analysis of the High/Scope Perry Preschool Program through age 40. *Educational Evaluation and Policy Analysis*, 27(3): 245–63.

Berezhkovskaya, E. (2009a). About the perception of space by the children of preschool age and primary school pupils. Paper presented at the Golden Key Summer School Program, Belay Kylavita, Russia, 22 June.

—— (2009b). The ideal child. Paper presented at the Golden Key Summer School Program, Belay Kylavita, Russia, 26 June.

Berk, L.E. (1994). Vygotsky's theory: The importance of make-believe play, *Young children*, 50(1): 30–9.

—— & Winsler, A. (1995). *Scaffolding Children's Learning: Vygotsky and early childhood education*. Washington, DC: National Association for the Education of Young Children.

Blaise, M. (2009). Revolutionising practice by doing early childhood politically. In S. Edwards and J. Nuttall (eds), *Professional Learning in the Early Childhood Settings*. Rotterdam: Sense Publishers, pp. 27–48.

Bock, J. (2002). Learning, life history, and productivity: Children's lives in the Okavango Delta, Botswana, *Human Nature*, 13, 161–97.

Bodrova, E. (2008). Make-believe play versus academic skills: A Vygotskian approach to today's dilemma of early childhood education. *European Early Childhood Education Research Journal*, 16(3): 357–69.

—— & Leong D.J. (1998). Development of dramatic play in young children and its effects on self-regulation: The Vygotskian approach. *Journal of Early Childhood Teacher Education*, 19(2): 115–24.

—— (2001). *Tools of the Mind: A case study of implementing the Vygotskian approach in American early childhood and primary classrooms*. Innodata Monographs – 7. Geneva: International Bureau of Education, UNESCO.

Bogoraz-Tan, N.G. (1934). *Chukchi*, part 1, Leningrad: n.p.

Bretherton, I. (1984). *Symbolic Play. The development of social understanding*. New York: Academic Press.

Brock, A. (2009). Curriculum and pedagogy of play: A multitude of perspectives? In A. Brock, S. Dodds, P. Jarvis and Y. Ousoga (eds), *Perspectives on Play. Learning for life*. Harlow: Pearson Longman, pp. 67–93.

Bruce, T. (1991). *Time to Play in Early Childhood Education*. London: Hodder & Stoughton.

—— (1997). Adults and children developing play together, *European Early Childhood Education Research Journal*, 5(1): 89–99.

Bruner, J.S. (1966). *Towards a Theory of Instruction*. New York: W.W. Norton.

—— (1968). *Processes of Cognitive Growth: Infancy*. Worcester: Clark University Press.

—— (1986). *Actual Minds, Possible Worlds*. Cambridge, MA: Harvard University Press.

—— (1999). Infancy and culture: A story. In S. Chaiklin, M. Hedegaard and U.J. Jensen (eds), *Activity Theory and Social Practice*. Aarhus: Aarhus University Press, pp. 225–34.

——, Jolly, A. & Sylva, K. (1976). *Play – Its Role in Development and Evolution*. New York: Basic Books.

Cannella, G.S. & Bailey, C. (1999). Postmodern research in early childhood education. In S. Reifel (ed.), *Advances in Early Education and Day Care*, vol. 10. Stamford: JAI Press.

Cannella, G.S. & Viruru, R. (2004). *Childhood and postcolonization: Power, education and contemporary practice*. London: Routledge Falmer.

Chaiklin, S. (2003). The zone of proximal development in Vygotsky's analysis of learning and instruction. In A. Kozulin, B. Gindis, V.S. Ageyev and S.M. Miller (eds), *Vygotsky's Educational Theory in Cultural Context*. New York: Cambridge University Press, pp. 39–64.

—— & Hedegaard, M. (2009). Radical local teaching and learning: A cultural–historical perspective on education an children's development. In M. Fleer, M. Hedegaard and J. Tudge (eds), *Constructing Childhood: Global–local policies and practices*. World Year Book 2009. New York: Routledge, pp. 254–78.

Coghlan, A. (2007). Babies overfed to meet flawed ideal. *New Scientist*, 28 April, 6–7.

Creche and Kindergarten Association (2006). *Building Waterfalls. A living and learning curriculum framework for adults and children (birth to school age)*. Brisbane: Queensland Studies Authority.

Cullen, J. (1996). The challenge of Te Whaariki for future developments in early childhood education, *Policy and Practice in Education*, 48(1).

—— (2009). The journey towards inclusion – co-constructing professional knowledge. In A. Anning, J. Cullen and M. Fleer (eds), *Early Childhood Education: Society and culture*. London: Sage.

Curriculum Development Council (2006). *Guide to the pre-primary curriculum*. Recommended for use in pre-primary institutions by the Education and Manpower Bureau, Hong Kong Special Administrative Region.

Dahlberg, G., Moss, P. & Pence, A. (1999). *Beyond Quality in Early Childhood Education and Care. Postmodern perspectives*. London: Falmer Press.

Darling-Hammond, L. (2000). Teacher quality and student achievement: A review of state policy evidence. *Education Policy Analysis Archives*, 8(1); retrieved from http://epaa.asu.edu/epaa/v8n1, 20 April 2009.

David, T. (1990). *Under Five – Under-educated?* Buckingham: Open University Press.

—— (2005). Questions of quality: The contribution of research evidence to definitions of quality in early childhood education and care practice. In H. Schonfeld, S. O'Brien and T. Walsh (eds), conference proceedings, international conference 2004, *Questions of Quality*, Dublin Castle, 23–24 September, pp. 22–9.

Davydov, V.V. (1983). Istoriceskie predposylki ucebnoj dejate'nosti (Historical conditions of learning activity). In V.V. Daydov (ed.), *Razvitie Psichiki Skol'nikov v Processe Ucebnoj Dejate'nosti*. Moscow: PN.

—— (1988a). Learning activity in the younger school age period. *Soviet Education*, 30(9): 3–47.

—— (1988b). Problems of developmental teaching. The experience of theoretical and experimental psychological research, *Soviet Education*, 30(8): 1–97.

—— (1988c). The mental development of younger school children in the process of learning activity, *Soviet Education*, 30(8): 48–83.

—— (1988d). Learning activity. *Multidisciplinary Newsletter for Activity Theory*, 1 / 2, 29–36.

—— (1990 [1972]). *Types of generalization in instruction: Logical and psychological problems in the structuring of school curricula. Soviet Studies in Mathematics Education*, vol. 2, trans. J. Teller. Reston: National Council of Teachers of Mathematics.

—— (1995). The influence of L.S. Vygotsky on education, theory, research and practice. *Educational Researchers*, 24(3): 12–21.

—— (1999a). What is real learning activity? In M. Hedeaard and J. Lompscher (eds), *Learning Activity and Development*. Aarhus: Aarhus University Press pp. 123–38.

—— (1999b). The content and unsolved problems of activity theory. In Y. Engestrom, R. Miettinen and R.-L. Punamaki (eds), *Perspectives on Activity Theory*, Cambridge, MA: Cambridge University Press, pp. 39–52.

—— (1999c). A new approach to the interpretation of activity structure and content. In S. Chaiklin, M. Hedegaard and U.J. Jensen (eds), *Activity Theory and Social Practice*, Aarhus: Aarhus University Press, pp. 39–50.

—— (2008). Problems of developmental instruction. A theoretical and experimental psychological study. *International Perspectives in Non-classical Psychology*. D. Robbins and V. Lektorsky (series eds). New York: Nova Science Publishers.

—— & Zinchenko, V.P. (1986). Vygotsky's contribution to the development of psychology. *Sovetskaya Pedagogika*, 11: 108–14.

—— (1993). Vygotsky's contribution to the development of psychology. In H. Daniels, *Charting the Agenda. Educational activity after Vygotsky.* London: Routledge, pp. 93–106.

Department of Education and Employment (2000). *Curriculum Guidance for the Foundation Stage.* London: Department of Education and Employment.

Diamond, A., Barnett, W.S., Thomas, J. & Munro, S. (2007). Preschool program improves cognitive control, *Science*, 318: 1387–8.

Dockett, S. & Sumsion, J. (2004). Australian research in early childhood education: Contexts, tensions, challenges and future directions, *Australian Educational Researcher*, 31(3): 3–18.

Duncan, R.M. & Tarulli, D. (2003). Play as the leading activity of the preschool period: Insights from Vygotsky, Leontiev, and Bakhtin, *Early Education and Development*, 14(3): 171–292.

Edwards, A. (2000). Research and practice: Is there a dialogue? In H. Penn, *Early Childhood Services. Theory, policy and practice.* Buckingham: Open University Press, pp. 184–99.

Edwards, D. & Mercer, N. (1987). *Common Knowledge.* Methuen: London.

Edwards, E. (2005). Talking about a revolution. Paradigmatic change in early childhood education: From developmental to sociocultural theory and beyond, *Melbourne Studies in Education*, 46(1): 1–12.

Edwards, S. (2003). New directions: Charting the paths for the role of sociocultural theory in early childhood education and curriculum, *Contemporary Issues in Early Childhood*, 4(3): 251–66.

—— (2009). Beyond developmentalism. In S. Edwards and J. Nuttall (eds), *Professional Learning in the Early Childhood Settings.* Rotterdam: Sense Publishers, pp. 81–96.

Einarsdottir, J. (1998). The role of adults in children's dramatic play in Icelandic preschools, *European Early Childhood Education Research Journal*, 6(2): 87–106.

—— (2003). Beliefs of early childhood teachers. In O.N. Saracho and B. Spodek (eds). *Studying Teachers in Early Childhood Settings.* Greenwich: Information Age Publishing, pp. 113–34.

Elkonin, D.B. (1978). *Psikhologiya Igry (Psychology of Play).* Moscow: Pedagogika.

—— (1993a). The crisis of childhood and foundations for designing forms of child development. *Journal of Russian and East European Psychology*, 31(3): 56–71.

—— (1993b). The nature of human action, *Journal of Russian and East European Psychology*, 31(3): 22–46.

—— (1999a). Toward the problem of stages in the mental development of children, *Journal of Russian and East European Psychology*, 37(6): 11–30.

—— (1999b). How to teach children to read, *Journal of Russian and East European Psychology*, 37(6): 93–117.

—— (1999c). On the structure of learning activity, *Journal of Russian and East European Psychology*, 37(6): 84–92.

—— (1999d). On the theory of primary education, *Journal of Russian and East European Psychology*, 37(6): 71–83.

—— (1999e). The development of play in preschoolers, *Journal of Russian and East European Psychology*, 37(6): 31–70.

—— (2005a). On the historical origin of role play, *Journal of Russian and East European Psychology*, 43(1): 49–89.

—— (2005b). The psychology of play, *Journal of Russian and East European Psychology*, 43(1): 11–21.

—— (2005c). The subject of our research: The developed form of play, *Journal of Russian and East European Psychology*, 43(1): 22–48.

Falmagne, R.J. (1995). The abstract and the concrete. In L.M.W. Martin, K. Helson and E. Tobach (eds), *Sociocultural Psychology. Theory and practice of doing and knowing.* Cambridge: Cambridge University Press, pp. 205–28.

Farquhar, S. (2003). *Quality Teaching Early Foundations. Best evidence synthesis.* Wellington: Ministry of Education.

Fein, G. (1981). Pretend play in childhood: An integrated review. *Child Development*, 52: 1095–118.

Flavell, J.H., Flavell, E.R. & Green, F.L. (1987). Young children's knowledge about the apparent-real and pretend-real distinctions. *Developmental Psychology*, 23: 16–22.

Fleer, M. (1999). Universal fantasy: The domination of Western theories of play. In E. Dau (ed.), *Child's Play*. Sydney: MacLennan and Petty, pp. 67–80.

—— (2002). Sociocultural assessment in early years education – Myth or reality? *International Journal of Early Years Education*, 10(2): 105–20.

—— (2005). Developmental fossils – unearthing the artefacts of early childhood education: The reification of 'child development', *Australian Journal of Early Childhood*, 30(2): 2–7.

—— (2006). Potentive assessment in early childhood education. In M. Fleer, S. Edwards, M. Hammer, A. Ridgway and J. Surman (eds), *Early Childhood Learning Communities. Sociocultural research in practice*, Sydney: Pearson Education, pp. 161–73.

—— (2008a). The significance of practice traditions in schools for shaping activities and generating motives in children's development. Paper presented at the ISCAR pre-conference workshop, Cultural–historical approaches to children's development section meeting. 8 September, San Diego; retrieved from www.iscar.org/section/chacdoc.

—— (2008b). Using digital video observations and computer technologies in a cultural–historical approach. In M. Hedegaard and M. Fleer (eds), *Studying Children: A cultural–historical approach*. Berkshire: Open University Press, pp. 104–17.

—— (2009a). Understanding the dialectical relations between everyday concepts and scientific concepts within play-based programs, *Research in Science Education*. 39(2): 281–306.

—— (2009b). Supporting conceptual consciousness or learning in a roundabout way, *International Journal of Science Education*, 31(8): 1069–90.

Fleer, M. & Hedegaard, M. (forthcoming). Development as participation in everyday activities across different institutions: A child's changing relations to reality. *Mind, Culture and Activity*.

—— & Tudge, J. (eds) (2009). Constructing childhood: Global–local policies and practices. *World Year Book 2009*, New York: Routledge, pp. 254–78.

Fleer, M. & Raban, B. (2006). A cultural–historical analysis of concept formation in early education settings: Conceptual consciousness for the child or only the adult?, *European Early Childhood Education Research Journal*, 14(2): 69–80.

—— (2007a). *Early Childhood Literacy and Numeracy: Building good practice*. Canberra: Commonwealth of Australia.

—— (2007b). Constructing cultural–historical tools for supporting young children's concept formation in early literacy and numeracy, *Early Years*, 27(2): 103–18.

Fleer, M. & Richardson, C. (2003). Collective mediated assessment: Moving towards a sociocultural approach to assessing children's learning, *Journal of Australian Research in Early Childhood Education*, 10(1): 41–55.

—— (2004a). *Observing and Planning in Early Childhood Settings: Using a sociocultural approach*. Canberra: Early Childhood Australia.

—— (2004b). Moving from a constructivist-developmental framework for planning to a sociocultural approach: Foregrounding the tension between individual and community, *Journal of Australian Research in Early Childhood Education*, 11(2), 70–87.

—— (2009). Cultural–historical assessment: Mapping the transformation of understanding. In A. Anning, J. Cullen and M. Fleer (eds), *Early Childhood Education Society* (2nd edn). London: Sage.

Fleer, M. & Robbins, J. (2004a). Yeah, that's what they teach you at uni, it's just rubbish: The participatory appropriation of new cultural tools as early childhood student teachers move from a developmental to a sociocultural framework for observing and planning, *Journal of Australian Research in Early Childhood Education*, 11(1): 47–62.

—— (2004b). Beyond ticking the boxes: From individual developmental domains to a sociocultural framework for observing young children, *New Zealand Research in Early Childhood Education*, 7, 23–39.

Freud, S. (1959 [1908]). Creative writers and daydreaming. In J. Strachey (ed.). *The Standard Edition of the Complete Psychological Works of Sigmund Freud*, vol. IX. London: Hogarth Press.

Frye, N. (1957). *Anatomy of criticism: Four essays*. Princeton: Princeton University Press.

Garbett, D. (2003). Science education in early childhood teacher education: Putting forward a case to enhance student teachers' confidence and competence, *Research in Science Education*, 33, 467–81.

Garet, M.S., Porter, A.C., Desimone, L., Birman, B.F. & Yoon, K.S. (2001). What makes professional development effective? Results from a national sample of teachers, *American Educational Research Journal*, 38(4): 915–45.

Garvey, C. (1977). *Play*. Cambridge, MA: Harvard University Press.

Gaskins, S. (1999). Children's daily lives in a Mayan village: A case study of culturally constructed roles and activities. In A. Göncü (ed.), *Children's Engagement in the World: Sociocultural perspectives*. Cambridge: Cambridge University Press, pp. 25–61.

—— (2007). The cultural relativity of Vygotsky's theory of play. Paper presented at the Invited Symposium on Play and Culture. Seville: International Society of Cultural Activity Research.

—— & Göncü, A. (1992). Cultural variation in play: A challenge to Piaget and Vygotsky, *Quarterly Newsletter of the Laboratory of Comparative Human Cognition*, 14(2): 31–5.

Gaskins, S., Haight, W. & Lancy, D.F. (2007). The cultural construction of play. In A. Göncü and S. Gaskins (eds), *Play and Development. Evolutionary, sociocultural, and functional perspectives*. New York: Lawrence Erlbaum, pp. 179–202.

Gaskins, S. & Miller, P.J. (2008). The cultural roles of emotions in pretend play. Paper presented at the International Society for Culture and Activity Research, San Diego, September.

Gesell, A. (1933). Maturation and the patterning of behavior. In C. Murchison (ed.). *A Handbook of Child Psychology*. Worcester: Clark University Press, pp. 209–35.

Gess-Newsome, J. & Lederman, N.G. (eds) (1999). *Examining Pedagogical Content Knowledge*. Dordrecht: Kluwer Academic, pp. 21–50.

Gibson, J.J. (1979). *The Ecological Approach to Visual Perception*. Boston: Houghton Mifflin.

Glick, J. (1997). Prologue. In L.S. Vygotsky, *The Collected works of L.S. Vygotsky*, vol. 4, *The History of the Development of Higher Mental Functions* (ed. R.W. Rieber), trans. M.J. Hall. New York: Plenum Press, pp. v–xvi.

Goldman, L. (1998). *Child's Play: Myth, mimesis, and make-believe*. New York: Berg.

Göncü, A. (ed.) (1999). *Children's Engagement in the World. Sociocultural perspectives*. Cambridge, MA: Cambridge University Press.

—— & Gaskins, S. (eds) (2007). *Play and Development. Evolutionary, sociocultural, and functional perspectives*. New York: Lawrence Erlbaum.

Göncü, A., Jain, J. & Tuermer, U. (2007). Children's play as cultural interpretation. In A. Göncü and S. Gaskins (eds), *Play and Development. Evolutionary, sociocultural, and functional perspectives*. New York: Lawrence Erlbaum, pp. 155–78.

Göncü, A., Mistry, J. & Mosier, C. (2000). Cultural variations in the play of toddlers, *International Journal of Behavioral Development*, 24(3): 321–9.

Gonzalez Rey, F.L. (2008). Subjectivity, and development in cultural–historical psychology. In B. van Oers, W. Wardekker, E. Elbers and R. van der Veer (eds), *The Transformation of Learning. Advances in cultural–historical activity theory*. New York: Cambridge University Press, pp. 137–56.

Goodfellow, J. & Sumsion, J. (2003). Transformative pathways in becoming an early childhood teacher. In O.N. Saracho and B. Spodek (eds), *Studying Teachers in Early Childhood Settings*. Charlotte: Information Age Publishing, pp. 59–78.

Groos, K. (1898). *The Play of Animals*. New York: Appleton.

—— (1901). *The Play of Man*. New York: Appleton.

Gulick, L.H. (1898). *A Philosophy of Play*. New York: Charles Scribner's Sons.

Haight, W. & Miller, P. (1993). *Pretending at Home: Development in sociocultural context*. Albany: State University of New York Press.

Hakkarainen, P. (2006). Learning and development in play. In J. Einarsdottir and J.T. Wagner (eds), *Nordic Childhoods and Early Education. Philosophy, research, policy, and practice in Denmark, Finland, Iceland, Norway and Sweden*. Charlotte: Information Age Publishing, pp. 183–222.

—— & Veresov, N. (1999). D.B. Elkonin and the evolution of developmental psychology (editors' introduction), *Journal of Russian and East European Psychology*, 37(6): 3–10.

Heckman, J.J. & Masterov, D.V. (2007). The productivity argument for investing in young children. Discussion paper 2725. Bonn: Institute for Labour Study.

Hedegaard, M. (1990). The zone of proximal development as basis for instruction. In L.C. Moll (ed.), *Vygotsky and Education. Instructional implications and applications of sociohistorcal psychology*, Cambridge: Cambridge University Press, pp. 349–71.

—— (1992). *Beskrivelse af Småbørn (Observing Children)*. Aarhus: Aarhus University Press.

—— (2002). *Learning and Child Development: A cultural–historical study*. Aarhus: Aarhus University Press.

—— (1995). The qualitative analysis of the development of a child's theoretical knowledge and thinking. In L.M.W. Martin, K. Nelson and E. Tobach (eds), *Sociocultural Psychology. Theory and practice of doing and knowing*. Cambridge, MA: Cambridge University Press, pp. 293–325.

—— (1999). The influence of societal knowledge traditions on children's thinking and conceptual development. In M. Hedeaard and J. Lompscher (eds), *Learning Activity and Development*. Aarhus: Aarhus University Press, pp. 21–50

—— (1998). Situated learning and cognition: Theoretical learning of cognition, *Mind, Culture and Activity*, 5 (2): 114–26.

—— (2004). A cultural–historical approach to learning in classrooms. Paper presented at the International Society for Cultural and Activity Research, Regional Conference, University of Wollongong, 12–13 July.

—— (2005a). Child development from a cultural–historical approach: Children's activity in everyday local settings as foundation for their development. Paper presented at the triennial conference of the International Society for Culture and Activity Research, Seville.

—— (2005b). Strategies for dealing with conflicts in value positions between home and school: Influences on ethnic minority students' development of motives and identity, *Culture and Psychology*, 11, 187–205.

—— (2007). The development of children's conceptual relations to the world, with a focus on concept formation in preschool children's activity. In H. Daniels, M. Cole, J.V. Wertsch (eds), *The Cambridge Companion to Vygotsky*. Cambridge, MA: Cambridge University Press, pp. 246–75.

—— (2008a) Developing a dialectic approach to researching children's development. In M. Hedegaard and M. Fleer (eds), *Studying Children: A cultural–historical approach*. Berkshire: Open University Press, pp. 30–45.

—— (2008b). A cultural–historical theory of children's development. In M. Hedegaard and M. Fleer (eds), *Studying children: A cultural–historical approach*. Berkshire: Open University Press, pp. 10–29.

—— (2009). Children's development from a cultural–historical approach: Children's activity in everyday local settings as foundation for their development, *Mind, Culture and Activity*, 16, 64–81.

—— & Fleer, M. (2009). Family practices and how children are positioned as active agents. In M. Fleer, M. Hedegaard and J. Tudge (eds), *Constructing Childhood: Global-local policies and practices*. World Year Book 2009, New York and London: Routledge, pp. 254–78.

—— (eds) (2008). *Studying Children: A cultural–historical approach*. Berkshire: Open University Press.

Hedegaard, M. & Chaiklin, S. (2005). *Radical-local Teaching and Learning: A cultural–historical approach*. Aarhus: Aarhus University Press.

Hedges, M. & Cullen, J. (2005). Subject knowledge in early childhood curriculum and pedagogy: Beliefs and practices, *Contemporary Issues in Early Childhood*, 6(1): 66–79.

Hetherington, E.M. & McIntyre, C.W. (1975). Developmental psychology, *Annual Review of Psychology*, 26: 97–136.

Higgins, J. & Nairn, K. (2006). 'In transition': Choice and the children of New Zealand's economic reforms, *British Journal of Sociology in Education*, 27(2): 207–20.

Holloway, S.D. & Yamamoto, Y. (2003). Sensei: Early childhood education teachers in Japan. In O.N. Saracho and B. Spodek (eds), *Studying Teachers in Early Childhood Settings*. Charlotte: Information Age Publishing, pp. 181–208.

Holzman, L. (1997). *Schools for Growth. Radical alternatives to current educational models*. Mahwah: Lawrence Erlbaum.

—— (2009). *Vygotsky at Work and Play*. London: Routledge.

Hutt, S.J., Tyler, S., Hutt, C. & Christopherson, H. (1989). *Play, Exploration and Learning. A natural history of the preschool*. New York: Routledge.

Janson, U. (2008). Togetherness and diversity in pre-school play. In E. Wood (ed.), *The Routledge Reader in Early Childhood Education*. New York: Routledge, pp. 109–19.

Kaplan, H.S., Lancaster, J.B., Hill, K. & Hurtado, A.M. (2000). A theory of human life history evolution: Diet, intelligence and longevity, *Evolutionary Anthropology*, 9: 156–83.

Karpov, Y.V. (2005). *The Neo-Vygotskian Approach to Child Development*. New York: Cambridge University Press.

—— (2003). Vygotsky's doctrine of scientific concepts. Its role for contemporary education. In A. Kozulin, B. Gindis, V.S. Ageyev and S.M. Miller (eds), *Vygotsky's Educational Theory in Cultural Context*. New York: Cambridge University Press, pp. 65–82.

Kosven, M.O. (1927). *Oskolok Pervobytnogo Chelovechestva*. Moscow: n.p.

Kozulin, A. (1998). *Psychological Tools. A sociocultural approach to education*. Cambridge, MA: Harvard University Press.

—— (2003). Psychological tools and mediated learning. In A. Kozulin, B. Gindis, V.S. Ageyev and S.M. Miller (eds), *Vygotsky's Educational Theory in Cultural Context*. New York: Cambridge University Press, pp. 15–38.

Kravtsov, G.G. (2006). A cultural–historical approach to imagination and will. *Journal of Russian and East European Psychology*, 44(6): 19–36.

—— (2008a). A cultural–historical view of play. Paper presented at the Vygtosky Symposium, Monash University, Peninsula campus, 12 December.

—— (2008b) Periodization. Paper presented at Vygotsky symposium, Monash University, Peninsula campus, 16 December.

—— (2008c). Cultural–historical theory and the theorization underpinning the Golden Key Schools in Russia. Paper presented at the Vygtosky Symposium, Monash University, Peninsula campus, 11 December.

—— (2009a) Periods of psychic development. Paper presented at the Golden Key Summer School Program. Belay Kylavita, Moscow, 26 June.

—— (2009b). Cultural–historical basis of the 'Golden Key' program. Paper presented at the Golden Key Summer School Program. Belay Kylavita, Moscow, 23 June.

—— & Kravtsova, E.E. (2009). Cultural–historical psychology in the practice of education. In M. Fleer, M. Hedegaard and Jonathan Tudge (eds), *Childhood Studies and the Impact of Globalization: Policies and practices at global and local levels*. World Yearbook of Education. New York: Routledge, pp. 202–12.

Kravtsova, E.E. (2005). The concept of age novel formation in modern developmental psychology, *Cultural–historical psychology*, 1(2): 23–4).

—— (2006). The concept of age-specific new psychological formations in contemporary developmental psychology, *Journal of Russian and East European Psychology*, 44(6): 6–18.

—— (2008a). Play and the arts. Paper presented at Vygotsky symposium, Monash University, Peninsula campus, 15 December.

—— (2008b). Using play for teaching and learning. Paper presented at Vygotsky symposium, Monash University, Peninsula campus, 15 December.

—— (2008c). Cultural–historical theory and preschool education. Paper presented at Vygotsky symposium, Monash University, Peninsula campus, 16 December.

—— (2008d). The problems and practices of communication. Subject positioning within the Golden Key program, Paper presented at Vygotsky symposium, Monash University, Peninsula campus, 17 December.

—— (2008e). Zone of Potential development and subject positioning. Paper presented at Vygotsky symposium, Monash University, Peninsula campus, 17 December.

—— (2008f). Experimental psychological theatre. Paper presented at Vygotsky symposium, Monash University, Peninsula campus, 12 December.

—— (2009a). On the formation of skills for seeing various materials and to understand and differentiate their properties. Paper presented at the Golden Key Summer School Program. Belay Kylavita, Russia, 24 June.

—— (2009b). The main principles of the Golden Key Program. Paper presented at the Golden Key Summer School Program, Belay Kylavita, Russia, 22 June.

—— (2009c). On the formation of the perception of time in the psyche of pre-schoolers and primary school students. Paper presented at the Golden Key Summer School Program, Belay Kylavita, Russia, 23 June.

—— (2009d). On the formation of the ability of preschoolers and junior schoolers to analyse their own and other people's activity (reflections). Paper presented at the Golden Key Summer School Program, Belay Kylavita, Russia, 25 June.

—— (2009e). Psychological problems of primary education. Paper presented at the Golden Key Summer School Program, Belay Kylavita, Russia, 21 June.

——, Berezhkovskaya, E., Shopina, Z., Novikova, T., Khovrina, G., Perelyghina, I. & Gorlova, E. (2009). Diagnostics and correction of psychic (mental) development. Paper presented at the Golden Key Summer School Program, Belay Kylavita, Russia, 24 June.

Kravtsova, E.E. & Rubashkina, E.N. (2009). Golden Key Program. Summer School Program, Belay Kylavita, Russia, 21 June.

Lather, P. (2007). Getting Lost. Feminists' efforts towards a double(d) science. Albany: State University of New York Press.

Latour, B. (2003). Do you believe in reality? News from the trenches in the science wars. In R.C. Scharff and V. Dusek (eds), Philosophy of Technology. The technological condition. An anthology. Oxford: Blackwell, pp. 126–37.

Lazarus, M. (1883). Die Reize des Spiels. Berlin: Ferd, Dummlers Verlagsbuchhandlung.

Lektorsky, V.A. (1999a). Activity theory in a new era. In Y. Engestrom, R. Miettinen and R.-L. Punamaki (eds), Perspectives on Activity Theory. Cambridge: Cambridge University Press, pp. 65–9.

—— (1999b). Historical change of the notion of activity: Philosophical presuppositions. In S. Chaiklin, M. Hedegaard and U.J. Jensen (eds), Activity Theory and Social Practice, Aarhus: Aarhus University Press, pp. 100–13.

Leontiev, A.N. (1978). Activity, Consciousness and Personality, trans. M.J. Hall. Englewood Cliffs: Prentice Hall.

—— (1978). Activity, consciousness, and personality, trans. M.J. Hall; retrieved from www.marxist.org/archives.htm, 9 June 2008.

—— (1981). Activity, Consciousness, and Personality, Englewood Cliffs: Prentice Hall.

—— (1997). The Psychology of Social Interaction, Moscow: Smysl; retrieved from www.marxist.org/archives.htm, 6 June 2006.

—— (2005a). Study of the environment in the pedagogical works of L.S. Vygotsky. A critical study. Journal of Russian and Eastern European Psychology, 43(4): 8–28.

—— (2005b). Paper presented at the all-union institute of experimental medicine, Journal of Russian and Eastern European Psychology, 43(4): 48–57.

—— (2005c). Language and consciousness, Journal of Russian and Eastern European Psychology, 43(5): 5–13.

—— (2005d). The structure of consciousness. Sensory fabric, meaning, personal sense, *Journal of Russian and Eastern European Psychology*, 43(5): 14–24.

—— & Luria, A.R. (2005e). The problem of the development of the intellect and learning in human psychology, *Journal of Russian and East European Psychology*, 43(4): 34–47.

Levykh, M.G. (2008). The affective establishment and maintenance of Vygotsky's zone of proximal development. *Educational Theory*, 58(10): 83–102.

Lillard, A. (1996). Body or mind: Children's categorizing of pretense, *Child Development*, 17: 17–34.

Maguire, S., Ball, S. & Macrae, S. (2001). Post-adolescence, dependence and the refusal of adulthood, *Discourse: Studies in the Cultural Politics of Education*, 22(2): 197–211.

Martin-Korpi, B. (2005). *The Foundation for Lifelong Learning in Children in Europe*, 9 September, Edinburgh.

Matthews, W. (1977). Mode of transformation in the initiation of fantasy play, *Developmental Psychology*, 13, 212–16.

McCain, M. & Mustard, F. (1999). *Early Years Study. Final report. Reversing the real brain drain*. Toronto: Founders Network.

—— (2002). *Early Years Study. 3 years later*. Toronto: Founders Network.

Ministry of Education (1996). *Te Whaariki, Early Childhood Curriculum*. Wellington: New Zealand Ministry of Education.

Ministry of Education (1999). *The National Kindergarten Curriculum*, trans. K.S. Lee and E. Park. Report commissioned by the Ministry of Education. Seoul: Ministry of Education.

Ministry of Education (2006). *The Kindergarten Program. Revised*. Toronto: Ministry of Education; retrieved from www.edu.gov.on.ca, February 2009.

Ministry of Education (2007). *Nurturing Early Learners. A framework for a kindergarten curriculum in Singapore*. Singapore: Pre-school Education Unit.

Ministry of Gender and Community Services (2003). *Parents' and Caregivers' Guide for Households and Communities. Child development practices*. Lilongwe: Government of the Republic of Malawi.

Mitchell, L., Wylie, C. & Carr, M. (2008). *Outcomes of Early Childhood Education: Literature review*. Report to the Ministry of Education. Wellington: Ministry of Education.

Nairn, K. & Higgins, J. (2009) 'In transition': How the children of the economic reforms articulate identities at the child–adult border, *Childrenz Issues*, 13(1): 30–4.

—— & Ormond, A. (2007). Post school horizons: New Zealand's neo-liberal generation in transition, *International Studies in Sociology of Education*, 17(4), 349–66.

National Agency for Education (2006). *Lpfo 98 (Curriculum for preschool)*, Stockholm: National Agency for Education.

National Research Council (2001). Eager to learn: Educating our preschoolers. Committee on Early Childhood Pedagogy. In B.T. Bowman, M.S. Donovan and M.S. Burns (eds), *Commission on Behavioral and Social Sciences and Education*. Washington, DC: National Academy Press.

—— and Institute of Medicine (2000). From neurons to neighborhoods: The science of early childhood development. Committee on Integrating the Science of Early Childhood Development. In J.P. Shonkoff and D.A Phillips (eds), *Board on Children, Youth, and Families, Commission on Behavioral and Social Sciences and Education*. Washington, DC: National Academy Press.

Nelson, K. (1995). From spontaneous to scientific concepts: Continuities and disconti-
nuities from childhood to adulthood. In L.M.W. Martin, K. Helson and E. Tobach
(eds), *Sociocultural Psychology. Theory and practice of doing and knowing.* Cambridge:
Cambridge University Press, pp. 229–49.

Nicolson, S. & Shipstead, S. (2002). *Through the Looking Glass: Observations in the early
childhood classroom* (3rd edn). Upper Saddle River: Prentice Hall.

Nixon, D. & Aldwinkle, M. (2003). *Exploring Child Development from Three to Six Years*
(2nd edn). Tuggerah: Social Science Press.

Nsamenang, A.B. & Lamb, M.E. (1998). Socialization of Nso children in the Bamenda
Grassfields of Northwest Cameroon. In M. Woodhead, D. Faulkner and K. Littleton
(eds), *Cultural worlds of early childhood.* London: Routledge, pp. 250–60.

OECD (2001). *Starting Strong. Early childhood education and care.* Paris: Organisation for
Economic Co-operation and Development.

—— (2006). *Starting Strong II. Early childhood education and care.* Paris: Organisation for
Economic Co-operation and Development.

Parten, M. (1932). Social participation among preschool children, *Journal of Abnormal and
Social Psychology*, 27: 243–69.

—— (1933). Social play among preschool children, *Journal of Abnormal and Social Psychology*, 28: 136–47.

Patrick, G.T.W. (1916). *The psychology of relaxation.* Boston: Houghton-Mifflin.

Patterson, C. & Fleet, A. (2003). Meaningful planning. Rethinking teaching and learning
partnerships, *Research in Practice Series*, 10(1), n. pp. Canberra: Early Childhood
Australia.

Peak, L. (1991). *Learning to go to School in Japan: The transition from home to preschool life.*
Berkeley: University of California Press.

—— (1986). Training learning skills and attitudes in Japanese early educational settings.
In W. Fowler (ed.), *Early Experience and Development of Competence.* San Francisco:
Jossey-Bass, pp. 111–23.

Peers, C. (2008). A post-developmental framework for the visual arts in early childhood?
How art and cognition intersect in early childhood educational discourse, *Journal of
Australian Research in Early Childhood Education*, 15(2): 87–98.

—— (2009). Twenty-first century bastards. Neo-liberalism, phallacracy and the Australian Early Development Index, unpublished position paper. Melbourne: Monash
University.

Petrova, A. (1925). Deti-primitivy. Psikhologicheskij analiz (Child-primitives. A psychological analysis). In M. Gurevich (ed.), *Voprosy Pedologii I Detskoj Psikhonevrologii
(Questions of Pedology and Psychoneurology)*, Moscow: Zhizn'I Znanie, pp. 60–92.

Piaget, J. (1945). *Play, Dreams, and Imitation in Childhood.* New York: W.W. Norton.

Power, T.G. (2000). *Play and Exploration in Children and Animals.* Mahwah: Lawrence
Erlbaum.

Raban, B. & Ure, C. (2000). Literacy in the preschool: An Australian case study. In J.
Hayden (ed.), *Landscapes in Early Childhood Education: Cross-national perspectives on
empowerment – a guide for the new millennium.* New York: Peter Lang. pp. 375–92.

Raban, B., Nolan, A., Waniganayake, M., Ure, C., Brown, R. & Deans, J. (2007). *Building
Capacity. Strategic professional development for early childhood practitioners.* Melbourne:
Social Science Press.

Reber, A.S. & Reber, E.S. (2001). *Dictionary of Psychology* (3rd edn), Harmondsworth:
Penguin.

Rodriguez, R. & Moro, Ch. (1999). *El Magico Numero Tres: Cuando los ninos aun no hablan (The Magical Number Three: When children do not yet speak)*. Barcelona: Paidos.

Rogoff, B. (2003). *The Cultural Nature of Human Development*. Oxford: Oxford University Press.

Rubin, K.H., Fein, G.G. & Vandenberg, B. (1983). Play. In P.H. Mussen (ed.), *Handbook of Child Psychology* (4th edn), vol. IV. New York: Wiley, pp. 693–774.

Sammons, P., Sylva, K., Melhuish, E., Siraj-Blatchford, I., Taggart, B. and Elliot, K. (2002). Technical Paper 8a – Measuring the impact of pre-school on children's cognitive progress over the pre-school period. London: London Institute of Education.

Sammons, P., Sylva, K., Melhuish, E., Siraj-Blatchford I., Taggart, B., Grabbe, Y. & Barreau, S. (2007). Effective pre-school and primary education 3–11 project (EPPE 3–11). A longitudinal study funded by the DfES (2003–08). *Influences on Children's Attainment and Progress in Key Stage 2: Cognitive outcomes in Year 5*. London: Institute of Education; retrieved from www.ioe.ac.uk/projects/eppe, December 2008.

Sawyers, J.K. & Carrick, N. (2008). Symbolic play through the eyes and worlds of children. In E. Wood (ed.). *The Routledge Reader in Early Childhood Education*. New York: Routledge, pp. 136–59.

Schieffelin, B. B. & Ochs, E. (1998). A cultural perspective on the transition from prelinguistic to linguistic communication. In M. Woodhead, D. Faulkner and K. Littleton (eds), *Cultural Worlds of Early Childhood*. London: Routledge, pp. 48–63.

Schultze, U., Rennecker, J. (2007). Reframing online games. Synthetic worlds as media for organizational communication, International Federation for Information Processing, vol. 236. In K. Crowston, S. Sieber and E. Wynn (eds), *Virtuality and virtualization*. Boston: Springer, pp. 334–51.

Schweinhart, L.J. & Weikart, D.P. (1997). The High/Scope Perry Preschool Curriculum comparison study through age 23, *Early Childhood Research Quarterly*, 12, 117–43.

—— (1998). Why curriculum matters in early childhood education, *Educational Leadership*, 55(6): 57–60.

—— (1999). The advantages of High/Scope: Helping children lead successful lives, *Educational Leadership*, 57(1): 76–8.

—— & Larner, M.B. (1986). Consequences of three preschool curriculum models through age 15, *Early Childhood Research Quarterly*, 1(1): 15–46.

Shore, R. (1997). *Rethinking the brain. New insights into early development*. New York: Families and Work Institute.

Siraj-Blatchford, I. (1999). Early childhood pedagogy: practice and principles. In P. Mortimore (ed.), *Understanding Pedagogy and its Impact on Learning*. London: Paul Chapman, pp. 20–45.

—— (2004). Educational Disadvantage in the Early Years: How do we overcome it? Some lessons from research, *European Early Childhood Education Research Journal*, 12(2): 5–20.

—— (2007). Creativity, communication and collaboration: The identification of pedagogic progression in sustained shared thinking, *Asia Pacific Journal of Research in Early Childhood Education*, 1(2): 3–23.

—— (2009). Quality teaching in the early years. In A. Anning, J. Cullen and M. Fleer (eds), *Early Childhood Education. Society and culture*. London: Sage, pp. 137–48.

—— & Manni, L. (2008) 'Would you like to tidy up now?' An analysis of adult questioning in the English foundation stage, *Early Years*, 28(1): 5–22.

Siraj-Blatchford, I. & Sylva, K. (2004). Researching pedagogy in English pre-schools, *British Educational Research Journal*, 30(5): 713–30.

——, Muttock, S., Gilden, R. & Bell, D. (2002). *Researching Effective Pedagogy in the Early Years*, research report no. 356, London: Department of Education and Skills, HMSO.

Siraj-Blatchford, I., Sylva, K., Taggart, B., Mehuish, E., Sammons, P. & Elliot, K. (2004). The effective provision of preschool education (EPPE) Project (1997–2003). Technical paper 10. *Intensive Case Studies of Practice Across the Foundation Stage*. London: Institute of Education, University of London.

Smilansky, S. (1968). *The Effects of Sociodramatic Play on Disadvantaged Pre-School Children*. New York: Wiley.

Smith, P.K. (2007). Evolutionary foundations and functions of play: An overview. In A. Göncü and S. Gaskins (eds), *Play and Development. Evolutionary, sociocultural, and functional perspectives*. New York: Lawrence Erlbaum, pp. 21–50.

Smith, P.K. & Connolly, K.J. (1980). *The Ecology of Preschool Behaviour*. Cambridge: Cambridge University Press.

Spencer, H. (1873). *Principles of Psychology* (3rd edn), vol. 2. New York: Appleton.

Stebnitskii, S. N. (1930). Koriatskie deti. *Sovetskii Sever*, 4.

Stetsenko, A. & Arievitch, I.M. (2004). The self in cultural–historical activity theory. Reclaiming the unity of social and individual dimensions of human development, *Theory and Psychology*, 14(4): 475–503.

Sutton-Smith, B. & Brice-Heath, S. (1981). Paradigms of pretense, *Quarterly Newsletter of the Laboratory of Comparative Human Cognition*, 3(3): 41–5.

Sylva, K., Melhuish, E.C., Sammons, P., Siraj-Blatchford, I. & Taggart, B. (2000). The Effective Provision of Pre-school Education (EPPE) Project. A longitudinal study funded by the DfEE (1997–2003). The EPPE Symposium at the British Educational Research Association (BERA), annual conference, Cardiff University, 7–9 September.

—— (2004). *The Final Report: Effective preschool education*. Technical paper 12. London: Institute of Education, University of London.

Tobin, J.J., Wu, D.Y.H. & Davidson, D.H. (1989). *Preschool in Three Cultures: Japan, China and the United States*. New Haven: Yale University Press.

—— (1998). Komatsudani: A Japanese preschool. In M. Woodhead, D. Faulkner and K. Littleton (eds), *Cultural Worlds of Early Childhood*. London: Routledge, pp. 261–78.

Tolman, E.C. (1932). *Purposive Behavior in Animals and Men*. New York: Century.

Traianou, A. (2006). Teachers' adequacy of subject knowledge in primary science: Assessing constructivist approaches from a sociocultural perspective, *International Journal of Science Education*, 28(8): 827–42.

Ugaste, A. (2005). The child's play world at home and the mother's role in the play. Jyvaskyla Studies in Education, *Psychology and Social Research 259*, Finland: University of Jyvaskyla.

Urban, M. (2005). Quality, autonomy and the profession. In H. Schonfeld, S. O'Brien and T. Walsh (eds), conference proceedings from *Questions of Quality*, international conference, Dublin Castle, 23–24 September 2004, pp. 30–47.

Van Der Veers, R. (2008). Multiple readings of Vygotsky. In B. van Oers, W. Wardekker, E. Elbers and R. van der Veer (eds), *The Transformation of Learning. Advances in cultural–historical activity theory.* New York: Cambridge University Press, pp. 20–37.

van Oers, B. (1999). Teaching opportunities in play. In M. Hedegaard and J. Lompscher (eds), *Learning, Activity and Development.* Aarhus: Aarhus University Press, pp. 268–89.

—— (2008). Inscripting predicates: Dealing with meanings in play. In B. van Oers, W. Wardekker, E. Elbers, R. van der Veer (eds), *The Transformation of Learning. Advances in cultural–historical activity theory.* New York: Cambridge University Press, pp. 370–79.

—— (2009) Developmental education. Improving participation in cultural practices. In M. Fleer, M. Hedegaard and J. Tudge (eds), *Childhood Studies and the Impact of Globalization: Policies and practices at global and local levels.* World Yearbook of Education, New York: Routledge, pp. 213–29.

Veresov, N. (2006). Leading activity in developmental psychology. Concept and principle, *Journal of Russian and East European Psychology,* 44(5): 7–25.

von Schiller, F. (1954). *On the Aesthetic Education of Man.* New Haven: Yale University Press.

Vygotskaya, G. (1999). On Vygotsky's research and life. In M. Hedegaard, S. Chaiklin and U.J. Jensen (eds), *Activity, Theory and Social Practice.* Aarhus: Aarhus University Press.

Vygotsky, L.S. (1991). *The Psychology of Art.* Cambridge: MIT Press.

Vygotsky L.S. (1929) The problem of the cultural development of the child II. *Journal of Genetic Psychology,* 36: 415–432; retrieved from www.marxist.org/archive/vygotsky/works/1929/cultural_development.htm, 27 January 2009, pp. 1–13.

—— (1930). *Imagination and Creativity in Childhood.* Abridged translation in unpublished manuscript by F. Smolucha. Chicago: Department of Education, University of Chicago.

—— (1933). The teaching about emotions: Historical–psychological studies. In *The Collected Works of L.S. Vygotsky,* vol. 6. New York: Plenum Press, pp. 69–235.

—— (1966). Play and its role in the mental development of the child. *Voprosy Psikhologii (Psychology Issues),* 12(6): 62–76.

—— (1978). *Mind in Society.* Cambridge, MA: Harvard University Press.

—— (1981). The instrumental method in psychology. In J.V. Wertsch (ed.), *The Concept of Activity in Soviet Psychology.* Armonk: Sharpe, pp. 134–43.

—— (1982). *Problems in the Theory and History of Psychology. Collected works, vol. 1,* Moscow: Izdatel'stvo Pedagogika.

—— (1987a). Thinking and speech. In L.S. Vygotsky, *The Collected Works of L.S. Vygotsky,* vol. 1, *Problems of general psychology,* R.W. Rieber and A.S. Carton (eds), trans. N. Minick. New York: Plenum Press, pp. 39–285.

—— (1987b). *Lecturers in psychology,* In L.S. Vygotsky, *The Collected Works of L.S. Vygotsky,* vol. 1, *Problems of general psychology,* R.W. Rieber & A.S. Carton (eds), trans. N. Minick. New York: Plenum Press, pp. 289–358.

—— (1987c). Imagination and its development in childhood. In L.S. Vygotsky, *The Collected Works of L.S. Vygotsky,* vol. 1, *Problems of general psychology,* R.W. Rieber & A.S. Carton (eds), trans. N. Minick. New York: Plenum Press, pp. 339–50.

—— (1997a). Problems of the theory and history of psychology. In L.S. Vygotsky, *The Collected Works of L.S. Vygotsky,* vol. 3, R.W. Rieber and J. Wollock (eds English translation), trans. R. van der Veer. New York: Plenum Press.

—— (1997b). The history of the development of higher mental functions. In L.S. Vygotsky, *The Collected Works of L.S. Vygotsky*, vol. 4, R.W. Rieber (ed.), trans. M.H Hall. New York: Plenum Press

—— (1998). Child Psychology. In L.S. Vygotsky, *The Collected Works of L.S. Vygotsky*, vol. 5, Robert W. Rieber (ed. English translation), trans. M.J. Hall. New York: Kluwer Academic and Plenum Publishers.

—— (2004). Imagination and creativity in childhood. *Journal of Russian and East European Psychology*, 42(1): 7–97.

—— & Luria, A. (1994). Tool and symbol in child development. In R. Van Der Veer & J. Valsiner (eds), *The Vygotsky Reader*. Oxford: Blackwell, pp. 99–174.

Wagner, J.T. & Einarsdottir, P. (2006). Nordic ideals as reflected in Nordic childhoods and early education. In J. Einarsdottir and J.T. Wagner (eds), *Nordic Childhoods and Early Education. Philosophy, research, policy, and practice in Denmark, Finland, Iceland, Norway and Sweden*. Charlotte: Information Age Publishing, pp. 1–12.

Webber, B. (compiler) (2002). *Teachers Make a Difference: What is the research evidence?* Conference proceedings. Wellington: New Zealand Council for Educational Research.

Wertsch, J.V. (1998). *Mind as Action*. New York: Oxford University Press.

Willis, S. (2002). Crossing borders. Learning to count. *Australian Educational Researcher*, 29(2): 115–29.

Wilson, E.O. (1978). *Sociobiology: The new synthesis*, Cambridge, MA: Harvard University Press.

Wood, E. (2008). Contestation, transformation and re-conceptualisation in early childhood education. In E. Wood (ed.), *The Routledge Reader in Early Childhood Education*, New York: Routledge, pp. 1–18.

—— & Attfield, J. (2005). *Play, Learning and the Early Childhood Curriculum* (2nd edn). London: Paul Chapman.

Wood, D., Bruner, J. & Ross, S. (1976). The role of tutoring in problem solving. *British Journal of Psychology*, 66: 181–91.

Wylie, C., Hodgen, E., Ferral, H. & Thompson, J. (2006). *Contributions of Early Childhood Education to Age-14 performance*. Wellington: New Zealand Council for Educational Research.

Wylie, C. & Thompson, J. (2003). The long-term contribution of early childhood education to children's performance – evidence from New Zealand, *International Journal of Early Years Education*, 11(1): 69–78.

Wyn, J. & Dwyer, P. (1999). New directions in research on youth in transition, *Journal of Youth Studies*, 21(1): 5–21.

—— (2000). New patterns of youth transition in education, *International Social Science Journal*, 5(164): 147–59.

Index